From History to Theory

From History to Theory

KERWIN LEE KLEIN

UNIVERSITY OF CALIFORNIA PRESS
Berkeley Los Angeles London

University of California Press, one of the most distinguished university presses in the United States, enriches lives around the world by advancing scholarship in the humanities, social sciences, and natural sciences. Its activities are supported by the UC Press Foundation and by philanthropic contributions from individuals and institutions. For more information, visit www.ucpress.edu.

University of California Press
Berkeley and Los Angeles, California

University of California Press, Ltd.
London, England

Library of Congress Cataloging-in-Publication Data

Klein, Kerwin Lee, 1961–
From history to theory / Kerwin Lee Klein.
p. cm.
Includes bibliographical references and index.
ISBN 978-0-520-26881-4 (cloth : alk. paper)
1. United States—History—Philosophy. 2. Historiography—United States—Methodology. 3. Historiography—United States—History. 4. Linguistic change—United States—History. 5. History—Terminology. 6. Religion—Terminology. 7. Discourse analysis. 8. Social change—United States—History. I. Title.
E175.7.K54 2011
901—dc22 2010033220

Manufactured in the United States of America

20 19 18 17 16 15 14 13 12 11
10 9 8 7 6 5 4 3 2 1

This book is printed on Cascades Enviro 100, a 100% post consumer waste, recycled, de-inked fiber. FSC recycled certified and processed chlorine free. It is acid free, Ecologo certified, and manufactured by BioGas energy.

Contents

Acknowledgments

This small book has left me with much debt. I should begin with the many students, at UCLA and Berkeley, in my seminars and lectures on history and theory, especially Kevin Adams, E.J. Kim, Heather McCarty, Giuliana Perrone, Kim Vu-Dinh, and Stephanie Young. Many friends and colleagues have read and commented on all or portions of the manuscript: Thomas Brady, Claudio Fogu, David Hollinger, Martin Jay, Michael Kammen, Dominick LaCapra, and Sabine Schindler. Stan Holwitz has been an inspiration. Niels Hooper is the best editor on skis. Beth Berry provided hours of entertainment and insight during our team teaching. Tom Laqueur pressed me to turn my skepticism of memory discourse into an article, and the *Representations* editorial collective provided a congenial environment. Looking back, I realize that two colleagues, now gone, were an important influence at critical moments: we all miss Bernard Williams and Mike Rogin.

I presented portions of this work at the Annual Senior Fellows Conference, the School of Criticism and Theory; the Department of History,

Tulane University; the Center for Humanities and the Arts, Colorado University, Boulder; the Center for Cultural Studies, University of California, Santa Cruz; the Doreen B. Townshend Center for the Humanities, University of California, Berkeley; and the Merits of Memory Symposium, Martin Luther Universität, Wittenberg. Thanks to all for invitations and support.

Earlier versions of some chapters, or portions of chapters, appeared in *Representations; History and Theory;* and Hans-Jürgen Grabbe and Sabine Schindler, eds., *The Merits of Memory: Concepts, Contexts, Debates* (Heidelberg: Universitätsverlag, 2007). A Faculty Research Grant from the University of California, Berkeley, helped me with research and writing.

Introduction

It's easier for a fat man to get through the eye of a needle than for a rich man to get into Heaven.

I cannot recall when I first learned this particular version of Matthew 19:24, but I can say that it was in southern Illinois. My family lived in the foothills above the confluence of the Mississippi and Ohio rivers, a tiny slice of the mid-South then peopled mostly by farmers and coal miners. Storytelling, jokes, and preaching were highly valued forms of art, and I watched masters of the craft almost every day. The Scots-Irish migrants of the late eighteenth and early nineteenth centuries who had marched from the Appalachians to the Ozarks had left their mark. This was (and remains) Bible Belt country, with dry counties and Dr. Pepper devotees, where Southern Baptists and Methodists assemble regularly at places like Bear Point Church (where my grandmother spent her Sunday mornings). The culture was strong enough that even those folks who lived in the small towns—many of them, like my father's side of the family, central, southern, or eastern European and Greek Orthodox—learned the speech patterns of rural Protestantism: King James with a twang.

Southern Illinois was also (and remains) a poor country, and as in most parts of rural America in the twentieth century, the road to upward mobility led out of town, typically via sports or the military. That was how my parents made their way, with my father picking up a baseball scholarship at Southern Illinois University and my mother working in a sewing factory (today we would say sweatshop) until he landed a job teaching history and coaching football in a farm-town high school. Later, when I was a teenager, my mother finished her college degree and my father completed a PhD in education, specializing in symbolic logic and language acquisition. So I learned at a young age to appreciate the aesthetics of the spoken word, and I gradually worked through an evolving family library that ran from scholarly works on the Civil War to cheap paperback editions of Wittgenstein. I also picked up a class identification that alternated between working class and rural petit bourgeois, despite the attempts of my parents to become respectably middle class and speak standard English.

My voyage in academia was something less than direct. I spent years working in construction, sports, and music, and my early college experience came at a small junior college in Southern California. For six years I worked full time and took courses on the side, primarily in biology, and to the extent that I imagined myself in a professional career, it was always one in the life sciences. Later, when I went to the University of California, Riverside, I studied both history and anthropology before finally settling on history. As late as my first year of graduate school, at the University of Arizona, I spent at least as much time with the poets and essayists in the MFA program as I did with my colleagues in history. When I moved to UCLA to do my PhD, I kept up with poetry and oral literature by studying ethnolinguistics. So I became a historian fairly late, and I spent a number of years being partly socialized into different academic traditions. As a result, although I happily identify as a historian rather than an anthropologist or literary critic or wildlife biologist, I am often reminded of the differences between the disciplines, and between academia and other corners of American life, in ways that shape my research in the theory and practice of history. I offer this bit of biography—an admittedly unlikely mixture of haying and coon-hunting, mobile homes and black lung, Cadillac preachers and propositional calculus—not to claim some spurious connection with the wretched of the earth, but to help to situate my aims and interests. The combination of rural childhood and eclectic disciplinary study may go some way toward introducing this book, a series of essays on the poetics, rhetoric, and logic of academic discourse on history in the twentieth century.

The chapter and verse with which I began does serve a larger point. Matthew's aphorism actually speaks of the difficulty of squeezing a camel, rather than a fat man, through the eye of a needle. Southern Illinois had a Lake of Egypt and a Cairo (pronounced KAY-row), but camels were hard to come by, and at some now forgotten point, someone translated the passage into a more recognizable metaphor. One task of intellectual history is to take metaphors made strange by distance in time or space and render them in vocabularies that have meaning for us. Another is to take the metaphors with which we feel most at home and trace out the ways in which they stand on generations of older, stranger meanings.

The epigraph for this introduction should remind us not simply of the enduring power of a particular religious tradition in American discourse but also of the subtle inflections involved in translating—even within a language—across differences of time, place, and position. As I have learned time and again, the English of rural southern Illinois is not quite the same as the English of most faculty clubs, and when moving through an intellectual landscape that takes in a variety of distinct languages, we need to pay close attention to word choice. Students of intellectual history have become familiar with the various ways linguistic and cultural settings shape the reception of particular intellectual traditions. It is something of a cliché to observe that the American psychiatrists who imported Freudian psychoanalysis produced a discourse less literary than that of the original Viennese German. Historians of the philosophy of Ludwig Wittgenstein and Karl Popper have frequently concluded that the Oxbridge admirers of both men transformed the idealist resonance of the original works by transposing them into a very British empiricist tradition. And still other writers have argued that the dominance of New Criticism in American departments of English reduced French deconstruction to another methodological formalism.[1]

The essays here chase the history of various words and phrases key to scholarly historical discourse in the twentieth century. My focus is upon English, especially English usage in North America, although the stories also weave in and out of Great Britain, France, and Germany. We need such a project largely because so much recent English-language writing on "history and theory" has been abstracted from modern French and German intellectual history with an occasional glance at England. That continental focus has served us reasonably well, since so many of the canonical events of global modern life swirl around the rise of fascism, communism, and imperialism. But our tendency to generalize from the intellectual history of modern western Europe has also limited our conversations, perhaps most obviously in dealing with Latin America, Asia, and Africa. Departmental battles between the "the West" and "the Rest" over appointments and curricula have become part of the seasonal round for most academic historians. A growing genre of literature influenced by postcolonial studies measures the relevance of Europe's historical keywords—*modernity, nationhood, subject,* and so on—for scholarship in other parts of the globe. And *Europe* takes in a good deal more cultural and geographic space than is fairly represented in most history departments in the United States, where the "modern" field is typically represented by appointments in French and German history.

The tendency to generalize from French and German intellectual history can also occlude the American settings in which so many of us produce and consume scholarship. I do not mean that William James is more important than Friedrich Nietzsche, or that we should write more books about Zora Neale Hurston than Martin Heidegger, but for students of history and theory the United States is the elephant in the corner. The sheer mass of the North American market means that even when "we" write about Franz Fanon or Hannah Arendt, we are likely to do so in English. As a result, even cloistered debates over fascism and historiography can sound remarkably Midwestern. We need not fret that we are debasing European or Asian or African ideas by translating them into American idioms. But we do need to attend carefully to that aspect of our craft, and I am speaking not only of our casual generalization from European examples but also of our tendency to imagine English-language terms primarily as they are used in the academy. We need to remember that we share many of our preferred words with much larger publics, where they can resonate in very different ways.

From History to Theory is an episodic history of history and theory in the twentieth century. The narrative that follows is not a tightly wound monographic account, but the chapters are more closely knit than is common for collections of occasional essays, and I believe that an essay form suits the subject. Since we have no institutional discipline called "history and theory" or even "philosophy of history," theoretical and empirical work on historical scholarship has been scattered across the campus and beyond. Lacking a central professional structure, history and theory has nothing like an institutional history of the sort that Peter Novick created for his account of the American Historical Association, *That Noble Dream*. Intellectual histories of the philosophy of history tend toward rational reconstructions of particular debates or the work of specific individuals. We still lack major biographies of many of the best-known figures, such as R. G. Collingwood, and although something like surveys of the field have appeared over the past few decades, and especially works attempting to explain "postmodernism" or "post-structuralism" to historians, we are far from the sort of textbook discourse that has become conventional for the related disciplines of history and philosophy. What follows, then, is a series of interwoven accounts of particular episodes in modern philosophy of history, mostly in the United States and largely concerned with academic rather than popular discourse. The central subjects of these essays, however, are words rather than institutions or individuals.

The key terms and phrases all relate to the critical but absent word *history*. Some of the keywords of *From History to Theory* are terms that function as contraries or antonyms of *history;* others are complements; still others have at least occasionally served as synonyms or similes. My intent is not to create a metahistorical lexicon, but rather to trace genealogies of especially important discursive moments. Some words and phrases may appear obvious choices (*historiography* or *memory*), while others are perhaps more obscure. A few likely candidates do not appear at all. *History* itself appears only through refraction, partly by design and partly because I spent much of my earlier book, *Frontiers of Historical Imagination,* on a history of academic usage in the United States. A few other terms—*historicism, modernism, postmodernity*—have been treated by other authors whose work I found sufficiently engaging that I decided not to rework that ground.[2] And one word, *culture,* has been so important as both contrary and complement to *history* that it has received a variety of book-length treatments, in addition to countless articles.[3] Like *history, culture* appears here primarily through refraction, but it remains a crucial player in the story that follows.

Simply the mention of *keywords* or *concepts* or *counterconcepts* suggests methodological or even political investments. Since recent intellectual history has been particularly engaged with debates over method and meaning, I should briefly situate this project. I like the term *keyword,* but the essays here do not share much methodological ground with Raymond Williams's famous book *Keywords,* a classic that I first encountered as an undergraduate fresh from reading Williams's *Culture and Society.* (I was so impressed with the Britishness of that study that I am always surprised to see it used as if it were a reliable guide to American English, let alone American history.) Williams probably did more than any other recent author to popularize the term *keyword,* but his book, as its subtitle indicates, attempts to provide a "vocabulary of culture and society," a program much broader than I could hope to undertake in these pages. Moreover, as Quentin Skinner pointed out in a trenchant critique, Williams's tight focus upon single words, rather than clusters of words or word strings or vocabularies, appeared to retreat from the most recent developments in linguistic analysis.[4]

Although each chapter in *From History to Theory* turns upon particular terms or phrases, they all grow out of a story in which linguists came to argue that no word could ever be studied in isolation—that to understand the meaning of a term, one must understand the language. Each discrete word thus leads to longer word strings. Keywords tend to carry lots of other words with them—antonyms, synonyms, complements, and related adjectival and adverbial phrases. Sometimes older meanings get conserved in strange places, only to resurface later. Some keywords function primarily as metaphors that open out into bigger shared stories. Others circulate within carefully crafted, enduring arguments. My approach here has been pragmatic rather than systematic. A few of these essays stay close to a single term; others branch well out into related words and phrases. A few venture into fairly traditional rational reconstructions of past arguments. Others instead track linguistic changes on a larger scale by examining changes in shared vocabularies. Most have been written in a narrative voice, rather than the present tense common in self-consciously philosophical or theoretical discourse. And the collection as a whole is deliberately selective. As a student of language, I am a chronic collector of lexical artifacts, from ethnographic word lists to the *Dictionary of the History of Ideas*, but that is not the primary tradition for this book.[5]

Another term, *genealogy*, became a new academic keyword during the period studied here, and it is sometimes used to refer to a hip new practice distinct from other sorts of intellectual history. The revival of interest in Friedrich Nietzsche's 1887 work, *Zur Genealogie der Moral*, helped to make the word available, but it was popularized via some of the later writing of the French philosopher Michel Foucault that so thoroughly shaped history and theory in the seventies and eighties.[6] Foucault's use of *genealogy* as an alternative to *history* suggested that one could practice genealogical criticism as a reproof to the metaphysical presumptions of historicism. Prior to Foucault, *genealogy* had typically referred to the tracing of family trees, one of the most conservative forms of historical research imaginable. I appreciate the fact that a term that conjures images of retirees swarming the Church of Jesus Christ of Latter-Day Saints—which, for reasons of Mormon theology, maintains one of the best archives for researching family histories—could become a keyword for hipster theorists decked out in black leather. I am less convinced that *genealogy* really refers to a distinct method. Nietzsche specialists still go to war over how to characterize even the formal elements of his original.[7] But I do like the word as an occasional synonym for some kinds of history, and one of our current uses—a history of discourse that eschews the search for some ultimate causal origin of historical phenomena—works well enough for my purposes.[8] Although some of the words I explore in this volume do indeed carry with them older meanings that can resurface at surprising times, I am not deeply interested in etymology or some Heideggerian notion that the primordial essence of a powerful term will shine through its modern surface.

At least some of these chapters fall more nearly into the genre of "conceptual history" frequently associated with the multivolume *Begriffsgeschichte* project in Germany. That series is best known in the United States through the work of one of its most skilled contributors, Reinhart Koselleck. Koselleck's virtuoso essays explore the imprint of modernity upon Europe through linguistic shifts visible in high culture.[9] Although I have been much impressed by *Begriffsgeschichte,* I am less committed to certain of its philosophical ambitions.

Begriff has a deep and divided history in German philosophy, and idealists once spent generations arguing over the use and comparative importance of *Begriff, Idee,* and related terms of art. Late in the nineteenth century, in the course of his attempts to make logical analysis more rigorous, Gottlob Frege pointed out that *Begriff* had come to be understood in various ways, ranging from psychological to logical senses to strange admixtures of the two. We have since come to imagine Frege's reformation of logical analysis, and his desire to create a "purely logical" usage for *Begriff,* as one of the canonical events in the creation of what we usually call analytic or linguistic philosophy. But Frege's critique did not spell the end of innovations for the word, including many that Frege would never have endorsed. Half a century later, Martin Heidegger's appropriation of *Begriff* for an ambitious hermeneutical program gave the word still another thick layer of gloss. In his 1941 seminar *Grundbegriffe,* or *Basic Concepts,* Heidegger came as close as ever he did to offering a historiographic account of the sorts of writing he did on language and philosophy. For Heidegger, *Grundbegriffe* always hinted at a sense of Being that had become unspeakable because it had grown so remote. The rise of a calculating modern world had hidden everything essential, and the task of the philosopher was to follow the "path of remembrance" through the thickets of metaphors past in an attempt to uncover the original ground of Being. Heidegger's students, from Hans-Georg Gadamer to Reinhart Koselleck, tended to follow somewhat more prosaic trails. But *Begriffsgeschichte* has often traded on those older associations, especially those derived from Heideggerian rather than Fregean approaches to language.[10]

In the areas of English-language philosophy that took up *concept* as a keyword, Frege was the more important influence. In 1979 Quentin Skinner, channeling Frege, described the failure to distinguish between "words" and "concepts" as one of the chief demerits of Raymond Williams's *Keywords.* If we wish to understand past authors, Skinner groused, "what we need to know is not what words they use but rather what concepts they possess." There is something to Skinner's plaint, and at least a few colleagues have objected that my concentration upon words and discourses misses the point. "No one cares about words," as some have put it. "What people care about are *ideas.*" There is something to this, too, and I cannot let it pass without comment. At this point in the history of philosophy, we are not going to make a strong claim about the priority of concepts or ideas over words and sentences without muscling up some appropriately beefy justification. Skinner described his own practice as derived from the Fregean analytic tradition. But that tradition had by midcentury grown less confident about the purity of "concepts." In *Philosophical Investigations* (1953), referring to Frege's insistence that "concepts" have hard and fast boundaries, Wittgenstein objected that his own concept of "language games" was blurry, but that this did not make it useless or meaningless.[11]

A more aggressive variety of analytic philosophy went a good deal further in asking such difficult questions as "What is an idea?" and "Where are ideas to be found?" Although we like to think that what we believe in are not sentences but something else, something more immediate and important, it is difficult to say exactly what that "something else" is. That the conventional sense of ideas as mental pictures survived the rise of forensic medicine is itself remarkable, and the mental-pictures account could appear quaint in the face of logical analysis and empirical psychology. By midcentury, *ideas* and *concepts* had begun to migrate out of some regions of analytic philosophy. In their place came *words, sentences,* and other bits of vernacular elevated to terms of art. Well before American academics had begun to think about reading Jacques Derrida in translation, some philosophers had translated the analysis of ideas into something like the analysis of words and sentences. By 1970 at least one textbook had drawn the obvious moral, that "whenever we are threatened by the philosophical question of objects of belief, we can gratefully retreat to the more explicit idiom which speaks of believing sentences true." One of the authors, W. V. O. Quine, had built a career out of the dissolution of the vocabularies of idealist philosophy, and had gone so far as to ridicule the "idea idea" as a "vaporous emanation" of premodern notions of language and cognition. "There is no place in science for ideas," he quipped.[12]

Quine's writing did not slam the door on the coffin, and empirical psychology and brain science have only expanded the possible uses of *concept* or *idea,* as well as potential critiques, but these new developments have also made it more difficult to straightforwardly claim to write a history of concepts. For those trained in the traditions of continental philosophy, the retreat to *words* and *sentences* rather than *ideas* or *propositions* amounted to a typically American evasion of philosophy, derived from pragmatism or empiricism or perhaps the result of the sheer coarseness of North American culture. But as my own sympathies lie with Quine and his successors, I am content to let words like *concept* and *idea* remain convenient bits of shorthand rather than jargon for a new idealist metaphysics. In *From History to Theory,* then, the words that most hold our attention might be described as concepts, provided we do not push too hard on that term, taking it rather as a useful label for words that do more abstracting and generalizing work than other words.[13]

So even though my own influences include German hermeneutics as well as French deconstruction and Anglo-American analytic philosophy, the work in this book owes at least as much to the sort of writing found in the best American ethnolinguistic and intellectual history traditions. Accordingly, I have tried to write in a style accessible to readers with a variety of different theoretical tastes. Those who prefer to imagine this work as a history of ideas or concepts are welcome to do so. Those who think of language as a tool or instrument of social forces should find the essays at least approachable. Those who imagine language as an endless play of signifiers, along with those who reckon it a sort of divinized ether, can simply bracket references to authors or events or imagine them as shorthand for particular textual moments. And although social historians may be disappointed that I do not ground linguistic shifts in a robust class analysis, they may nonetheless read these essays as studies in collective linguistic behavior. Those who insist that the only possible way to study the meaning of words and discourse is by reference to the self-conscious intent of the individual author or speaker as each instance occurs—those who, in other words, have decided not to avail themselves of all the riches accumulated during two centuries of rigorous, disciplined inquiry into linguistics—can write their own books.

Language and linguistics feature here because they proved among the most important topics of the twentieth century. In philosophy, language emerged as a focus of scholarly inquiry as early as the works of Frege and Bertrand Russell on the one hand, and Friedrich Nietzsche on the other. The early work of Frege, Russell, and Wittgenstein was quickly recognized as a distinctly modern moment in philosophy, and by midcentury the serious study of logic and language preoccupied elite journals and institutions in North America. As Gustav Bergmann put it in 1953, philosophy had taken a "linguistic turn."[14] Philosophy was not alone in this—in anthropology, English, and sociology, a new enthusiasm for linguistic analysis produced stacks of new work on dialects, language standardization, poetics, form, and semantics, ranging from obscure monographs to best-selling paperbacks. Few accounts of history and theory, though, have focused on that broader set of habits and traditions. Our most popular story instead reduces the "linguistic turn" to a handful of texts associated with the French generation of 1968—Roland Barthes, Michel Foucault, Jacques Derrida, Jean-François Lyotard, and a few others—received in the United States as poststructuralism or postmodernism or theory or as a cultural or aesthetic turn. Variants of the popular story sometimes seek out key precursors for the radical revolution: recent histories-of-ideas that trace this or that Derridean or Foucauldian theme back through its Heideggerian influences and into the Nietzschean dark. And battles over the politics of "theory" or the "linguistic" or "cultural" or "memorial" or "aesthetic" turn have become the stuff of legend. Yet the vocabulary we employ for describing these transitions suggests more questions. How did *language* come to substitute for *culture,* and vice versa? How did *linguistics* come to be associated with *aesthetics* and *memory*?

While each essay in *From History to Theory* has particular points to make, the essays are tied together by a larger argument, namely, that our standard story is misleading. The standard story portrays historiography as a bastion of positivism, aside from a few flickers of relativist doubt in the manner of Charles Beard or Carl Becker, until the arrival of linguistic radicalism in the sixties. Then cultural revolutionaries from France or Germany or Berkeley (take your pick) led the world to either hell or New Cultural History. *From History to Theory* argues that the conditions of possibility for these changes emerged out of earlier developments in historical and linguistic discourse in North America. What we have sometimes taken as French debates over writing, language, textuality, semiotics, signs, culture, and aesthetics arrived in an English-language landscape already saturated with discourse about language and linguistics and decorated with American idioms. It is not that the earlier North American debates over language were the real source of, say, deconstruction or postmodernism, if we could even imagine those as coherent intellectual movements. But older American habits of talking about language both made possible the reception of new linguistic turns and shaped the ways in which the new vocabularies could resonate, circulate, and proliferate.

In the twentieth century, history's engagements with a variety of self-consciously a- or antihistorical traditions created new narrative and analytical vocabularies. Two midcentury linguistic habits proved especially significant in the reworking of historical discourse. First, an increasingly narrow scientism invited reaction and opened the door to a more aesthetic language, as well as, in some cases, to vocabularies traditionally associated with religious discourse. Second, decolonization pressed historical discourse in new directions, even as most historiographers avoided direct engagement with colonial peoples and places. Ethnographic language played a leading part in this development, and the popularization of the word *culture* was only the most visible of a series of larger semantic shifts. These movements, toward aesthetic and post-secular discourses on the one hand, and a more ethnographic discourse on the other, were contemporaneous, but neither entailed the other. They were contingently related, rather than the necessary products of some obscure logic of cultural production.

Although *From History to Theory* is primarily an account of linguistic shifts in the English-speaking academy, and especially in North America, the story I tell about history talk in the academy does overlap with other sections of American historiography not focused upon language. Here I will point up one of the most important, namely, the large body of work that examines the transition in intellectual and cultural life from the late nineteenth century to the twentieth, as a Victorian culture built upon Protestant piety and bourgeois convention gave way to a recognizably modern or even modernist world that was more secular, consumerist, and culturally diverse. Whether we are speaking about intellectuals—as in Henry May's classic study *The End of American Innocence* (1959)—or the popular world of American movies mapped by Lary May's *Screening Out the Past* (1983), most of us have come to imagine the twentieth century as a place rather different from its predecessors. The middle decades of the century have received less scrutiny from historians, but David Hollinger's *Science, Jews, and Secular Culture* (1996) goes some way toward arguing that the transition from a Victorian to a modern cultural regime was especially visible in higher education. Prior to World War II, scholarly discourse was heavily white, male, and Protestant, but a sustained critique, coming first from the physical sciences and often led by secular Jewish academics, reworked the academic environment. The humanities departments held out the longest, but by the 1980s Jews, women, and other ethnic and racial minorities had dramatically altered the ways we talk about history and other academic disciplines in North America.[15]

The transformation of research universities from bastions of WASP culture to places far more diverse—and less churchy—matters for our story. Only after the academy had been sufficiently "secularized," so as to allow significant participation by religious and racial minorities, could a secular discourse come to feel oppressive. Only after a basic degree of "secularity" had been normalized could some academics begin to describe secularism as a constraining or possibly colonial discourse even within the university.[16] By century's end, it had become possible for some serious scholars to argue that only an escape from history, or perhaps the creation of an historical discourse grounded in aesthetics or open to more religious languages, could help to emancipate the wretched of the earth. Ironically, that reenchantment of academic discourse about history coincided with a far more threatening reenchantment of American public culture.

Chapter 1 follows the rise and fall of one of the older English words used to discuss the practice and theory of history. Around the middle of the twentieth century, *historiography* came to be associated with both a new type of intellectual history and the training of new historians. The advent of historiography courses, textbooks, and teaching anthologies created a tradition in which the word could reference an eclectic mix of practices ranging from philosophy to source criticism. By the seventies, though, both the term and the courses appeared to have grown dated, and it was unclear how historians could best engage the theoretical challenges raised by feminism, structuralism, postcolonialism, and other intellectual movements. *Historiography* itself had frequently come to connote beginner work, rather than a serious research program.

Chapter 2 tracks the emergence of "philosophy of history" as both a research specialty and a term of art in cold war North America. Before the Second World War, essentially no respectable academic in Canada, Great Britain, or the United States identified as a philosopher of history. By 1960 the subject had grown specialists, monographs, and teaching anthologies. Yet *philosophy of history* remained popularly identified with old-fangled universal history. And new conceptions of science, especially those developed in analytical philosophy, posed special challenges, as philosophers came to suspect that history could never attain the logical precision of a true science. By the mid-1960s, *history and theory,* a more nearly "scientific" phrase, threatened to displace *philosophy of history,* just as the failure of historical discourse to conform to idealized conceptions of scientific method opened the possibility that history might be redefined as an aesthetic practice.

Chapter 3 begins with the New Cultural History, a movement commonly described as history's response to the growing influence of radical, continental conceptions of language. This chapter argues that cultural history's reception of French structural linguistics and post-structuralism was shaped by earlier linguistic turns in American anthropology and analytic philosophy. *Language,* along with *culture,* perhaps the most important keyword of the human sciences in the twentieth century, had a lengthy history in North America, where academic and popular studies of linguistics were strongly shaped by ethnographic encounters with racial difference. Some of the most radical renditions of language came not from the deconstructive inclinations of literary critics but from analytical philosophy's encounters with popular anthropology. As a result, when historians began to borrow idioms and phrases from anthropology, they entered a semantic field in which language, art, and racial difference had grown tightly together.

Chapter 4 unpacks the claims of certain strains of postmodern or post-structural discourse to engage global history without falling back into the sort of universal history that had been practiced by Hegel or Marx. Decolonization forced academics to recognize that the increasing economic integration of the globe had not produced a homogenous global culture. And so something like a new, skeptical philosophy of history emerged, in which a variety of new words and phrases—*master narrative* and *metanarrative* among them—created narrative forms and political labels for a radical but post-Marxist mode of discourse. But these new stories and terms drew far more heavily on the old universal history than many had hoped, breathing new life into the bad, old idea of peoples without history. In the event, both skeptics and speculators converged on a shared narrative in which modernization generated antimodern social forces.

Chapter 5 is a polemical account of the emergence of new uses for an old word, *memory*. In the eighties and nineties, a term abandoned by the midcentury academy returned as a keyword for history and theory. Many of the justifications for the new usage turned upon the term's utility for articulating the experience or subject positions of minority and colonized peoples in a traumatic, postmodern age. And yet *memory* carried with it a host of associated words drawn from predominantly religious discourses that could resonate in mysterious and possibly dangerous ways.

Chapter 6 takes off the gown. Where the previous chapters concentrate upon academic usage, this chapter examines one strand of popular and political discourse about the past in the recent United States. For an emergent Christian conservative movement, *memory* and related linguistic forms helped to open nominally secular public spaces to Judeo-Christian constructions of the past. Here, memory talk helped a newly muscular Christianity reduce history to eschatology.

The afterword briefly looks back upon the politics of linguistic change and our investments in narratives of progress and declension. *Theory* has become a battle flag, despite the notorious vagaries of the term. Recent accounts of the rise of *theory* have blamed either reactionary European imports or the segmentation of the academic market for leading us astray. *From History to Theory* argues that earlier changes in the ways we talk about language, history, and culture prepared the ground for the ways we think about history and theory today.

ONE The Rise and Fall of *Historiography*

One way to get at a big question like "What is history?" is to pose smaller, related questions. How do historians survey the property lines of the profession? How do we train our students? How do we trace our own genealogy? According to Hans Kellner, history, like other disciplines, works largely by imprinting students with particular sets of anxieties.[1] If so, these questions are roundabout ways of asking, What makes us anxious? Kellner's argument has special resonance for those members of the guild with the greatest cause for anxiety: graduate students, junior faculty, and the growing numbers of nontenured temporary lecturers and staff. Anxieties seldom run higher than when money is on the line. My own fading memories of my time in the job market include a talk I gave at a big school. The talk went well enough, as best I can recall, but afterward, at a meeting with the graduate students, one of them declared, with a bit of hostility, that it took some nerve to present a "historiography" paper as a job talk. I had just finished a dissertation on historical imagination in American academia and had learned not to tell anyone who asked that I was interested in "historiography." Instead, depending on the question, I would describe my research interests in "philosophy of history" or "history and theory" or mumble something about "cultural studies." Like many other graduate students, as part of my socialization into the profession I had learned that historiography was not something to which "real" historians aspired. In letters, interviews, and even hall talk, I treated the term cautiously.

Historiography may have loomed especially large in my particular landscape, but it is a surprisingly ambiguous and highly charged term. It is also a word that historians cannot do without. It is one of those drab bits of professional furniture that has become so familiar, it is virtually invisible, at least until someone bumps into it. In his 1938 review essay "What Is Historiography?" Carl Becker measured the common meanings of this "unlovely word." His assessment remains recognizable today:

> What precisely is Historiography? It may be, and until recently has for the most part been, little more than the notation of the historical works since the time of the Greeks, with some indication of the purposes and points of view of the authors, the sources used by them, and the accuracy and readability of the works themselves. The chief object of such enterprises in historiography is to assess, in terms of modern standards, the value of historical works for us. At this level historiography gives us manuals of information about histories and historians, provides us, so to speak, with a neat balance sheet of the "contributions" which each historian has made to the sum total of verified historical knowledge now on hand. Such manuals have a high practical value. To the candidate for the Ph.D. they are indeed indispensable, since they provide him at second hand with the most up-to-date information. From them he learns what were the defects and limitations of his predecessors, even the most illustrious, without the trouble of reading their works.

Becker hoped that historiography could mature into a more analytical and thoughtful enterprise ("a phase of intellectual history"). The mercenary approach to scholarship that disturbed Becker was scarcely unique to history. He spent much of his career decrying the decline of the liberal arts. But what was common in Becker's day has become dominant in ours, partly because we have so many more monographs and specialties. Half a century after Becker, the historiographic essay had become a boilerplate exercise in which students reduce each monograph to a summary paragraph; criticize the book as reductionist; string together enough summaries to fill out the requisite number of pages; and conclude with a call for a new paradigm. For most graduate students, "historiography" means the synoptic reduction of a variety of monographs on a given topic to a narrative march out of the darkness and into the intellectual light of their own dissertation.[2]

Becker's account suggests the ways that the meanings of *historiography* have narrowed. In 1938 *historiography* had at least three discrete meanings. First, and most commonly, the word meant the writing of history in the abstract. In this broadest category, it simply meant written historical discourse of any sort. Second, *historiography* could refer to the critical study of the writing of history. This was the meaning Becker had in mind, and it included what other writers called "the history of historical writing" as well as philosophical discussions of historical method and exercises in source criticism. Finally, *historiography* could refer to a specific body of historical scholarship, such as "the historiography of Progressivism." In recent years, this last meaning has predominated, and few historians who specialize in the study of historical discourse refer to the practice as historiography or identify themselves as historiographers. Along the way, historiography has acquired the odor of beginner work, appropriate to entry-level graduate students preparing for exams rather than to a serious intellectual inquiry.

Although Becker imagined historiography as an analytical enterprise, by the 1960s historians had begun to use other words, especially *theory*, to refer to the reflective study of historical discourse. Word substitution may seem a trivial matter, but since key words of historical method are at issue, our linguistic habits deserve a closer look. The politics of word choice can tell us a good deal about other sorts of politics, and *historiography*'s semantic shifts may help to sketch a history of the way we imagine history as a discipline. Here I would like to follow Carl

Becker's lead by chasing semantics into pedagogy. A history of the use and abuse of *historiography* will lead us into the situations where the word has most resonance—places where we write about and teach the history of historical discourse. That focus, though, creates peculiar obstacles. The historian's reference to the profession as a "guild" is not purely a bit of nostalgic hope. Graduate students typically learn teaching by observing mentors, and that process has not been well represented in the reflective work on the discipline. Simply put, try as we might to collect old syllabi or survey old course catalogues, we have no guarantee that these documents give us a truly reliable guide to classroom practice. Despite the recent emergence of the "scholarship of teaching and learning," we know remarkably little about the history of historical training.[3] Since *historiography* has probably circulated more frequently in seminars and hall talk than in published documents, my semantic history here is necessarily brief and impressionistic. But while the particulars remain murky, we can trace out a narrative arc.

Historiography is indeed an unlovely word, and its homeliness is reflected in its absence from a wide array of dictionaries and encyclopedias. *Historiography* appeared only briefly in the 1933 and 1989 editions of the *OED*. There, it served chiefly as a synonym for *history* in the sense of a written narrative, mainly to distinguish history as a linguistic artifact from history as actual events. Another related word, *historiology,* "the knowledge or study of history," denoted the actual study of historical discourse, rather than the general body of written history. The most recent usage dated to 1813: "Erudition has been divided by a German professor into glossology, bibliology, and historiology." In a footnote to his 1988 social history of the American Historical Association, *That Noble Dream,* Peter Novick lamented the disappearance of this "once respectable word." And a recent attempt by Hayden White to bestow the kiss of life on the term has apparently failed. Still, *historiology* at least has its mourners, unlike the other archaic alternatives, *historiognomer, historionomer,* and *historionomal*. For good and ill, historians ended up with *historiography,* a word that survived its early years as a synonym for historical writing and, having cannibalized *historiology,* expanded to encompass metahistorical reflection.[4]

Most accounts of the rise of historiography as the study of historical discourse focus upon the German origins of "scientific" history in the eighteenth and nineteenth centuries. German historians could use the term *Historiographie,* but the language generated a host of other words that one might translate as "historiography": *Geschichteswissenschaft, Geschichteschreibung, Geschichtesphilosophie, Geschichtestheorie,* and Johann G. Droysen's preferred term, *Historik.* What these terms connoted ranged from exercises in source criticism to critical readings of monographs to philosophical hermeneutics. English and American historiographers tamed this linguistic wilderness by telling the story of "scientific history," a narrative in which modern methods of source criticism, as exemplified by the writing of Leopold von Ranke, created professional history and, with it, historiography. Herbert Butterfield's 1955 classic, *Man on His Past,* noted that Renaissance humanists had written both histories of historiography and treatises on historical method, but that such works amounted to little more than "ropes of sand," lists of titles with no analytical content. The real "history of historiography" began at Göttingen in the late eighteenth century. As early as 1760, J.C. Gatterer had called for a "History of History." According to Butterfield, the papers of the youthful Lord Acton suggest that, by the end of the 1850s, the subject "was already a familiar thing."[5]

By the end of the nineteenth century, professional historians in England and the United States had a substantial list of titles to consult for direction on historical method, narrative tradition, and philosophy of history, and the possibility, if not yet the habit, of referring to such works as "historiography." How-to books on source criticism mingled promiscuously with evolutionary stories of the history of historical discourse and philosophical speculation upon historical substance. German works decorated these early bibliographies. One of the more suggestive bibliographies appeared as an appendix to Frederick Jackson Turner's 1891 essay "The Significance of History." Turner listed Lord Acton's 1886 essay "German Schools of History," but also detailed a long line of German works ranging from methods texts, such as Ernst Bernheim's *Lehrbuch der historischen Methode und der Geschichtsphilosophie* (1889), to surveys of philosophy of history, such as Rudolf Rocholl's *Aufbau einer Philosophie der Geschichte* (1878). Turner's own essay narrated the transition in historical discourse from romantic narratives of the lives of great men to more socioeconomic approaches to history that he embraced as his own. And he drew heavily upon one of his featured texts: J.G. Droysen's *Grundriss der Historik.*[6] Turner's essay was the one of the first important historiographic works by an American, and we should mark its form: it was at once a philosophical reflection upon historical practice, a narrative account of the evolution of historical discourse, and a manifesto for a new history.

We should pause, briefly, to remark the text that became Turner's preferred exposition of method. Droysen's *Grundrisse* differed dramatically from other period choices, such as Charles Victor Langlois and Charles Seignobos, *Introduction aux études historiques,* in that it offered far more philosophical ambition. Droysen's text appeared in English language translation as *Outline of the Principles of History* (1897), and it mixed a broadly Hegelian epistemology and universal history with an infinitely practical account of the investigative and imaginative tasks of historical research. The book was at once a philosophy of history; a practical account of the mechanics of source criticism; an analysis of the various modes of historical interpretation; and a treatise upon the formal differences among various types of historical exposition, from essay to narrative to monograph. Droysen's work was also arguably the last important study to imagine all of these topics in a synthetic manner, as parts of an organic whole, each of which necessarily informed the others in a dialectical fashion. Much subsequent writing on historiography would systematically dismantle that architecture, pulling out particular pieces and discarding others. That the *Outline* appeared at all in North American practice is surprising. And in Turner's hands it had influence, if only because it invited reaction. Carl Becker and Merle Curti were only two of the future historiographers to pass through Turner's seminar.[7]

Thanks to Turner's diligent biographers and many students, we probably know more about his seminars at the University of Wisconsin than we do about other training situations of that period. Most of Turner's students appear to have encountered their mentor's preferred historiographic texts, Droysen in particular, in one of the famous research seminars. Here, Turner worked in the fashion he had learned at Johns Hopkins, immersing himself and his students in a shared body of archival and primary materials, with each student producing a paper on an assigned topic relevant to Turner's own research. For instance, while he worked on his *Rise of the New West,* the seminar would focus on a few counties in a particular decade or two matched to census data. Turner would assign each student a topic—mining or immigration or agriculture—and at seminar's end, the collective project could produce something like a total history for a specific locale during a specific period. On the one hand, the seminar was a residue of German idealism as it materialized in Wisconsin public education, elevating the enthusiasms for local antiquities to something like universal history. On the other hand, it was also the beginning of a peculiarly North American approach to history as a social science. We do not know if *historiography* was even a key word, but the easy blend of philosophy of history, source criticism, and historical research was a hallmark of early Turnerian practice. The idea that source criticism and historical method had philosophical as well as practical significance proved attractive to an early generation of historians and helped to underwrite a growing body of technical literature.[8]

By the early twentieth century, *historiography* could refer to a wide variety of commentaries upon historical discourse. Most professional historians were introduced to research methods through such texts as Droysen's *Outline,* Langlois and Seignobos's *Introduction aux études historiques,* and Bernheim's *Lehrbuch.* They could consult a growing number of annotated bibliographies. They could piece together the manifestos of predecessors ranging from von Ranke to Charles Beard. They could read and write critical reviews of contemporary scholarly works. More reflective thinkers could read Droysen or Croce. And new monographs narrated the march of historical science. In 1913 George P. Gooch's *History and Historians in the Nineteenth Century* became the first book-length history of historical discourse published in English. In 1922 James Shotwell's *Introduction to the History of History* appeared. In 1938 Harry Elmer Barnes's *History of Historical Writing* turned up on the book review desk at the *American Historical Review.* The editors sent it to Carl Becker, and his lengthy review became a classic in its own right partly because its reckoning of historiography as a form of intellectual history proved timely.[9] James Westfall Thompson's survey of historical writing from antiquity to the twentieth century appeared in 1942, quickly followed by a long list of titles, including Butterfield's lectures and the Social Science Research Council's Committee on Historiography publications of 1946, 1954, and 1962. Three years later, in 1961, John Higham's *History: Professional Scholarship in America,* noted that, where the 1931 AHA *Guide to Historical Literature* listed only ten works on the philosophy of history (only one of which had appeared after 1875), the 1961 *Guide* listed fifty-nine titles. Historiography had arrived, or so we might presume.[10]

In retrospect, we can imagine Carl Becker distilling a relatively new and fragile usage. Where Gatterer had spoken of a "History of History" and Benedetto Croce of the "history of historiography," Barnes and Becker simply said "historiography." That usage could appear when it did because of the growing number of monographs and even teaching texts that treated the history of historical discourse. And these changes in usage tracked changes in professional training. As Becker noted, the word tended to get used most often in teaching situations, and as the profession grew, so did the need for historiography. In the United States, the postwar expansion of higher education facilitated the development of methods courses and subsidized the market for texts. The increase in students and in available monographs also changed the way the subject could be taught. Where Frederick Jackson Turner had learned historiography in Herbert Baxter Adams's famous seminar at Johns Hopkins University, imported directly from Droysen's Germany, Turner's grandstudents—his students' students—frequently encountered general historiography in a lecture hall in courses taught by American scholars or European émigrés who assigned English translations of classic works of continental philosophy and history.[11]

We cannot speak with too much authority upon the precise content of these historiography courses, but we can reasonably conjecture that a significant percentage drew upon that postwar publishing innovation the teaching anthology. If the nineteenth century introduced treatises upon source criticism and histories of historical writing, the teaching market provided a rich context for publications that sampled representative texts useful for the undergraduate and graduate classroom. By the early 1960s, Fritz Stern's *Varieties of History* (1956), Hans Meyerhoff's *Philosophy of History in Our Time* (1959), and Patrick Gardiner's *Theories of History* (1959) were readily available. Of those three works, the Meyerhoff anthology presented the clearest argument in its editorial comment and textual selection. For Meyerhoff, a professional philosopher, the story of the last century was the story of the collapse of historicism as a philosophical project and the rise of antihistorical challenges from positivism, existentialism, and Christianity: Meyerhoff began with Wilhelm Dilthey and ended with Karl Jaspers and the neoorthodox theologian Reinhold Niebuhr.[12]

The Stern and Gardiner anthologies followed a trajectory very different from that traced by Meyerhoff. Each made his selections so as to tell a story of the increasing disciplinization and secularization of historical thinking from Voltaire or Vico to the cold war. Stern, a historian of modern Europe, emphasized the writings of professional historians. Gardiner, a philosopher, anthologized mostly philosophical texts. There was virtually no overlap in selection. Only one text (and author) appeared in both books—an excerpt from Karl Marx's *German Ideology,* although that convergence scarcely tilted either text toward radicalism. Each book, rather, complemented the dominant narrative of historiography as told by Butterfield and other historiographers.

Fritz Stern's book proved popular with historians, and by 1963 *The Varieties of History* had reached its ninth printing, an impressive record for a teaching anthology. Stern organized his text as a history of the evolution of source criticism. His very first author, Voltaire, appeared as a "pioneer of a new type of history," based upon the careful examination of primary sources, and Stern's second selection was Barthold Niebuhr, exemplar of the "critical method." That editorial decision helped to impart a certain conservative cast to such courses, as students learned basically Whiggish stories about the evolution of source criticism from either the ancient Greeks or the Enlightenment, right on up to their own sorties into the archives. Stern was not, of course, a vulgar

Rankean. "History springs from live concern, serves life, deals with life," he declared, warning readers that future historians might have to "struggle to preserve a sense of the freedom of man." Stern's colleague Jacques Barzun, in his concluding essay on cultural history, agreed. Historical writing demands an *"esprit de finesse."* "The rest," said Barzun, "is footnotes."[13]

That footnotes and esprit might go together was one of the morals students were likely to draw from another popular teaching text, Marc Bloch's elegant defense of historical studies, posthumously published and translated into English in 1953 as *The Historian's Craft.* Bloch's work had served as a defense of historical discourse against the demands of the sciences and social sciences. Learned, casual, and stylish, the book described the "critical method" as the true legacy of historical studies, the genuine contribution that historians had made to the creation and survival of a human civic order. For students, that claim must have had a special resonance, for one of the most memorable features of *The Historian's Craft* was that its author had died at the hands of the Nazis while fighting for the Resistance. Here, historiography set itself in a global context, although by the time North American readers encountered Bloch's treatise, the curriculum had become more cold war than world war. But craft still served as an instrument of freedom.[14]

By the end of the 1950s, many departments of history in the United States expected graduates and sometimes undergraduates to suffer through at least one course in general historiography. A 1962 American Historical Association survey, *The Education of Historians in the United States,* reported that, of 376 four-year colleges, 35 percent offered coursework in "methodology"; 33 percent in "historiography"; and another 15 percent in "philosophies of history." It is not clear if these represented distinctly different courses or if the three fields could be compressed into a single course. Intriguingly, "Catholic colleges" and "Colleges for Negroes" offered methodology courses at a higher rate than did other institutions. Of the 77 "Ph.D.-training Institutions" surveyed, all offered "historiography" courses, although 66 percent offered them only to graduate students. Seventy-seven percent offered "methodology" courses," and 36 percent courses in "philosophies of history." Still, the authors of the survey doubted that this instruction was sufficiently broad. They recommended that undergraduates, as well as graduate students, receive a better grounding in the "classics of historical literature," in "philosophies of history," and in historical method. Recent graduates seemed sympathetic to such suggestions; 90 percent of recent history PhDs told the committee that a course in "historiography" or "philosophies of history" should be required of all doctoral candidates.[15]

Although most PhD-granting universities offered historiography courses, it is difficult to divine what was actually taught. The three rubrics used by the committee—historiography, methodology, and philosophies of history—suggested the topical variety. The course could focus strictly upon methods: how to assemble a bibliography, distinguish primary and secondary sources, subject sources to textual criticism, abstract the relevant information on index cards, and piece together the story. Alternatively, a historiography course might introduce students to classics of historical literature. Or the historiography course could explore the philosophical analysis of historical discourse. In actual teaching situations, the blend of topics depended heavily upon departmental traditions and even more upon the whims of the teacher. The same course at Columbia University produced texts as different as Shotwell's narrative of the evolution of historical discourse, *History of History;* Barzun and Graff's *Modern Researcher,* with its chapters on bibliographies, source criticism, and outlining; and Fritz Stern's *Varieties of History,* which anthologized classics of historical literature from Voltaire to Huizinga.

Even those texts that attempted to synthesize historiography's many tendencies suggested how impossible the task had become. Houghton Mifflin found enough buyers for Wood Gray's 1956 primer, *Historian's Handbook: A Key to the Study and Writing of History,* that the publisher released a second edition in 1964. In eighty-eight pages the text introduced the nature of history, catalogued bibliographical resources for various periods and all the major continents, introduced source criticism, and offered a tutorial on prose. No page was wasted, for the back cover included a graphic guide to the arcane symbols of proofreading. Even the authors recognized that the subject had been so condensed that students would need to read each and every word: "*Don't skim!*" That the warning was needed said something about the evolving reading habits of young historians. Meanwhile, Norman F. Cantor and Richard I. Schneider's *How to Study History* (1967) attempted to give undergraduates the basics they needed to survive lecture courses and undertake their own research. Chapter 6, "A Practical Lesson in How to Read a History Book," offered an early step-by-step guide to "gutting" a history monograph. With "creative" technique, one could acquire a thorough grasp of a secondary scholarly study in half-an-hour's time, primarily by concentrating upon introductions, conclusions, and topic sentences while avoiding the bulk of the prose. Following chapters on evidence and historical prose, the authors closed with a quick survey of "historiography and philosophy of history." The radical compression of topics hinted at the difficulties that could appear in the classroom.[16]

For those attempting to integrate all three of historiography's possible applications—methods, history of discourse, and philosophical analysis—in a single semester, the strain could be severe. In the late sixties, Robert D. Cross described Columbia's compulsory course as "an uneasy balance between methodology, historiography, and the philosophy of history." By 1970, when Walter Rundell Jr. published *In Pursuit of American History,* a survey of graduate training that doubled as a jeremiad, the courses had grown increasingly segregated and specialized. Methods and historical literature increasingly were taught as an aspect of a specific field. One learned research method in the research seminar on American Progressivism; one learned historiography in a colloquium that surveyed important writings on American slavery; one learned philosophy of history not at all or else in a specialized course on great thinkers in sociology or literature. According to the unhappy Rundell, most graduate programs had turned to specialized topical seminars rather than general historiography courses that stressed source criticism: "When professors hold widely diverging views on methodological training, the danger exists . . . that some students may escape this training altogether."[17]

Whatever vocabularies Turner and his students had used to describe those early seminar sessions, the days had gone in which a single course would smoothly blend philosophy of history, older monographs, and serious investigation of archival materials. Those three different historiographic practices had once fit into a single linguistic and practical space, but by the 1960s, discipline had taken its toll. The sort of breezy generalist work common in Victorian scholarship in the United States had come to look like amateurism. The time had past in which one would write a twenty-eight-page dissertation, in longhand, as Turner had done, or confidently set out Droysen's *Historik* as a text for explicating and legitimating the analysis of census data. Scholars truly engaged with Hegel or similar authors found new specialties for their work and began to speak with greater frequency of "philosophy of history" or "history and theory." And the accumulation of specialties, collections, and monographs meant that even the most energetic scholar could no longer keep abreast of the scholarly literature within a single field, let alone across fields. Was it really possible to offer a "general" introduction to source criticism when different fields could use sources so far apart? Mastering the National Archives was of little instrumental value to the medievalist who needed to polish her Latin. Reading Dilthey in translation offered little utility to the social historian anxious to collate data from early modern tax rolls. The physical separation of source criticism and research from serious reflection on historical discourse was more nearly a logistical necessity than a philosophical demand, but the separation of source criticism from critical historiographic work could have more subtle consequences.

Historiography spent a century gradually expanding its usage to encompass *historiology;* now its usage began to constrict. Historiography courses grew more specialized, and the number of courses actually introducing students to classics of historical literature declined, but the profession held on to a vague expectation that students would learn a simple creation tale that stretched from the origins of historical thinking (located anywhere from Herodotus to Herder) to the emergence of history as a discipline in nineteenth-century Germany and culminated in one's favorite (and usually American) predecessors. Insofar as the remaining courses on the history of historical discourse placed source criticism at the center of historiographic progress, they complemented the more numerous courses in which graduate students learned to do their own specialized research. At worst, the historiography course was an empty formal exercise allowing its professor to rant at length upon a topic in which he (seldom she) had little or no special competence.[18] At best, it introduced students to a wide range of important texts and encouraged them to think historically—and critically—even of history.

In the late 1980s I was an undergraduate student at the University of California, Riverside, and one of the last for whom History 102: Historiography was a required course. My experience there was probably fairly representative. It was a lecture course taught by an older British historian, who organized the syllabus along fairly traditional lines by mixing treatises on method with overarching narratives of discursive evolution. Ernst Breisach's textbook, *Historiography,* was the core text, and the lectures followed that book's organization fairly closely. I can also remember reading E.H. Carr's *What Is History?* And our essay assignment was also a holdover: we were to read the entire works of a single historian. (My professor was not stodgy—he allowed me to write on Bernard DeVoto.) The course was not a popular one. The materials were not sexy, and few lecturers kindle the flames of undergraduate excitement with such topics as the Magdeburg Centuries. But once the quarter had ended, even those students who hated the course grudgingly confessed that the experience and reading had been useful. That did not prevent the department from removing His102 from the list of courses required for the major. With that move, the University of California, Riverside, joined the mainstream of American departments of history, most of which had done away with the course many years earlier.[19]

The reasons for the disappearance of Introduction to Historiography are legion. Given the traditional resistance of most professional historians to anything approaching philosophical reflection, it is a surprise that the course was ever offered anywhere; its disappearance is less surprising than the fact of its existence. Nor can we safely imagine that there existed a hard, reliable core of "historiographic contents" in such courses—the label was sufficiently general that virtually anything could happen. In the sixties, some of those who demanded an end to the historiography requirement were actually student radicals who believed the course too frequently served as a site of ideological production. By the late seventies, many historians had a somewhat different reason for objecting to historiography courses—in such places students might be exposed to theory, especially of the feminist and French post-structural varieties, and thereby lose their enthusiasm or fitness for doing "real" history.

Something was clearly cutting into history. In 1960, history had been one of the three most popular undergraduate majors in the United States. Between 1971 and 1980, the number of American undergraduates majoring in history declined 57 percent.[20] During the restructuring of the university system in the 1970s and '80s, job lines were hard to come by and historiography could appear to both radicals and conservatives alike as a politically suspect luxury. By the end of the 1980s, historiography as an undergraduate requirement and a job specialty verged on extinction. A survey in fall 2000 of course catalogues from the top twenty-five departments of history in the United States found only two that required its majors to take a historiography course. No major department had advertised a tenure-track position in historiography since the early seventies.[21]

Historiography's disappearance was untimely. Even if students, lacking a background in the history of historical discourse, still could learn the rudiments of source criticism in occasional exercises in lecture courses or specialized seminars, such exercises threatened to become ahistorical. And the disappearance of classics of historical literature and philosophy of history—or rather their removal to specialized corners—could incline history toward anti-intellectualism. The intellectual upheavals of the late 1960s and the 1970s—structuralism, post-structuralism, feminism, postcolonialism, and multiculturalism—hit campus just as departments of history eliminated the one place in the curriculum that seemed especially adaptable to engagement with such a variety of topics. If history students were to learn anything about any of these innovations, they would have to do so as individuals and specialists, picking up a piece here or there from other departments, depending upon their course schedules and personal inclinations.

Engagement with classic historical literature and philosophy of history did not end with historiography courses, much less with the decline in the popularity of the actual word. But it did divide itself into two distinct traditions. In one, reflection or historicization of historical practice became a sort of beginner's task, to be carried out as briefly and unself-consciously as possible, separated off from real historical work in a few prefatory and invariably Whiggish paragraphs. In the other, reflection became a specialty all its own. Or more accurately, rigorous historiographic discussion threatened to become a subspecialty of a subspecialty, namely, modern European intellectual history or, more recently, South Asian history.

The lexical shift has implications aside from questions of curriculum. In the usage of most professional historians, the shift away from *historiography* to *history and theory* implies that history is one thing and theory quite another. Where the single term *historiography* subsumed a wide range of meanings, *history and theory* may put events and writing on one side and reflection on another—*history and theory* easily slips into *history* or *theory*. In everyday practice, the separation of history and theory frequently translates into divisions of intellectual labor and narrative form. Many who identify as "working historians" treat theory as a mysterious black box filled with occult instruments. From time to time, we might run over and pull out some specific theoretical tool and then scurry back to history to see if it can be applied. In such applications, *theory* typically shows up in an introduction or an occasional present-tense sentence or paragraph stuck amid the larger narrative flow. For historians who think of themselves as theorists, the separation of history from theory is equally useful, since it allows them to imagine what they do as a practice more rarefied than the dismal fact-grubbing of their colleagues. For them, theory is different from—and somehow better than—simple intellectual history. The creation and maintenance of theory thus serves both philic and phobic tendencies even as it reflects and facilitates the bureaucratization of our intellectual life. We might expect all historians to do historiography, but we cannot have the same expectation about theory.

The shift from *historiography* to *theory* has also made it easier for both historians and theorists to avoid historicizing their own preferred practice. Those who identify as "working" or "real" historians routinely excoriate "theorists" for writing obscure, ahistorical treatises in the present tense, but "real" history has not been routinely rigorous about imagining its own pasts. Against the ahistorical senses of *theory* stand equally ahistorical varieties of *practice*. As Walter Rundell noted, historians have long responded to demands for theoretical reflection with a simple but effective Deweyan rejoinder: one learns history through practice rather than through speculation. But as Dewey would have reminded us, we cannot responsibly beg the question of where "practice" comes from. Historical discourse is the one subject we refrain from historicizing; instead we teach modern research method as if it were the stuff of timeless revelation. Despite an eternal round of "new histories," our historical sense of both theory and practice remains fairly rudimentary. Lacking a mediating third term, we suspend history between theory on the one hand, and practice on the other, and then leave each of these terms thoroughly unhistoricized. We may practice new historicisms, but our sense of scholarly selfhood remains, as Lowie once said of civilization, a "thing of shreds and patches."[22] We piece together our intellectual genealogies from bits of hall talk, salacious gossip, random grad school memories, oral legend, and chronicles culled from oral exam lists, the entirety wrapped in decorative but transient jargon.

The story of historiography, then, is partly the story of the inability of scholarly discourse to develop a third term or space that mediates theory and praxis. Although I do believe that the shift from *historiography* to *history and theory* facilitated intellectual bureaucratization and segregation, I do not believe that a simple return would restore a golden age of intellectual community, or even that a "return" to historiography is possible. As far as the word goes, we may doubt that *historiography*, a term with a thoroughly checkered past, has much of a future. As far as curriculum, there are signs, if only in the form of a number of new teaching texts, of new interest in teaching the history of historical practice, if only under some other rubric.[23] We should hope for a more engaging and dialogical course than the cold war curriculum that dominated our postwar historiography. As a logistical matter, however, it is much easier to reduce than to increase requirements for graduate and undergraduate study, and bureaucratic inertia alone makes it unlikely that we will see a dramatic rise in the number of departments of history requiring historiography. As for that unlovely word, when colleagues ask about my research, I tell them I am hard at work on a book about history and theory.

TWO From *Philosophy* to *Theory*

In the 1990s, pundits announced that, after decades spent wandering in the formalist wilderness, the human sciences had taken a historical turn. After nearly a century of functionalism, behaviorism, structural linguistics, and other hopeless expeditions in search of timeless axioms of cultural order, humanists and social scientists had finally come to their historical senses. One might reasonably expect philosophy of history to figure prominently in academia's return to historical consciousness, and the titles of at least two important books in history and theory—Frank Ankersmit and Hans Kellner's anthology, *A New Philosophy of History* (1995), and Ewa Domenska's collection of interviews, *Encounters: Philosophy of History after Postmodernism* (1999)—seemed to promise as much. But of the twenty-four authors or interviewees represented in these works, only Arthur Danto was a professional philosopher.[1] Asked to speak to the future of the philosophy of history, Danto replied, "The subject so far has been pretty marginal." As editor of the flagship *Journal of Philosophy,* he estimated contributions on "any aspect" of the philosophy of history at "a rate of one per thousand submissions." He could not recollect a single important title in philosophy of history more recent than the midseventies.[2] A brief survey of the top ten ranked departments of philosophy in the United States in the fall of 2000 confirmed Danto's intuition. Only one had any permanent faculty listing philosophy of history as a research interest. None listed a philosophy of history course in their 2000–2001 catalogues.[3] At the end of the twentieth century, it appeared that American philosophers rarely thought about philosophy of history, and historians had more than matched that disinterest. Few historians had much contact with modern philosophy, and fewer still had the technical competence to seriously engage much of the last century's worth of analytical philosophy. Today, it remains unusual to hear a historian use *philosophy of history* in a sentence. Instead, *history and theory* has become the terminology of choice.

How do we get a "new" philosophy of history in which philosophers seldom participate? How did we go from *philosophy of history* to *history and theory*?

We do not yet have a monographic account of the philosophy of history in the twentieth century, but something like a standard story is beginning to emerge in hall talk, prefatory statements, and brief synoptic gestures. Michael Roth's introduction to *History and ... Histories within the Human Sciences* (1995) is a fair example. In this account, after nearly a century of assaults on history as a mushy, unscientific inquiry, literary criticism, anthropology, sociology, and even philosophy began to think again about history. As a result, the human sciences had begun to think more carefully about what *historical knowing* means. But *historical knowing* had its own history, and philosophy of history was a prime example. Between the 1940s and 1960s, philosophers concentrated upon history as a "form of knowledge." Carl Hempel's 1942 article "The Function of General Laws in History" set the tone. Hempel had made two key claims: First, scientific explanations worked by subsuming specific events under general, or covering, laws. Second, historical explanation did—or must, if it was to be scientific—meet the same logical criteria. For two decades, philosophers and historians argued over whether historical discourse did, could, or should employ covering laws. In the late 1960s, however, philosophers shifted to a focus on history as "a kind of writing." Thus did philosophy of history turn from logical analysis to literary theory. In Roth's words, analytical philosophy had taken "a linguistic turn." Or as Ankersmit and Domenska put it, philosophy of history had turned toward "aesthetics." The bibliographic essay appended to *A New Philosophy of History* even offered a brief, Whiggish genealogy of the new aestheticism that began with J.G. Droysen and Friedrich Nietzsche.[4]

Where the standard story stresses aestheticism as the major player in the transformation of philosophy of history, an alternative account concentrates upon changes in philosophical conceptions of science. In "The Decline and Fall of the Analytical Philosophy of History," Arthur Danto told a story that began at the same point as Roth's but led to a very different ending. Hempel's 1942 article effectively marked the origin of analytical philosophy of history. For some twenty years, philosophers of history fought over covering laws, but that ended in the 1960s with the reception of Thomas Kuhn's *Structure of Scientific Revolutions* (1962). In place of Hempel's account of scientific reason governed by predictive syllogisms, Kuhn offered a science governed by the messy, workaday business of inquiry. Danto did not believe that Kuhn had convinced everyone that the covering law model was incorrect or logically flawed; he had simply made it seem irrelevant. Philosophers had moved away from a "world according to Hempel," oriented to debates over whether or not historical discourse did or could construct the sort of covering laws that defined scientific explanation, to a "world according to Kuhn," in which even science looked historical. That world held little room for analytical philosophy of history.[5]

Both of these tales began in 1942 and ended in the 1960s. In the aesthetic narrative, literary theory effectively dispensed with the logicians' debates; in the science story, history of science did so. Either story might explain the end of analytical philosophy of history, and each might complement the other. But since other forms of analytical philosophy, including analytical philosophy of science, continued on their merry way, the decline of the analytical philosophy of history still seems fairly mysterious. The 1960s were, after all, the years in which Richard Rorty's anthology, *The Linguistic Turn* (1967), made that phrase popular; and analytical philosophers from Nelson Goodman to Donald Davidson did some of their best and most famous work in the 1970s.[6]

Why was analytical philosophy of *history* so vulnerable to literary critics and historians of science? How could language and linguistics come to be identified with aesthetics? And what precisely is the relation between these tales of two cultures?

As it turns out, neither of our standard stories can give us a compelling answer to those questions. And where our standard stories place the key moment in the late 1960s and the 1970s, my story is going to focus on the events that immediately preceded the celebrated revolutions that brought literary criticism and social construction to philosophy of history. Instead of giving a rational reconstruction of the arguments that defined philosophy of history between 1942 and 1962, I mean to track the linguistic changes that made *philosophy of history* possible. This will be a history of a two semantic shifts: in the 1940s a phrase given up as a dead letter returned as both a genre of best-sellers and a new academic specialty; in the early 1960s, *history and theory* displaced *philosophy of history.* Those events were not merely rhetorical. Philosophy of history emerged from midcentury debates about science and liberalism and dissolved, little more than two decades later, in a remarkable set of theoretical disputes over aesthetics and ideology. By the early seventies, history had been effectively expelled from the "sciences," and philosophy of history had been exiled by leading departments of philosophy.

When Henri Berr and Lucien Febvre contributed the essay "History" to the 1937 edition of the *Encyclopedia of the Social Sciences,* they referred only briefly to "philosophy of history." The phrase had been tainted by association with Christian theology and German idealism, but "if the term is in bad repute it is because of the use which has been made of it; the concept is still legitimate." They noted that in Germany, where the phrase remained current, practitioners distinguished *materiale Geschich-*

tsphilosophie, which "pretends to disentangle the skein of history," from *formale Geschichtsphilosophie,* which reflected upon historical discourse and involved the study of *Geschichtslogik.* The distinction, though, had no common counterpart in English, and although later writers would indeed speak of "material " and "formal" philosophy of history, it is no accident that this account ran only a few apologetic paragraphs and was written by two French historians about German philosophical scholarship.[7]

As a phrase, *philosophy of history* reaches back at least to Voltaire's *philosophie de l'histoire.* Despite that Enlightenment pedigree, *philosophy of history* has had a checkered career in American academic and popular discourse. American historians have seldom shown informed interest in any sort of philosophy. *History,* on the other hand, has long had a tenuous place in departments of philosophy. As Bruce Kuklick has noted, the disciplining of philosophy in the United States turned, to a great degree, upon the displacement of a nineteenth-century tradition, often Hegelian and broadly historicist, rooted as deeply in local philosophical societies and theological seminaries as in the universities. The move out of the provinces and into the profession was largely a move out of history. Unlike their German counterparts, American academic philosophers in the early twentieth century did not suffer through a crisis of historicism simply because, aside from Josiah Royce or John Dewey, few of the major figures invested in historical accounts of philosophical practice, let alone claimed to be historicists. Even the phrase *philosophy of history* was rare. Many academics associated it with the German metaphysics they had put behind them, not least because of John Sibree's Victorian translation of Georg W. F. Hegel's *Philosophy of History.*[8]

Prior to World War II, few works in English claimed to be philosophy of history. J. G. Droysen's *Grundriss der Historik* was translated into English in 1897 and found a readership among historians, but then Droysen had claimed that his study was "not a Philosophy of History." Benedetto Croce's *Teoria e storia della storiografia* was translated into English in 1920 and delighted many readers with its carefully italicized claim that *"philosophy of history is dead."* Michael Oakeshott's 1933 book, *Experience and Its Modes,* had included a remarkable chapter on "historical experience," but Oakeshott referred to "philosophy of history" as a "hybrid and homeless form of thought." Raymond Aron's important 1938 text, *Introduction à la philosophie de l'histoire,* did not appear in English translation until 1961 and so had little circulation in the United States and England. In 1938 Maurice Mandelbaum's *Problem of Historical Knowledge* used the phrase only in brackets and specifically to refer to what he saw as outmoded teleologies. He called his own book a "methodological inquiry." In England, R.G. Collingwood was hard at work upon a manuscript at the time of his death in 1940, but *The Idea of History* was not released until 1946. It immediately became the single most important English-language work in philosophy of history, but significantly, Collingwood did not attempt to clear a field of inquiry that might correspond to the phrase *philosophy of history.* As Louis Mink has noted, in Collingwood's mature usage, *philosophy* and *history* were essentially the same thing. Virtually no English language text prior to the Second World War used *philosophy of history* to refer to epistemological or analytical practices. *Philosophy of history,* in brackets more often than not, designated metaphysics, plain and simple.[9]

As a disciplinary specialty in Canada, Great Britain, and the United States, philosophy of history was a postwar novelty. When William H. Walsh, Collingwood's successor at Oxford, published his *Philosophy of History: An Introduction* in 1951, he opened with this sentence: "A writer on philosophy of history, in Great Britain at least, must begin by justifying the very existence of his subject." So, he asked, "if philosophy of history is thus generally despised, why venture to revive it?" Walsh's first response to this hypothetical objection was quintessentially midcentury and instrumentalist—traditional philosophy of history had not ended with Hegel but rather had continued on in Spengler, Toynbee, and importantly, Marx. Walsh did not linger over the political implications, but hurried on to a more academic justification for his subject, namely, that philosophy of history was the natural counterpart to the respected field of philosophy of science. But even slow readers could grasp the subtext—that one should study philosophy of history in order to understand the world-historic struggle between communism and liberalism.[10]

Philosophy of History distinguished two types of philosophizing. Just as the word *history* had two common meanings, one referring to the "totality of past human actions" and the other to the "narrative account of those actions," so too did philosophy of history divide into "speculative" and "critical" halves. The first, properly rejected by most philosophers, attempted to construct metaphysical accounts of the totality of human events; the second dealt empirically with the attempts of professional historians to scientifically reconstruct the human past. These types of theorizing appeared to reiterate the political division between communist dogma and democratic science, but Walsh stepped gingerly when it came to speculative philosophy of history. He did not demonize Marx or deny the potential usefulness of theories that attempted to elaborate "the meaning of history." The question of whether certain factors, such as the economic, were the key causal agents in historical process struck Walsh as a question for professional historians rather than philosophers.

Walsh's 1951 publication was not quite the first to survey the conceptual frontier between professional philosophy of history and priestcraft. Morton G. White's 1950 essay "Toward an Analytic Philosophy of History" distinguished between a "Toynbeean, speculative" study and "an analytical philosophy of history." The distinction paralleled C. D. Broad's formula of "speculative" and "critical," or Rudolf Carnap's "metaphysics" and "logical analysis," and suggested a proper object of philosophical inquiry: "The analytic philosopher ought to approach history as a mode of discourse, as a kind of language which needs clarification." Historical discourse itself divided into at least two kinds of expressions. The first, *object-language,* involved names and phrases that historians used when writing directly about the object of their investigation, such as *the Renaissance.* The second, *metalanguage,* involved those terms and sentences specifically employed to discuss actual historical writing, such as *history* or *chronicle*. White described this second metalanguage of the historian—"metahistorical expression"—as the most likely field in which philosophers could contribute to historical study. Since few philosophers had the competence to intervene in debates over such object-language terms as *the Renaissance,* "the major, though not the sole task of the analytic philosopher of history, is that of defining or clarifying terms in *metahistory*." For White, analytical philosophy of history was to be part of what Gustav Bergmann, three years later, called the "linguistic turn."[11]

At the outset, then, postwar philosophy of history offered itself as a new analytical or critical practice distinct from the old Hegelian and Spenglerian metaphysics. White's essay had nothing like the impact of Walsh's text, and it took a decade for *analytical* to acquire the same adjectival popularity as *critical*. Those grounded in the British idealist tradition, from Walsh to Louis O. Mink, called their practice "critical" philosophy of history. Those trained in the post-Wittgensteinian linguistic tradition, from Carl Hempel to Morton White, spoke of the "analytical" philosophy of history. Together, though, these linguistic innovations, dividing analytical and critical from speculative philosophy of history, were unusually successful and helped to recuperate *philosophy of history* as a phrase while defining the bounds of philosophy of history as a field.

We should mark the moment, since most efforts to create a new field or specialty fail, and it is especially rare for such a movement to resuscitate an archaic label. But by 1965 two other books with the title *Philosophy of History* graced library bookshelves, one a textbook by Walsh's student William H. Dray, the other a teaching anthology edited by Alan and Barbara Donagan. Each emphasized the difference between critical and speculative philosophies of history.[12] Philosophy of history had become a recognized specialty with its own practitioners, problems, and even a realistic hope of reaching a popular audience.

The separation of critical and speculative philosophy of history quickly became canonical, in part because popular culture of the period invested so heavily in historical metaphysics. In the twenties and thirties, such writers as Oswald Spengler had served as objects of ridicule, but after the war, universal history and speculative historicisms found a place in the spotlights. Even a brief chronicle of titles makes the point plain. A two-volume abridgement of Arnold J. Toynbee's *A Study of History* made the best-seller lists in 1947. The homiletics of neoorthodox theologian Reinhold Niebuhr earned him a place on the cover of *Time* in 1948, and the following year his *Faith and History* hit the stores. In 1950 Roderick Seidenburg's *Posthistoric Man* argued that the world had entered into a new posthistoric era of bureaucratic stasis. In 1959 Norman O. Brown's *Life Against Death* built Freud's notion of the death instinct into a universal history of the nuclear age. Nor did celebratory accounts of progress disappear entirely, for in 1960 Walt Rostow's modernization theory decorated weeklies. The market was sufficiently robust that it stimulated the translation of a variety of important texts in the continental tradition. The variety here was remarkable, ranging from the 1949 edition of Karl Löwith's *Meaning in History,* with its account of the theological origins of historical materialism, to Franz Rosenthal's 1959 translation of Ibn Khaldun's *Muqaddimah: An Introduction to History.* C.J. Friedrich introduced Dover's 1956 paperback edition of Hegel's *Philosophy of History* with the claim that "there is at present a vastly increased interest in the 'philosophy of history,'" although even Friedrich viewed that development as so novel that he enclosed the phrase in quotes.[13]

Critiques of speculative historicizing also made best-sellers out of academic authors from Isaiah Berlin to Daniel Bell. Here, the division of philosophy of history into critical and speculative halves frankly served to align liberal science against communist metaphysics. In 1944 the first portion of Karl Popper's *Poverty of Historicism* appeared in the journal *Economica;* and in 1945 his sequel, *The Open Society and Its Enemies,* found a mass audience and reviews in the glossies. Seven years later Popper dedicated the trade edition of *The Poverty of Historicism* to the "memory of the countless men and women of all creeds or nations or races who fell victims to the fascist and communist belief in Inexorable Laws of Historical Destiny." By 1961 Popper's polemic had gone through three editions, and in 1964 Harper Torchbooks released a paperback edition. Although most philosophers avoided Popper's highly idiosyncratic use of *historicism* as a synonym for *metaphysics,* other aspects of his account had more impact. By the early sixties it had become common to follow Popper's lead in describing speculative philosophies of history as a category mistake: the displacement of the logic of scientific inquiry, which required predictive laws, onto the substance of historical events.[14]

Such titles suggest the way that philosophy of history articulated with global discourses. We will not successfully insulate the 1956 reissue of Hegel's *Lectures* from period concerns with the cold war state, much less separate the 1959 translation of Khaldun's *Muqaddimah* from decolonization or even neocolonialism. Nor should we imagine the debates in philosophy of history as simple responses to the real events of the cold war. Popper's work was not a response to the cold war—his attempt to provide a clear, principled division between ideology and science was also an attempt to provide a clear, principled division between epistemic practices under totalitarianism and those under Western democracies. Certainly the new academic specialty of philosophy of history could not detach itself from these broader semantic fields. At any moment, philosophy of history could suddenly break away from disciplined inquiry and shoot toward either *Pravda* or the *Reader's Digest.* So far as professional philosophy was concerned, it was hard to say which was worse: the totalizing biases of speculative philosophy of history or its success on the book club circuit. If the popularity of *philosophy of history* made it possible to use the phrase in polite company, it also forced academics at cocktail parties to point to Toynbee or Marx and declare, "I am a philosopher of history, but this is precisely the sort of thing that I do *not* do." As William Dray stated in his Prentice-Hall textbook, *Philosophy of History,* "It was *Time* and *Life* magazines, rather than serious academic journals, which received Toynbee's *Study of History* with enthusiasm." But that complaint became one of the specialty's defining anxieties. As late as 1965, Arthur C. Danto's magisterial *Analytical Philosophy of History* devoted an introductory chapter to distinguishing its subject from "substantive philosophy of history" or "philosophical history" à la Hegel and Marx. The need for the adjectives suggests the continuing concern for separation from various popular and subversive alternatives.[15]

Public interest in universal history made it impossible for philosophy of history to break entirely free of its speculative other. "Critical" and "analytical" discourse continued to parasitize the older forms, partly because of the sort of boundary construction that allows a community to create an identity for itself, but also because of other forms of sustenance. The rapid expansion of the postwar university system and the emergence of a boom market in paperbound books facilitated the recuperation of *philosophy of history*. At the most vulgar level, the phrase could circulate in numbers and at speeds unimaginable just fifteen years earlier. No longer relegated to the dustiest corner of the research library, *philosophy of history* spun around on the racks at the corner drugstore. As late as 1965 such philosophers as Morton White and Jack W. Meiland found major publishers for technical works in philosophy of history. Walt Rostow was a player in national policy; Isaiah Berlin gave a seminar on philosophy of history to the Kennedy White House; and a young Henry Kissinger (who had written his Harvard undergraduate thesis on Toynbee, Spengler, and Kant) decorated his essays on nuclear strategy with allusions to universal history. On campus, that sort of popular interest helped serious analytical philosophy of history to find a space in the curriculum as students fresh from skimming Toynbee or Niebuhr leafed through course catalogues in search of electives. Ironically, a look at pedagogy suggests that the very popularity of philosophy of history helped to ensure its marginality as a scholarly enterprise, for the new field opened out between a speculative past and a positivist future.[16]

One of the ways that a specialty defines itself is through the creation of a canon for teaching as well as research, and here the metaphysicians evinced a remarkable staying power. Classroom dynamics seldom show themselves in the brief black-and-white lines of catalogues, but we may glean a sense of the possibilities from the sourcebooks. By the early 1960s, instructors could assign readings from among various anthologies. Patrick Gardiner's selections and introductory essays in *Theories of History* (1959) outlined a historical account of scientific development. The earliest modern philosophers of history, like Vico, had mixed speculative and critical approaches to history, but the story of philosophy of history was that of the increasing separation of speculation and analysis. Gardiner's text ended with the contemporary analytical tradition from Hempel to Morton White. The Donagan anthology, *Philosophy of History*, provided a similar storyline with a slightly more idealist flavor, opening with Collingwood's account of early Christian history and then excerpting great texts from Augustine to Hempel and Dray. Gardiner's book used *analytical* where the Donagans said *critical*, but each reinforced the division between modern scientific philosophy of history and the old metaphysical variety while still providing enough speculative moments to satisfy intellectual tourists.[17]

The textbooks also provided plenty of space for speculative interests. Both Walsh and Dray, despite their suspicion of metaphysics, devoted roughly half of their textbooks to exposition of metaphysicians past and present. Dray's 1965 text had a chapter each on Hegel, Toynbee, and Niebuhr. As he noted with some irritation, academics writing textbooks on philosophy of science did not feel a comparable need to include chapters on speculative cosmology. No text on philosophy of science would devote half its chapters to a respectful debunking of Aristotelian physics and Linnaean biology. But the philosophy of history texts did precisely that. Over and over, in tedious and repetitive detail, analytical philosophers identified the category mistakes, propositional leaps, and inductive meltdowns of Vico, Hegel, Marx, Spengler, Niebuhr, Toynbee, and, inevitably, each other. Unlike mainstream analytical philosophy, which constituted itself as a field of inquiry simply by expelling the metaphysicians from introductory courses in favor of scientized readings of more legitimately critical thinkers—Descartes, Hume, Locke, and Kant—analytical philosophy of history kept reprinting its speculative past.[18]

A comparison with other analytical textbooks of the period is instructive. William P. Alston's *Philosophy of Language* (1964) and Richard Rudner's *Philosophy of Social Science* (1965)—though published in the same Prentice-Hall series as Dray's textbook—devoted virtually no space to older, speculative philosophies in their fields. Alston, for instance, devoted only two introductory pages (out of 106) to "metaphysics." John Hospers's popular textbook, *An Introduction to Philosophical Analysis* (1953), did include a chapter titled "Some Metaphysical Problems" and another titled "The Philosophy of Religion," but *history* did not even appear in the book's index. The closest the textbook's many bibliographies came to a work in philosophy of history was Henri Bergson's *Creative Evolution.* The omissions reflected the antihistorical slant of linguistic analysis, but the failure of philosophy of history to overlap significantly with dominant problems of analytic philosophy at large did not augur well for the new specialty. Most philosophers imagined analytical philosophy of history as, at best, a minor subspecialty. Hempel, author of the single most important monograph in the area, described himself as a philosopher of science. Virtually no major departments in the United States hired philosophers of history, critical, analytical, or otherwise. Danto at Columbia and White at Harvard were exceptions, but each also published widely in fields remote from history. For continental philosophers, who were more likely to take history seriously, the situation was even worse, as major departments purged their faculties of specialists in what many regarded as an antiquarian exercise in the reconstruction of intellectual error.[19] A closer look at logical positivism, the most conspicuously "analytical" philosophy of history, is telling.

The very label *positivism* raised questions. Although many historians have come to use the term casually, as a synonym for vulgar empiricism of the sort frequently (if glibly) attributed to von Ranke—in which the historian ostensibly eschewed hypothesis and theory in order to let the plain facts speak for themselves—the word had often pointed in very different directions. August Comte's sociological work in search of "positive laws" of social development had arrived in English translation as a program of positivism in sociology, and it did not take long for the word to surface in pejorative as well as probative ways. Still another and somewhat different trajectory came out of the German Hegelian tradition, where the Frankfort school's suspicion of both Weberian sociology and analytic philosophy would surface in the 1960s as the *Positivismusstreit*. But by midcentury, the phrase *logical positivism* had gained some notoriety in English as a nomination for a particularly aggressive form of analytic philosophy that used language as a medium for placing philosophy on a sound scientific footing.[20]

Many English readers encountered the term through the popular work of analytic philosopher A. J. Ayer, who enthusiastically promoted the linguistic analysis of Wittgenstein and a cluster of other German and Austrian philosophers. Ayer's 1936 work, *Language, Truth and Logic*, helped to launch its author as a public intellectual, and Ayer worked to promote his own, sometimes idiosyncratic translation of the new scientific approach to philosophy. In a popular teaching anthology titled

Logical Positivism (1959), Ayer described the movement as one devoted to the destruction of the lingering metaphysical tendencies of both the idealist and British empirical traditions. The key essay, Rudolf Carnap's "Overcoming of Metaphysics through Logical Translation of Language" (1931), argued that all metaphysical claims (Carnap employed Martin Heidegger's recent work as example) were really pseudostatements, as they could neither be tested empirically nor fitted into a class of sentences that were true in and of themselves, such as tautologies. Instead, such sentences were simply meaningless. For the flamboyantly atheistic Ayer, this sort of philosophy offered the possibility of cleansing English and other languages of all sorts of spiritual residue.[21]

It was not always easy to tell what counted as logical positivism, as many of those associated with the movement disagreed on basic issues or even rejected the label itself. The overweening scientism of logical positivism, though, remained constant regardless of its forms of expression. In the Vienna Circle, an informal seminar presided over by Carnap and others, the fierce pursuit of metaphysics became so intent that, whenever an analysis appeared to stray into error, critics would shout out "Metaphysik" or, eventually, simply "M!" Introduced by such colorful anecdotes, logical positivism and its sometimes synonyms—*logical analysis, logical empiricism,* or at times simply *empiricism*—materialized in English-language philosophy as an aggressive, rigorous, and purifying linguistic force with a strong antihistorical edge.[22] The antihistorical flavor of the new positivism drew partly upon tone and partly upon actual semantics. The ruthless dismantling of philosophical tradition struck a particularly modern chord, but more than this, logical positivism seemed to open little hope for a serious historiography. If mathematics and theoretical physics were the best models of cognition, then historical writing would have to change dramatically. Since the verification of empirical statements depends on actions that take place in the present or the future, statements about the past could seem suspiciously squishy. In his best-selling text *Language, Truth and Logic,* Ayer even appeared to cast doubt on the very possibility of verifying any past event. Later editions would retreat from some of the original's incautious language, but there seemed little doubt that present and future, rather than the past, constituted the key temporal realm for linguistic analysis.[23]

The radical futurity of the new sense of scientific method probably surfaced most clearly in the very few writings on philosophy of history contributed by any of the authors associated with logical positivism. Ironically, two figures from the periphery of logical positivism would prove most influential in the subfield of philosophy of history. In the 1934–35 issue of *Economica,* Karl Popper argued that scientific truth claims did not in fact work by verifying empirical propositions, since all empirical cases produced exceptions, ambiguous cases, and disputable data that always left verification a matter of some doubt. Instead of a fixed world of verified truths, science produced predictive hypotheses that might eventually be falsified and then discarded or amended, but never definitively settled. Popper would later extend this argument in spectacular and public ways, but few North American philosophers or historians took note of his effort in *Economica,* and by the time it appeared in English, as *The Logic of Scientific Discovery* (1959), he had been scooped. In 1942, Carl Hempel published a similar account as "The Function of General Laws in History" in the premier English-language journal, the *Journal of Philosophy,* and the covering law model became available just in time for the emergence of a new disciplinary specialty, philosophy of history.

Although it took a decade for the logical positivist account of historical explanation to really enter into the conversation, once there it fairly set the terms of debate.[24] This shift in focus and interest was important for the field, but it had its own ironies: At the moment that logical positivist accounts of language and science began coming under serious fire in other arenas, one of their variants became a key element of philosophy of history. From roughly 1952 forward, *analytical philosophy of history* meant essentially one thing: endorsement or criticism of the covering law account of scientific explanation as set forth in Carl Hempel's 1942 article. The various other works suggested by Morton White in 1950 never became part of the canon. White had singled out Morris R. Cohen's *Meaning of Human History* (1947) for praise, but Cohen's work effectively disappeared from 1950s debates in philosophy of history. And of the analytic thinkers listed in White's footnotes, only two, Hempel and Popper, found their way into the important arguments, let alone textbooks. The others—Rudolf Carnap, Gottlob Frege, Alfred Tarski, and W. V. O. Quine—loomed large in philosophy of language, science, and even social science, but in history they remained minor figures whose influence was highly mediated. Even works that seemed directly relevant to history—Elizabeth Anscombe's *Intention* (1950) or Quine's *From a Logical Point of View* (1953) or Peter Winch's *Idea of a Social Science* (1958)—went missing. By the early 1960s, analytical philosophy of history whirled compulsively round the covering law model and pushed other analytical matters to the periphery.[25]

The dominance of logical positivist philosophy of science had several effects on the philosophy of history. For a start, the covering law debate provided a clear set of problems and thus a research program. Concentrating upon a handful of figures—Hempel, Popper, and possibly Nagel—kept the conversation moving in something like a straight line. The analytical or critical portions of arguments, seminars, and lecture courses could be turned into an extended debate between the covering law theorists and those "intentionalists" or "rationalists" who stressed the reconstruction of the intentions of human agents. An entire course could be reduced to two founding texts: Hempel's "Function of General Laws in History" and Collingwood's *Idea of History.* By redescribing Collingwood along narrowly epistemological lines as a preemptive response to logical positivist accounts of historical knowledge, critical philosophy of history avoided the English idealist's embarrassing claim that there was no justifiable boundary "between epistemology and metaphysics." (Which meant, by extension, that there was no ground for distinguishing "critical" from "speculative" philosophy of anything.) By excluding other problems in analytical philosophy—over, say, Quinean meaning holism, or Wittgensteinian arguments about "events-under-description"—the new specialty kept its conversations under control. Significantly, the excluded voices were precisely those that criticized the logical positivist notions of language and scientific inquiry. As a result, philosophy of history naturalized logical positivist conceptions of scientific method.

An endless series of monographs in philosophy of history argued for or against the applicability of the covering law model to historical discourse, but all tacitly accepted the general model as normative for science. Philosophers of history never asked whether the covering law model was in fact generalizable—an important question since many of the physical sciences—biology, for instance—seemed much closer in actual practice to the sort of hermeneutic enterprises common in historical inquiry. Instead, philosophers of history simply assumed the validity of the positivist account and then proceeded to their real concern: does or can or should historical discourse meet the logical positivist criteria for scientific explanation? In other words, is history a science? The image of science projected by philosophy of history thus verged on a pop culture stereotype. *Science* meant those practices most removed from interpretive inquiry and likely to translate into spectacular forms of military hardware (namely, theoretical physics); and it meant those practices as interpreted by the most scientistic of available analytical accounts.

Ultimately, the acceptance of positivist understandings of scientific explanation helped many "critical" philosophers of history to shore up older varieties of humanism while still claiming to avoid metaphysics. The dynamic worked in this way: Critical philosophy of history stood speculative metaphysics to one side as an example of muddy thinking and totalitarian politics. But to the other side it placed positivist science and all it seemed to portend for historical inquiry—including the intellectual threats from behaviorism, functionalism, and (after the late 1950s) structuralism. Critical philosophy of history thus could represent itself as a last redoubt of freedom between two types of determinism, one metaphysical, one methodological. By the end of the fifties, those who denied the applicability of the covering law model to historical inquiry tended to justify their objections in suspiciously old-fashioned ways, and some began dredging the neo-Kantian gulf between the *Naturwissenschaften* and the *Geisteswissenschaften.* Claims about the "autonomy" of historical understanding or arguments that history was sui generis proliferated and often took the unanalytical form of moral exhortation. A positivist would argue that scientific explanation demanded covering laws; an intentionalist would reply that historians clearly did not use syllogisms in their prose; the positivist would respond that historians needed to reform their prose if they wished to be scientific; and the intentionalist, hard pressed, would retreat to *ought:* historians ought not to use covering laws.

Many philosophers of history found scientistic accounts of history as terrifying as communist metaphysics. When William Dray contended that his critical philosophy of history—which emphasized the rational reconstruction of the intentions of free historical agents—exemplified a "humane curiosity," he had Hempel as well as Marx in mind. The positivist desire to subsume human acts under natural laws was tyrannical in its own way, and behaviorists could threaten rationality as thoroughly as Stalinists. "Even if we are not libertarians," said Dray, "we are ourselves, and believe others to be, agents.... My chief complaint against acceptance of the covering law doctrine in history is not the difficulty of operating it, in either fully deductive or mutilated form. It is rather that is sets up a kind of *conceptual barrier* to a humanistically oriented historiography." Other varieties of analytical philosophy had humanists and conservatives aplenty, but it is difficult to imagine Quine or Anscombe anchoring a semantic analysis with such an appeal. But Dray's invocation was not unusual in philosophy of history. The tendency to concede the accuracy of the logical positivist account of scientific explanation while denying that history did or should follow the same course suggested yet another meaning for the continuing vitality of the speculative tradition. In sourcebooks, textbooks, and weekly glossies, Augustine, Hegel, Marx, and Toynbee helped to legitimize the critical philosopher's refusal to join other logicians in giving up the very traditional question of free will.[26]

So far as they followed any of these debates, historians in the fifties and early sixties tended to sympathize with the intentionalists, but few paid attention. Even the phrase *philosophy of history* seemed not to have lived up to its postwar promise. Having failed to find a place in the most dynamic conversations in academic philosophy, it found even less interest in departments of history. In 1962 Sydney Hook organized a conference at New York University to bring prominent historians and philosophers together. There was not much common ground. In his preface to the published proceedings, Hook observed that the difficulties extended to the most basic lexical level: "The subject was phrased as history *and* philosophy because of the ambiguity in the expression 'philosophy of history,' whose connotations embrace notions ranging from theology to epistemology." The problem wasn't just that historians largely ignored the covering law debates. Even the crucial distinction of *critical* or *analytical* versus *speculative* philosophy of history eluded them. In his 1965 book, *History: Professional Scholarship in America,* John Higham surveyed the recent interest in philosophy of history, but lumped Hempel with Hegel as he described all approaches to the topic—from logical positivist to neoorthodox theological—as "theoretical and speculative." Critical philosophers of history must have been depressed to note that Higham was one of the most philosophically disposed historians of his generation; indeed he cited Walsh's *Philosophy of History.* But philosophy of history was running out of adjectives.[27]

Analytical and critical philosophy of history had made itself as dependent—and parasitic—upon logical positivism as upon speculative metaphysics. Each served as a conceptual border that defined what could count as a respectable critical position. In retrospect, it is easy to see the strategic mistake. Already besieged by ordinary language philosophy and Quinean neopragmatism, logical positivism would not long survive Kuhn's historicist account of scientific revolutions. Appeals to the "autonomy" of history or the "humane" qualities of historical inquiry would not impress behaviorists, functionalists, and structuralists, let alone the critics associated with feminist theory and post-structural linguistics. Having essentially conceded that history was not a science, and having failed to connect philosophy of history with the analytical debates that ran through Quine, Kuhn, and later, Donald Davidson, philosophy of history left itself only one place to turn: the ancient notion of history as Art.

Art was not what it had been. The Kantian habit of dividing the world into epistemic, ethical, and aesthetic thirds had always threatened to leave history homeless. But the rise of logical positivist models for defining the third of the universe accessible to scientific knowledge had also shifted the boundaries for ethical and aesthetic inquiry. If the logical positivist model appropriated by philosophy of history had attempted to shed epistemic claims of affect, it also had a related tendency, namely, to strip the "aesthetic" of any epistemic ambition. Carnap's *Logical Construction of the World* had made the point plain: Either one made scientific claims or one made art. Claims had be warranted scientifically, or they were meaningless. *Meaningless* did not mean "useless"—many of the purest logicians enjoyed a painting or musical performance—it was the mixing of aesthetic and scientific realms that led to trouble. Carnap, famously, had enjoyed Nietzsche's writing as an aesthetic performance while denouncing Heidegger's work as metaphysical twaddle. If one accepted the logician's broader claims about science, and if history could not reform itself along truly scientific lines, then there was no place for a discipline that claimed to blend science and art.

In 1960, debates over the disciplinary status of historical scholarship still recalled the Victorian and Edwardian disputes that had ranged the devotees of hard science, such as J. B. Bury, against the defenders of a belletristic tradition. In "Clio, A Muse," George M. Trevelyan had famously argued that history was both science and art, that its claim to artistic quality lay in its use of narrative, and that truly great history could thus transcend the changes of methodological fashion and the revelations of new empirical research. But the fights that materialized in the 1960s could take much nastier turns. In England, the famous "two cultures" exchange between chemist-turned-novelist C. P. Snow and the English professor F. R. Leavis served as a form of class warfare, as Snow held up the meritocratic and democratic models of the natural sciences against the reactionary gentility of Oxbridge humanities. In Germany, Theodor Adorno's critique of Karl Popper articulated a radical suspicion of the ideological tendencies of analytic philosophy of science. In North America the stakes were murkier, but here, too, the divide between science and art had deepened, and nowhere more than in philosophy of history.[28]

Historians and analytic philosophers may have spoken past one another, but the rise of social science discourse helped to guarantee the emergence of a certain amount of shared vocabulary. H. Stuart Hughes, in a series of essays attempting to mediate the clash between historians committed to older humanistic models and a younger generation enthusiastic about quantification and behavioral analysis, encouraged historians to assimilate the new vocabulary of *generalization, explanation,* and *causal reasoning*. But what the new analytic philosophy showed, he believed, was that art and science were not so far apart as many humanists feared. "History can become more scientific," he claimed, "without losing its aesthetic quality." That was a moderate and soothing judgment. But even Hughes conceded that the logical analysis and "mathematical modeling" of the new social sciences posed a far different challenge than had the old discursive models of Freud, Durkheim, and Weber. Since terms of art served as terms of allegiance to different communities of inquiry, the new vocabulary connoted more than a simple shift away from literary habits, for it suggested wildly different patterns of capitalization for research and pedagogy. A move out of logical analysis and into literary or art critical ways of speaking meant more than a simple swap of language games or a short trot across the quad to a shared High Table.[29]

Philosophy of history's inability to constitute its subject as a science according to the logical positivist model, and its continuing investments in old-fangled humanisms, made history an obvious target for critics. In 1962, when Claude Lévi-Strauss characterized history as "a method with no distinct object," he meant to highlight an invidious comparison with his own practice of structural linguistics, a science aimed at "discovering general laws." As one admirer observed, the new "modernist" approach to historical discourse created the possibility of writing "antihistory." In an important 1966 article, Hayden White argued that logical positivism's "expulsion" of history from the true sciences, and modern art's hostility toward historical consciousness, suggested that historians ought to revise the old Romantic notion of history as literature so as to participate in the "liberation of the present from *the burden of history.*" In a lengthy polemical reckoning of the new contest of the faculties, White pieced together an intellectual history of literary and artistic modernism's contempt for history and historians. History had lost its moral authority and its privileged place on campus because it no longer mediated, as once it had, between the natural sciences and art. History had always claimed to be both art and science, but the rise of new conceptions of scientific method, together with revolutions in the practice of the arts, had revealed the essential parochialism of the discipline: For historians, science materialized as a fetish of facts, while historical narratives clung to the realist novel as a model of presentation. Historians mixed eighteenth-century science with Victorian art. No wonder they had earned the contempt of physicists and artists alike.[30]

The obligation of the new generation of historians, White argued, was to follow the lead of the historians of the discipline's golden age—Tocqueville, Michelet, Burckhardt—who had taken up both the scientific and the artistic avant-garde of their day. For history in the 1960s, that meant accepting the logical positivist claim that science was simply hypotheses all the way down rather than a fixed or fixable body of knowledge. More important, it also meant picking up the glove thrown down by modernists from Schoenberg to Cage, Picasso to Proust, modeling historical discourse upon the fragmented aesthetics of high modernism and thereby returning history to its preeminent place as the discipline most responsible for revealing the truth of "man's fate." The result would relinquish the quaint Victorian notion of history as a mode of discourse that could be judged by its scientific contribution. No longer could historians credibly claim epistemic privilege. Rather, each must commit to choosing a dominant metaphor that could be taken up or dropped as the situation demanded, and those choices depended upon ethical and aesthetic rather than epistemic criteria.

Already in 1966 we can see the basic outlines of the story with which we began: the marginality of philosophy of history as a disciplinary practice; the naturalization of logical positivist conceptions of the scientific method; the endurance of older humanist investments; the imprint of cold war campus politics; the gradual demotion of logical analysis and the elevation of the metaphorical aspects of language; and the turn toward self-consciously aesthetic rather than epistemic criteria as guides for critical judgment. Here we have already in place the conditions of possibility for the redescription of historiography as a primarily aesthetic practice whose products are primarily literary artifacts. But we need to recognize an additional linguistic innovation with which these changes would be strongly associated. We should underscore, here, the provenance of White's manifesto, "The Burden of History." This article (which would eventually lead to a contract for an ambitious and provocative book, *Metahistory*) appeared not in the *American Historical Review,* nor in the *Journal of Philosophy,* but in a new specialty journal titled *History and Theory.*

By the early seventies, literary criticism had largely displaced logical analysis as the preferred form for theorizing historical discourse, and *theory* was the new keyword. In 1960 George Nadel began editing a new journal, *History and Theory,* based at Wesleyan, a small liberal arts college, which was the first specialized quarterly for philosophers of history.[31] We should linger, briefly, over the word choice. Neither Nadel nor anyone else was willing to call a journal by the name *Historiography,* and that fact might be reducible to the clunkiness of the word. But the avoidance of another obvious title is curious—to this day, there is no periodical in English that calls itself *Philosophy of History.* If *history and theory* offered to bridge history and philosophy as disciplines, it also avoided the unhappy middlebrow and totalizing connotations that *philosophy of history* carried in everyday English, even though Nadel intended the journal to define what could count as philosophy of history.

Theory in 1960 did not have the metaphysical baggage of *philosophy of history* and had not yet acquired its later associations with sixties radicalism. *Theory* sounded much more scientific, or at least social-scientific, than it would just twenty years later. *History and Theory* was sober, respectable, and modestly onomatopoeic. As Richard Vann has noted, *History and Theory* was one of the journals that helped to change the resonance of *theory* as the journal began moving away from analytical philosophy to behaviorist and structuralist social science and on to literary criticism. In the 1950s, the most influential studies of historical discourse were written by analytic philosophers who focused on logic while ignoring aesthetics; twenty years later the most influential studies of historical discourse were written by intellectual historians and literary theorists who concentrated upon aesthetics to the exclusion of logic.[32]

We need not linger, here, over the details of that final shift from *philosophy* to *theory* in North America. The story has been told often enough that the years between the emergence of *History and Theory* and the appearance of Hayden White's *Metahistory* (1973) have been chronicled with obsessive detail, if only in rational reconstructions mixed with memoir. We need only note that the horizon of possibility for those years had opened by the early 1960s: history could be treated as art, at least by its leading theorists. And as an aesthetic object, historical discourse found its metahistorians not in departments of philosophy but in literature, comparative literature, anthropology, and the intellectual history corner of the historian's guild. What sort of art was at issue? Hans Meyerhoff's 1959 anthology, *The Philosophy of History in Our Time,* had chosen the appropriate image for its cover: Pablo Picasso's *Guernica.* Modernism's notorious mistrust of history echoed in metahistorical discourse.

In retrospect, it is clear that one of the principal effects of philosophy of history's cold-war engagement with logical positivism and metaphysical speculation was to create the horizon of reception for structural linguistics and post-structuralist literary theory. Professional historians, most of whom had ignored the covering law controversy, found these new critiques sufficiently disconcerting that, in departments of history, the phrase *linguistic turn* quickly came to mean "structuralism" and "post-structuralism" rather than the German, British, and American "analytical philosophy," from Frege to Hempel, that had inspired the name. The "linguistic turn" became a "literary turn" and then, by century's end, an "aesthetic turn" that seemed to have no necessary connection to linguistic analysis.[33] The move from philosophy to theory could carry metahistorians from a hopelessly scientistic expectation for historical discourse to an equally narrow aestheticism.

THREE Going Native

HISTORY, *LANGUAGE*, AND CULTURE

Near the end of his 1989 book, *Soundings in Critical Theory,* intellectual historian Dominick LaCapra complained about a historiographic movement commonly identified as New Historicism or New Cultural History. LaCapra, who had been closely identified with the American reception of deconstruction and its emphasis upon close readings of canonical texts, found in the New Cultural History a "tendency to turn away from patient, subtle, and painstaking analysis of texts or particular artifacts" and even "to dismiss textual analysis as an anachronistic residue of bourgeois liberalism." In place of close reading, New Cultural History substituted a "weak montage" that used undertheorized conceptions of "culture" to glue together motley assemblages of high and low texts and artifacts. With this method, "contexts from popular, commodified, and high culture are reduced to set pieces, and their relations to texts are 'negotiated,' 'thought,' or 'stitched' together in a precious tableaux through relatively facile associationism, juxtaposition, or pastiche." Warming to his topic, LaCapra lamented the dilution of political critique by New Cultural History's dependence on conceptions of "power" and "ideology" that were so generalized as to result in a "gallows functionalism."[1]

As if in realization of the intellectual historian's worst fears, that very year the New Cultural History, rather than responding to LaCapra's criticisms, simply swallowed him whole. In a popular collection of methodological essays, *The New Cultural History,* LaCapra surfaced not as one of New Cultural History's most trenchant critics but as a "model" and "exemplar" who had expanded the bounds of cultural history. And he was not alone. Intellectual history, never the most crowded specialty, began to shrink as "cultural history" flexed its muscles, making its way through review essays, job descriptions, and the self-identifications of historians old and new. By the 1990s, Hayden White—who had built a career upon the highest of high intellectual history and was known, along with LaCapra, as a leading exponent of radical approaches to textuality—was calling himself a cultural historian. Even the dead were not safe. With a few strokes of the keyboard, E. P. Thompson, long claimed as one of the founders of New Social History (a movement now grown a bit elderly), became a founder of New Cultural History, and his classic 1962 book, *The Making of the English Working Class,* a "bridge" to the new school, if not to an actual paradigm.[2]

A good decade after the appearance of *The New Cultural History,* it had become conventional to associate the new school with the linguistic turn, generally understood as a theoretical movement originating in 1960s France, or occasionally Germany, that had undermined the old scientistic approaches to the study of history. In hall talk, one could hear the facile equation History + Theory = New Cultural History. In more formal settings, much as New Cultural History promised to consume intellectual history, so, too, could the cultural turn gobble up the older linguistic turn. Lynn Hunt's introduction to *The New Cultural History* had observed that, while cultural historians differed in their preferences for either anthropological or literary models, they shared one central tendency: "the use of language as metaphor. Symbolic actions such as riots or cat massacres are framed as texts to be read or languages to be decoded." In a 1999 collection, *Beyond the Cultural Turn,* editors Victoria E. Bonnell and Lynn Hunt looked back on the older anthology and observed that it had captured a series of exciting new developments in historiography that "we now place under the general rubric of 'the linguistic turn' or 'the cultural turn.'" Throughout both the introduction and many of the collected essays, *linguistic* and *cultural* appeared as synonyms or near synonyms, and by the time readers arrived at Hayden White's afterword they had been well prepared for his coinage of *culturalism* and its contents—"linguisticism," "textualism," "constructivism," and "discoursivism."[3]

The conflation of *language* and *culture* had become one of the new discoursivistic habits of historians, and it deserves a closer look. To some critics, the hegemonic bent of New Cultural History and the apparent circularity of its definitions—culture is a language, and language is culture—betrayed a conservative reaction against more radical forms of interpretation. Dominick LaCapra's critiques may have been especially pointed, but at least a few other historians shared his larger concerns. One of Hayden White's students, Sande Cohen, repeatedly denounced New Cultural History for its "violence towards deconstruction" and its tendency toward "aestheticism." For Cohen, the new forms of historical theory had appropriated some of the trappings of linguistic radicalism while carrying forward the most reactionary habits of old-fashioned historicism. Still others, Frank Ankersmit among them, argued that historical theorists should trade textual for visual models of the past and redescribe the debates over language and history in terms of aesthetics.[4] Such critiques suggested that historiography had not arrived at anything like a consensus about what an authentic linguistic turn might mean for historical discourse. If we set aside the related words and phrases, such as *deconstruction* or *theory* or even *culture,* one of the most investigated terms in the English language, we still need to ask, just what was the linguistic turn?

That phrase had not had a terribly long career in historiography. John Toews's 1987 article "Intellectual History after the Linguistic Turn," in the flagship journal of the discipline in the United States, *American Histori-*

cal Review, had given many readers their first glimpse of the tag in print, but Toews had not been the first historian to use it. In 1982, Martin Jay's "Should Intellectual History Take a Linguistic Turn? Reflections on the Gadamer-Habermas Debate" deployed the phrase somewhat differently to describe the conflict of interpretations between the hermeneutics of Hans-Georg Gadamer and the critical theory of Jürgen Habermas. Jay, like Toews, used the phrase casually rather than with any serious technical intent, and his opening paragraphs invoked Ludwig Wittgenstein. Indeed, the phrase had been popularized in Anglo-American analytical philosophy by the 1967 anthology *The Linguistic Turn.* The book's editor, Richard Rorty, had taken the title to describe a "revolution" in which "linguistic philosophy" displaced older ways of philosophizing. By *linguistic philosophy,* Rorty meant, "the view that philosophical problems are problems which may be solved (or dissolved) either by reforming language, or by understanding more about the language we presently use." The actual phrase *linguistic turn* had first appeared in Gustav Bergmann's 1953 essay "Logical Positivism, Language, and the Reconstruction of Metaphysics" and found a new audience with Rorty's collection. Bergmann had coined the phrase by way of describing logical positivism as a movement whose members were united in "philosophical style": "They all accept the linguistic turn Wittgenstein initiated in the *Tractatus.*"[5]

In the span of two decades, *linguistic turn* had come to refer to competing movements. From its coinage as a reference to the work of logical positivists, such as Carl Hempel, *linguistic turn* had landed in departments of literature and history as a label for the arguments of poststructural philosophers, such as Jacques Derrida. Finally, it had become a banner for cultural historians pursuing anthropological treatments of historical events and literary texts. Much as analytic philosophers might have chastised historians for misappropriation of the legacy of Bertrand Russell and Wittgenstein, so might a generation of deconstructionists come to resent the assimilation of the work of linguistic revolutionaries into histories of kitsch. But the weird career of *linguistic turn* offers more than an object lesson in semantic confusion.

The New Cultural History's conflation of *culture* and *language* may have been more instinctive than analytical, but we may tease other meanings out of that prosodic convergence. Were we simply to list the attempts at formal definitions of *language* or *linguistic* or even *linguistic turn,* we would quickly burn through both patience and pages. Instead I have in mind something a bit humbler, an episodic history of key moments in the rethinking of "language," "linguistic," and related concepts. If we are to grasp the resonance of the phrase *linguistic turn,* we will need to step out beyond the bounds of analytical philosophy and French post-structuralism. Language was one of the most engaged research topics of the twentieth-century academy, and the new and obscure specialties of linguistics and semantics reached into popular and mass culture well before Foucault or even Wittgenstein had found English translations. In North America, modern ethnography's engagements with racial and cultural difference helped to shape and facilitate the better-known analytic and post-structural linguistic turns.

Most recent accounts of New Cultural History begin with Clifford Geertz's 1973 collection of essays, *The Interpretation of Cultures.*[6] Perhaps only Hayden White's *Metahistory* or Michel Foucault's work had the same reach, and a quick scan of monographs in literary and cultural history since the 1980s demonstrates that Geertz's essays had far more impact on the level of prose. The colorful opening anecdote had long been a staple of historical essays, but Geertz's virtuosity raised it to an art form. Monograph after monograph began with the apparently inscrutable event or parade or picture or other bit of cultural arcana that, when properly analyzed, opened out on a new world of meaning. That stylistic influence was pervasive, and it tended to work on a subconscious level. Things were different, though, with what academic readers thought of as Geertz's methodological contribution; and especially in departments of history and literature, the ethnographer's tendency to read events and cultural artifacts as if they were Shakespearean sonnets was a revelation: "The culture of a people is an ensemble of texts," Geertz had written. Many readers assimilated *Interpretation of Cultures* to other books that treated the world as a text, works with titles like *Of Grammatology* or *The Order of Things,* but Geertz's essays, written between 1957 and the early 1970s, footnoted theorists that appeared decidedly old-school in comparison. The most famous passage, "Man is an animal suspended in webs of signification that he himself has spun," which Geertz attributed to Max Weber, appeared near the end of his introductory essay, "Thick Description: Toward an Interpretive Theory of Cultures."[7]

Although *thick description* became almost an academic bumper-sticker in the eighties, few will easily remember that this key phrase was borrowed from the analytic philosopher Gilbert Ryle, or that the essay opened with still another reference today untimely, to Susanne Langer's 1942 book, *Philosophy in a New Key: A Study in the Symbolism of Reason, Rite, and Art.* Langer was a favorite, and in another of Geertz's pleas for a more interpretive approach to cultural anthropology, he cited Langer's 1956 essay "On a New Definition of 'Symbol'": "If Langer is right that 'the concept of meaning, in all is varieties, is the dominant philosophical conception of our time,' that 'sign, symbol, denotation, signification, communication . . . are our [intellectual] stock in trade,' it is perhaps time that social anthropology, and particularly that part of it concerned with the study of religion, became aware of the fact." If we wish to associate Geertz's ethnography with a linguistic turn, we should look here. Langer's name surfaced throughout Geertz's essays, frequently at crucial methodological moments, usually to support Geertz's sense that questions of symbolic interpretation dominated other contemporary fields of intellectual life. Specifically, Geertz appealed to Langer to authorize that feature of *The Interpretation of Culture* that most influenced historiography: the ethnographer's predilection for reading social behavior as if it were a linguistic artifact.[8]

So far as "influence" is concerned, we might make two general points about Geertz's use of Langer. First, that Langer, like Geertz himself, tended to mix and match all human behaviors and artifacts—music, gesture, art, speech, writing—in ways that allowed one to glide easily from language to culture and back again. The German-born philosopher saw that broad conception of semantics as philosophy's new key. Langer attributed that interpretive turn to Ernst Cassirer's *Philosophie der symbolischen Formen,* a work that suggested that the privileged languages of science were simply "special cases" of a broader human impulse toward symbolization that reached much deeper than reason. In Langer's synopsis of Cassirer, from "On a New Definition of 'Symbol,'" "a sound, mark, object, or event could be a symbol to a person, without that person's consciously going from it to its meaning." The breadth of this new conception of semantics allowed Langer to speak even of feelings and intuitions in symbolic terms and helped her essays gracefully to bridge the seemingly distant worlds of formal logic and modern art. We should not infer from this chain of citations that Clifford Geertz and the New Cultural Historians he influenced were all closet neo-Kantians; but to Geertz, Langer's reading of language, music, art, and rituals as symbolic events sanctioned the reading of culture, broadly, as if it were another text. That slippage helped to underwrite *The Interpretation of Cultures,* as the anthropologist alternatively analyzed ritual events, material artifacts, conversations, and literary texts as if they belonged to a single discursive field.[9]

The second point I want to stress is that *Philosophy in a New Key* and *Philosophical Sketches* were indeed synthetic texts aimed at a general audience to introduce the idea that the problems of symbolism and signification had become the dominant themes of modern philosophy. Langer's books may have struck an especially sympathetic chord with the young anthropologist, but they had a much bigger audience, and they remain important partly as representatives of a larger genre of literature. Her work resonated deeply with the period's fascination with semantics and linguistics, and *Philosophy in a New Key,* especially, was but one of a host of popular books aimed at explicating language and its academic study to a general audience. From Margaret Schlauch's *Gift of Tongues* (1942, 1955) to Mario Pei's *Story of Language* (1949, 1965) or Robert A. Hall Jr.'s *Linguistics and Your Language* (1948, 1950) or Edward T. Hall's *Silent Language* (1959), linguistics and semantics found a mass market in midcentury America. By the end of the 1950s, linguistics had become *the* hot topic for teachers of English, and educators accordingly reorganized the curriculum of reading and language instruction. By the time a young scholar named Noam Chomsky published his first book, *Syntactic Structures,* in 1957, linguistics had become sufficiently hip that it might serve as a jumping-off point for a life as a public intellectual.[10]

Today, *Philosophy in a New Key* is all but forgotten, but as late as the 1980s the back shelves of used bookstores groaned under the weight of old paperback editions, testimony to the book's wide circulation, especially in higher education. Originally published by Harvard University Press in 1942, *Philosophy in a New Key* appeared as a Mentor paperback in 1948 and went through ten printings in its first two years, en route to a run of more than a half million. *Philosophical Sketches* appeared in 1956 and proved almost as popular. Langer's *Form and Feeling* (1953) and *Introduction to Symbolic Logic* (1937) similarly graced thousands of student bookshelves, and the first volume of her three-volume study, *Mind,* written between 1967 and 1982, was nominated for a National Book Award and favorably reviewed in the *New Yorker.* Thus did the more esoteric work of philosophers as different as Ernst Cassirer and Rudolf Carnap find a wider circle of readers in North America. Langer, though, was more than a popularizer, and she pulled traditions in aesthetics and logic into conversation with academic anthropology.[11]

One of the recurring themes of *Philosophy in a New Key*—and indeed of the genre—was its insistence upon language as a cultural universal that simultaneously illustrated cultural diversity. I quote this passage in full, both for the remarkable content and for a sense of the midcentury style that helped to make the book into a best-seller.

> Language is, without a doubt, the most momentous and at the same time the most mysterious product of the human mind. Between the clearest animal call of love or warning or anger, and a man's least, trivial *word,* there lies a whole day of Creation—or in modern phrase, a whole chapter of evolution. In language we have the free, accomplished use of symbolism, the record of articulate conceptual thinking; without language there seems to be nothing like explicit thought whatever. All races of men—even the scattered, primitive denizens of the deep jungle, and brutish cannibals who have lived for centuries on world-removed islands—have their complete and articulate language. There seem to be no simple, amorphous, or imperfect languages, such as one would naturally expect to find in conjunction with the lowest cultures. People who have not invented textiles, who live under roofs of pleated branches, need no privacy and mind no filth or roast their

> enemies for dinner, will yet converse over the bestial feasts in a tongue as grammatical as Greek, and as fluent as French!

If this passage today seems to lack the cultural sensitivity one might hope to find in a philosophical essay, it nonetheless reveals the imprint of a peculiarly modern ethnographic sensibility in its insistence that, however much material objects and manners may evolve, language everywhere marks *civitas.* The ancient distinction between those civilized peoples who could speak properly and those who could not was truly dead and buried, and Langer held out linguistic virtuosity as an index of a universal humanity. Moreover, the universal impulse here was not simply the instrumental need for communication but something more primordial and yet more elevated. Langer quoted from Edward Sapir's 1933 essay "Language" in the *Encyclopedia of Social Sciences:* "The primary function of language is generally said to be communication.... The autistic speech of children seems to show that the purely communicative aspect of language has been exaggerated. It is best to admit that language is primarily a vocal actualization of the tendency to see reality symbolically." For Langer, Sapir's formulation pointed out the true meaning of the new semantic key in modern philosophy, for it replaced the old borders between humans and animals—tools, speech, or reason—with symbolism.[12]

In drawing heavily upon a linguistic tradition derived from Boasian anthropology, Langer placed herself in good company. In the first half of the twentieth century, much linguistic research came out of departments of anthropology, and the two most important general works on language, Leonard Bloomfield's *Language* (1933) and Edward Sapir's *Language: An Introduction to the Study of Speech* (1921), were written by students of Franz Boas. Bloomfield's book proved so influential that, as late as 1955, Archibald A. Hill, in an essay titled "Linguistics since Bloomfield," described Bloomfield as "the real founder of American linguistics." We may get a sense of the importance of anthropology's domination of American linguistics from Hill's account: "From Boas, Bloomfield got the realization of the importance of so-called primitive languages as the laboratories in which the principles of investigation later applied to English could be worked out." That application had political consequences, for as grammarian W. Nelson Francis put it, "a long overdue revolution is at present taking place in the study of English grammar—a revolution as sweeping in its consequences as the Darwinian revolution in biology. It is the result of the application to English of methods of descriptive analysis originally developed for use with languages of primitive people." The influence of anthropology, and especially Boasian anthropology, upon American conceptions of language set linguistics in the United States apart from European linguistics and had important consequences for other fields of study.[13]

As linguistics matured as a discipline, it became conventional to place the origin of linguistics, or at least "modern" (later, "structural") linguistics, in the late eighteenth and early nineteenth centuries. At the Linguistic Society of America, founded in 1929, many linguists traced their own practice back to the rise of comparative studies of the Indo-European languages and the discovery, by Orientalists of that period, that Sanskrit was related to Greek and Latin. The realization that Indian and European languages had an ancient familial relation opened up new sorts of inquiry, notably comparative research methods that departed from earlier traditions of language study, especially the older scholarly approaches to grammar and philology.[14] Unlike traditional grammar, linguistics could use a variety of different structural features for describing a given language, and unlike classical philology, with its antiquarian etymologies, linguistics might treat modern languages in an entirely ahistorical mode. But the relationship between linguistics and history was complicated, and it differed from continent to continent.

In Europe, the canonical texts, such as Hermann Paul, *Prinzipien der Sprachgeschichte* (1880), and Ferdinand de Saussure, *Cours de linguistique générale* (1915), drew primarily upon research in Indo-European languages. De Saussure, for instance, taught German and did much of his empirical work in Sanskrit. But since these languages belonged to a greater Indo-European linguistic tradition, it was possible to treat even the most ahistorical analyses of Sanskrit verb stems as a window on the history of modern European languages. Casual readers could easily imagine de Saussure's researches into Sanskrit as revealing a chain of continuities linking modern Swiss life to the deep past of Indo-Aryan ancestors. In American linguistics, the situation was rather different, for although Sapir and Bloomfield freely drew upon Sanskrit or French or Old English for illustrations of one point or another, they were more nearly experts in a variety of Native American languages. Bloomfield did much of his early important work on Algonquin and later studied Menominee. Sapir was best known for his linguistic work with Athabascan. And each had grown up, scholastically speaking, with the work of other colleagues on Native American or Pacific Island indigenous languages, so those examples leapt readily to the pen. In these years, Franz Boas's revelation that "Eskimo" Inuit speakers had more than fifty words for snow became an intellectual cliché. The constant iteration of indigenous exemplars, and the peculiarly cultural turn given them by the problems of modern American ethnography, imparted a very different tone to the study of language in the United States. Where the general European reader of European work on linguistics might find in Sanskrit the echo of familiar ancestors and a connection to history, most readers of American works encountered a long string of exercises in cultural and racial difference.[15]

Boasian linguistics thus echoed Boasian ethnography's critiques of biological racialism and social evolution. Indeed, the celebrated "cultural relativism" of Boasian ethnography may have found its sharpest tongue in ethnolinguistics. There would be no grading of languages as "higher" or "lower." As Langer had noted, no matter how "primitive" the material culture of a given people, language invariably displayed astonishing complexity. Of all cultural artifacts, language seemed the most resistant to social evolutionist valuation, and the most profitable for espousing cultural relativism. As Sapir put it, "When it comes to linguistic form, Plato walks with the Macedonian swineherd, Confucius with the head-hunting savage of Assam." This sort of historical assemblage typified not simply Sapir's prose style but also the larger conceptual mode of ethnography of the period that imagined humans as divided not by national borders or biological racial groupings but by cultural boundaries, and then placed the various self-contained cultures side by side, rather than linking them together in a long narrative sequence. The result tended to privilege spatial over temporal metaphors and contrast over continuity. Removing modern European culture from its privileged place atop social evolution removed the most conventional rationale for describing European civilization as superior to other cultures. And that strong relativist tendency proved especially important in the specialties that would later become socio- and ethnolinguistics, where specialists studied the contexts of speech use of particular language communities. By midcentury, it had become common to find linguists claiming that "proper" English usage was simply the name given to the peculiar habits of a particular class and racial group, and such works as Martin Joos's classic "Five Clocks" delivered scathing dissections of those "prescriptivist" approaches to English that judged some particular form of expression as "correct."[16]

The tendency to relativize or democratize varieties of English usage materialized well outside the walls of the Linguistic Society of America, and it also turned attention to aspects of language that philosophers had traditionally thought of as aesthetic rather than epistemic. Mark Twain offered perhaps the most famous case. Widely criticized through the early twentieth century for his reliance upon vernacular speech and the subliterary genre of humor, by the 1950s the Missourian had been rehabilitated and placed atop the canon of American English as the most ethnographic and inventive of authors. Twain's special affection for African American speech and oral literature, too, found academic parallels, from the writing of Zora Neale Hurston (another Boas student) to William Labov's influential 1972 book, *Language in the Inner City*. And as these cases suggest, the democratizing arc also tended to shift linguistic analysis subtly away from the logic, conceptualization, and warranting of truth claims and toward figurative language of all sorts, especially metaphor. By the early 1960s the systematic study of the metaphorical aspects of literary language and vernacular speech had interwoven with older analytical conversations. Max Black's work on logic and figural language, including his influential book *Models and Metaphors* (1962), simply exemplified a larger trend in the field. Nor was this strictly an American exercise, as language studies in Great Britain followed similar lines. British linguistic anthropology, especially in the work of Bronislaw

Malinowski and John Firth, was widely read as sharing the general thrust of Boasian linguistics. And we might place such works as C.K. Ogden and I.A. Richards's seminal study in semantics, *The Meaning of Meaning* (1923), and Richards's extensive studies in usage along a path curving toward Richard Hoggart's *Uses of Literacy* (1955) and what would later be known as British Cultural Studies. But alongside these democratizing tendencies, the new linguistics tended toward another, somewhat different end, namely, the corrosion of confidence in the ability even of linguistics to achieve anything like a scientific understanding of the world.[17]

Linguistic anthropologists, as well as the philosophers, had run up against two related conceptual problems. The first was that it had become essentially impossible to imagine reason or thought apart from what most people thought of as its linguistic expression. The idealist tradition, in which a prelinguistic intuition or thought or concept simply found a spoken or literary form, had collapsed. As Sapir put it in his 1929 essay "Linguistics as a Science," "The time is long past when grammatical forms and processes can be naively translated by philosophers into metaphysical realities." The consequences of this new view could be startling. If reason took flight only in language, then our knowledge of the world was itself linguistically conditioned. In a remarkable passage, Sapir sketched the situation in which linguists and philosophers found themselves: "It is quite an illusion to imagine that one adjusts to reality essentially without the use of language and that language is merely an incidental means of solving specific problems of communication or reflection. The fact of the matter is that the 'real world' is to a large extent unconsciously built up on the language habits of the group." From this first difficulty, that reality is given to us or even constituted in language, came the second and rather urgent difficulty: "No two languages are ever sufficiently similar to be considered as representing the same social reality. The worlds in which different societies live are distinct worlds, not merely the same world with different labels attached." How then, would one choose between contrasting accounts of the world? Or rather, adjudicate competing worlds?[18]

We should linger awhile over Sapir's passage, for it was an amazing formulation. We have grown so accustomed to the talk about the "social construction of reality" and "absent presence" and the "deferral of meaning" that such claims have come close to being naturalized or else have been cast into a simple great history of 1968 or perhaps focused upon a single prophetic moment, say Friedrich Nietzsche's Zarathustra or William James's cash-dollar account of truth. Sapir's claims here, especially his claim that different linguistic communities live in "distinct worlds, not merely the same world with different labels attached," came four years before Wittgenstein had begun to dictate his *Blue and Brown Books,* and ten before Benjamin Lee Whorf used Sapir's passage as the epigraph for "The Relation of Habitual Thought and Behavior to Language." But we are close to what later scholars would somewhat glibly refer to as the Sapir-Whorf hypothesis, or linguistic relativity. Sapir and his colleague and student Whorf were trained as anthropologists rather than philosophers, and their most dramatic statements about language and knowledge tended to appear in less formal talks or even popular essays rather than monographs, so it is no easy matter to abstract a straightforward proposition from any of their writings. But Sapir's "Linguistics as a Science" introduced, albeit in a fairly informal way, two of the recurring problems that occupied much postwar analytical philosophy: the empirical underdetermination of all theory, and the indeterminacy of translation. A brief tour through those debates will eventually bring us back around to our starting point, historiography and the linguistic turn.[19]

One way of engaging the developments in linguistic anthropology is to place them with developments of the period in analytic philosophy as precursors to the explosion of talk about rationality and relativism in the sixties, especially in the history of science. If we sketch a brief history of the debates over language and translation, beginning with Sapir's account of language as a constructive agent, we may develop a better sense of how the revolution in linguistics of the 1920s and 1930s helped to clear the ground for later revolutions.

We should start by highlighting the terrific impact that ethnography had upon American vocabularies, both in and out of academia. The partial displacement of *race* by *culture* was the single most dramatic event, but a host of related terms and new usages found their way into casual and technical conversations. *Coming of Age in Samoa* (1928) helped to make Margaret Mead into a major public intellectual and struck at the common belief that childhood development was inevitably and eternally everywhere the same. Ruth Benedict's *Patterns of Culture* (1934) probably achieved its greatest circulation in the late 1940s; it suggested that different cultures were as unified and formally organized as any work of art and, therefore, "essentially incommensurable." And the preeminence of linguistic anthropologists in the new field of linguistics helped to make anthropology monographs common reading for analytic philosophers. So we should not be too surprised to learn that, when philosopher Willard Van Orman Quine vacationed in Oaxaca in 1941, he took along as his guidebook not the current Baedeker but ethnographer Robert Redfield's monograph on Mexican village life, *Tepoztlán.*[20]

Quine, who had come to analytic philosophy through a chance reading of a popular book on historical linguistics, George H. McKnight's *English Words and Their Background* (1926), had actively participated in the Vienna Circle. A lifelong friend of Rudolf Carnap and Carl Hempel, and mentor to the philosopher of history Morton White, Quine would also write the single most devastating critique of logical positivism, "Two Dogmas of Empiricism" (1951). In that essay, Quine took up ethnographic metaphors for his demolition of logical positivism's foundational principles of verificationism and the analytic-synthetic distinction. His account of science as a "language" or a "conceptual scheme" whose objects—commonly imagined by scientists and logicians as physical things—were really "cultural posits" already hinted at how ethnolinguistic vocabularies might influence logical analysis. And Quine's fascination with the figure of the field linguist, an image he introduced in various essays of the 1950s, derived partly from his reading and partly from his own experiences. In 1941, the highlight of Quine's Mexico trip came when, as he was walking about the street, *Tepoztlán* in hand, one of the passing locals recognized a photo of one of Redfield's informants. Quine spent the evening with the man, hearing stories of the village and listening delightedly to the household converse in Nahuatl. For the multilingual philosopher and dedicated traveler, amateur ethnography served as the accompaniment to a career in linguistic analysis, and Quine's most important book, *Word and Object* (1960), centered upon the problems of translation as they had developed both in analytic philosophy and linguistic anthropology.[21]

Quine's key words and phrases, especially *radical translation* and *indeterminacy of translation,* helped readers to grasp the epistemological difficulties of an idealized ethnographic experience. The sort of translation Quine had done in Oaxaca, where he and his guest had shared enough Spanish to help each other bridge the unrelated languages of English and Nahuatl, was by far the most common sort of interpretive enterprise, but by *radical translation* Quine meant "translation of the language of a hitherto untouched people." The fantasy of a lost tribe had driven plenty of ethnographic research, to say nothing of the movies and other works of fiction in mass culture, but in philosophy it served as a modern alternative to the old state-of-nature scenarios that had adorned so much Enlightenment and Romantic speculation. Where "natural man" had served Hobbes or Locke as a subject for thought experiments, *Word and Object* canonized a new figure: the analytic philosopher as field linguist.[22]

Quine's account of the ultimate ethnographic encounter drew linguistic anthropology and the new philosophy of language into a strange dialogue. His opening hypothetical example quickly became famous: "A rabbit scurries by, the native says 'Gavagai', and the linguist notes down the sentence 'Rabbit' (or 'Lo, a rabbit') as tentative translation, subject to testing in further cases." But the testing of such sentences would create endless difficulties, from the problems of interpreting gestures ("gestures are not to be taken at face value; the Turks' are nearly the reverse of our own") to the more substantive problems of deciding if the native language even conceptualizes the world in a way that the linguist could recognize. Even if the linguist eventually concludes (based on "intuitive judgment") that he and the native were indeed pointing at the same stimulus, and not at the movement of the grass or the buzzing of a hypothetical rabbit-fly, it may be that *gavagai* applies not simply to "rabbit" but to "mere segments, or brief temporal stages, of rabbits," or perhaps "rabbithood" or some other term unimagined in English. Nor could a bit of pointing and questioning conclusively resolve the issue.

> We cannot even say what native locutions to count as analogues of terms as we know them, much less equate them with ours term for term, except as we have also decided what native devices to view as doing in their devious ways the work of our own various auxiliaries to objective reference: our articles and pronouns, our singular and plural, our copula, our identity predicate. The whole apparatus is interdependent, and the very notion of term is as provincial to our culture as those associated devices.... Occasion sentences and stimulus meaning are general coin; terms and reference are local to our conceptual scheme.

Stimulus or occasion sentences ("Gavagai") and traditional observation sentences ("Bachelor"), proved tricky, yet these were far and away the most straightforward and manageable. Messier bits of language, such as logical connectives or theoretical sentences ("Neutrinos lack mass"), could prove close to impossible. Here one would have to do far more than point and query.[23]

Translations, Quine contended, invariably depended upon the linguist's hypotheses about which domestic constructions matched which native constructions. But those hypotheses necessarily remained hypothetical. Even if they seemed to function in a practical setting, one could never quite be sure of avoiding "mishaps." More, a different set of translation hypotheses could produce alternative and possibly conflicting translations. Or as Quine parsed the indeterminacy of translation, "manuals for translating one language into another can be set up in divergent ways, all compatible with the totality of speech dispositions, yet incompatible with one another." There was no "fact of the matter" to which one could appeal when deciding between functional but mutually incompatible manuals.[24]

Quine believed that this principle of indeterminacy clarified the problems formulated by Sapir and other linguistic anthropologists and sometimes inflated into metaphysics. "One frequently hears it urged that deep differences of language carry with them ultimate differences in the way one thinks or looks upon the world," he observed. "I would urge that what is most generally involved is indeterminacy of correlation. There is less basis of comparison—less sense in saying what is good translation and what is bad—the farther we get away from sentences with visibly direct conditioning to non-verbal stimuli and the farther we get off home ground." As the analytic philosopher saw it, these conclusions pointed in fairly pragmatic directions, but other readers would find them nearly apocalyptic, and Quine's own argument would prove almost as tough to parse as the Sapir-Whorf hypothesis. Part of the difficulty was that *Word and Object* introduced the indeterminacy of translation thesis in tandem with another, better-known issue. Or as Quine put it, indeterminacy of translation was simply a clearer example of a more general problem of interpretation. What was true abroad ("in the darkest archipelago") was true at home: "To the same degree that the radical translation of sentences is underdetermined by the totality of dispositions to verbal behavior, our own theories and beliefs in general are underdetermined by the totality of possible sensory evidence time without end." Indeterminacy of translation simply pointed up the way that all interpretation rested on squishy experiential ground.[25]

The appropriation of ethnographic metaphors remade American philosophical discourse. Quine's images and arguments in particular, with their exotic locales and heroic field linguists, helped to make conversations previously imagined in terms of racial difference into paradigms of epistemological debate. We should not rush to describe that language as postcolonial, and Quine's own politics were notoriously conservative. But where a generation of logical positivists and empiricists had formulated their questions in terms of the differences between different mathematical languages or perhaps the nationalistic flavor of modern European languages, Quine and his contemporaries turned instead to the metaphorical vocabulary of colonial encounter. The shift was not trivial. By the end of the 1950s, both popular literature on language and the cutting edge of linguistic philosophy had made the ethnographic association of race, culture, and language a familiar thing. And the questions generated by the field linguist quickly made their way into that intellectual domain commonly reckoned as the glory of modern civilization and the one that continued to set apart civilized and savage peoples, the natural sciences.

The indeterminacy of translation and the underdetermination of theory quickly resurfaced in a more empirical setting. In 1962, Thomas Kuhn, one of Quine's friends and readers, published a book that eventually outreached even *Word and Object* in audience and impact. The making and reception of *The Structure of Scientific Revolutions* has grown into one of the creation tales of science studies, but we need not linger here over the story or its countless retellings. The argument that science works not in a smooth, evolutionary progression but rather through occasional and cataclysmic "revolutions" in which one "paradigm" or theoretical conception of the world abruptly displaces another has become a graduate student truism. Kuhn's more provocative and murky reckoning of the morals of that story, though, generated decades of controversy, partly because of the ambiguous prose that seemed to imply that there is no neutral external world to which one can appeal in cases of conflicting paradigms.[26]

What we should note here is Kuhn's vocabulary, or rather that portion of it that looks most familiar. For instance: "The normal-scientific tradition that emerges from a scientific revolution is not only incompatible but often actually incommensurable with that which has gone before." Or: "In so far as their only recourse to that world is through what they see and do, we may want to say that after a revolution scientists are responding to a different world." Or: "Communication across the revolutionary divide is inevitably partial." Or: "In a sense that I am unable to explicate further, the proponents of competing paradigms practice their trades in different worlds." This was not the vocabulary of Alexandre Koyré or Arthur Lovejoy, frequently cited (and by Kuhn himself) as crucial influences. *World* and *incommensurable* were not keywords for Koyré or Lovejoy. But we have seen them before; and even without making any strong biographical claims about Kuhn's reading or intent, we can recognize the linguistic habits of *Patterns of Culture* ("essentially incommensurable") or Sapir's essays ("the 'real world' is to a large extent unconsciously built up on the language habits of the group"). Even certain translations of German philosophical and psychological terms—*worldview* is one of Kuhn's favorites—had been thoroughly popularized in the United States by authors like Meade and Benedict. And the individual words were frequently strung together in ways that had been opened by earlier generations of anthropological prose. In his postscript to the second edition in 1969, Kuhn invoked *Word and Object:* "To translate a theory or worldview into one's own language is not to make it one's own. For that, one must go native, discover that one is thinking and working in, not simply translating out of, a language that was previously foreign."[27]

Going native had unforeseen consequences. Much as scholars of English had applied linguistic anthropology to the study of ordinary English, philosophers and historians of science went "ethnographic," or at least borrowed loan words from the anthropologists, but with results that the Boasians would never have predicted. And much as ethnographic vocabularies tended to relativize descriptions of English usage, once transferred into philosophical discussions of science, those lexicons and stylistic tendencies opened out on a world more radical than that imagined by the Sapir-Whorf hypothesis.

Sapir and Whorf's strongest claims about language as a way of world-making had always been directed toward ordinary usage. As Sapir saw it, only in literature was translation genuinely impossible—scientific language, in contrast, was perfectly translatable. "A scientific truth is impersonal," Sapir had written in 1929; "in its essence it is untinctured by the particular linguistic medium in which it finds expression." Since science ultimately based itself on a universal language of mathematics, "one can adequately translate scientific literature because the original scientific expression is itself a translation." By inverting that judgment and making theoretical scientific expression the least translatable of linguistic forms, Quine had radicalized Sapir and Whorf's views of language even as he refuted what he saw as their metaphysical tendencies. By treating conceptual schemes or theories or paradigms as languages, as the Boasians had never done, the new science studies had opened the door to increasingly radical claims about the relativity of scientific method, including interpretations that neither Quine nor Kuhn would sanction. *Incommensurability,* in particular, became an instant keyword for claims that competing conceptual schemes or languages could not be meaningfully intertranslated, a view that, in its boldest forms, held that the world consisted of an anarchistic array of mutually hostile languages in which modern science held pride of place only through the violent expression of its will to power.[28]

Of all the furious argumentation that surrounded Quine's translation argument and Kuhn's incommensurability claims, we may single out Donald Davidson's critiques as an appropriate end point for our brief history. In 1941, Davidson, then a graduate student, had accompanied Quine on the trip to Mexico, leading his mentor up Popocatepetl and following him round the streets of Tepoztlán, arguing points of translation over tequila and lime. His 1974 essay "On the Very Idea of a Conceptual Scheme," which was developed from a series of talks in the early seventies, brought to a close several strands of argument that we have traced out of linguistic anthropology and analytical philosophy. For Davidson, "conceptual relativism"—the notion that reality was relative to a particular conceptual scheme or language—simply could not be sustained without recourse to some old, bad linguistic habits that now belonged to outdated conceptions of science.[29]

Although Davidson conceded that one could identify conceptual schemes with languages, as Quine and Kuhn had done, strong claims of incommensurability were incoherent. Translation was frequently difficult or bad, and what came easily in one language might come hard in another, but none of these distinctions amounted to a difference so great that it could not be described in one language or the other.

> Whorf, wanting to demonstrate that Hopi incorporates a metaphysics so alien to ours that Hopi and English cannot, as he puts it, "be calibrated," uses English to convey the contents of sample Hopi sentences. Kuhn is brilliant at saying what things were like before the revolution using—what else?—our post-revolutionary idiom. Quine gives us a feel for the "pre-individuative phase in the evolution of our conceptual scheme," while Bergson tells us where we can go to get a view of the mountain undistorted by one or another provincial perspective.

The very idea of a conceptual scheme already involved translation—simply recognizing an alternative language as a language meant that the process of translation was already under way. A truly "incommensurable" or alien language could not even be recognized as a language.[30]

As Davidson drew out the argument, the only way for one to make sense of the idea of competing conceptual schemes was to imagine that some sort of neutral world—usually rendered in philosophical discourse as *experience* or *sensation* or *sense stimuli*—offered a stable content that could be differently organized by different conceptual schemes. Thus the observed rabbit would take one form in Hopi and another in English; one form in Newtonian physics and another in quantum mechanics. But Davidson contended that the scheme-content distinction was simply a holdover from logical positivism. Much as Quine had tossed out the old distinction between analytic and synthetic propositions along with the positivist dogma of verificationism, so Davidson jettisoned the "third dogma of empiricism," the distinction between experience on the one hand, and language on the other. For without verificationism and the analytic-synthetic distinction, one could not intelligibly defend the appeals to some neutral middle ground of experience or sense data anymore than one could defend old-fashioned appeals to substance. If we wanted to improve our sense of the differences between our language and the native's language, then we could do so by enlarging the "basis of shared (translatable) language or of shared opinion." But if we could make no intelligible sense of "schemes," at least as a hard and fast demarcation of conceptual borders, neither could we make grandiose claims about incommensurability or even commensurability: "It would be equally wrong to announce the glorious news that all mankind—all speakers of language, at least—share a common scheme and ontology. For if we cannot intelligibly say that schemes are different, neither can we intelligibly say that they are one."[31]

Davidson's critique of philosophical scientism drew attention from all sides, but we should note here the dependence of that critique upon an equally radical reworking of conceptions of language. If one outcome of Quinean thought experiments in field linguistics was to erode hard and fast distinctions between different sorts of sentences, another was the subversion of traditional philosophical reckonings of linguistic difference. For if one could identify schemes with languages, and if tossing the scheme-content distinction also meant tossing any warranted claims about hard differences between schemes, then linguistic philosophy had really become something completely different. A few years later, Davidson drew one of the morals of his story. "We should realize that we have abandoned not only the ordinary notion of a language, but we have erased the boundary between knowing a language and knowing our way around the world generally. For there are no rules for arriving at passing theories that work.... There is no such thing as a language, not if a language is anything like what philosophers, at least, have supposed." It may seem impossibly convenient, but the end of our sketch of linguistic anthropology and analytical philosophy is also something like the end of linguistic philosophy, at least as far as one of its traditions was concerned. Among analytic philosophers, Davidson's essay virtually concluded the argument over translation and commensurability, whether because Davidson's arguments appeared irrefutable or simply because, as so often happens, the particular conversation had exhausted itself. But the close affiliation of linguistic and ethnographic metaphors had become part of the larger discourse on language and the world.[32]

What appears to be a simple category mistake—the conflation of ethnographic research and linguistic analysis—actually helps us to think about changes in historical discourse. One may criticize the New Cultural History's lack of precision in the conflation of "linguistic" and "cultural" adjectives for characterizing a motley assortment of intellectual events. Or one might criticize Geertz for relying so much upon archaic varieties of language study, or even attempt to trace some strand of his footnotes that might lead into, say, Roland Barthes rather than Max Black and thereby find the true "source" of linguistic conceptions of culture that would transform so much of historical discourse in the 1970s and 1980s. But the belief that one could exchange *culture* for *language* demonstrates, however faintly, the imprint of colonialism and decolonization upon academic vocabularies. Here we may reach back through *The Interpretation of Cultures* and thus outward into the linguistic reformation of the human sciences in North America for a sense of the ways that colonial encounters impressed *language* and *linguistics* in the twentieth-century academe. I am not claiming that the linguistic turn was "really" about decolonization—but decolonization shaped the variety of historical events that we have since, sometimes, come to mean when we say *the linguistic turn.*

The casual identification of the adjectives *cultural* and *linguistic* in accounts of the rise of New Cultural History may have been intuitive rather than reasoned, but the association of those terms fit into older patterns. And without the earlier linguistic shifts of modern ethnography, the impact of continental philosophy of mathematics and logic would have taken different forms. Geertz himself was a cultural anthropologist, rather than an ethnolinguist, and his explication of philosophy's new key may have mixed his specialized acquaintance with linguistic anthropology with a more impressionistic understanding of talk about language in other disciplines, but we cannot dismiss it as idiosyncratic or provincial. In the twentieth century, technical terms borrowed from German and French, problems translated out of symbolic logic and into ordinary English, and even the framing of new research questions, all entered into a discourse profoundly influenced by anthropology's engagement with cultural and racial difference. More reflective usage also carried on that new tradition. Quine's philosopher-as-ethnolinguist and Davidson's deflation of language became set pieces in the more popular writing of another American philosopher, Richard Rorty, where they served the neopragmatist author of "Postmodernist Bourgeois Liberalism" in his debates with other public intellectuals, including Geertz, over the meanings of democracy in a postmodern global world.[33]

In both the strong claims for incommensurability that emerged in postwar philosophy, and the antifoundationalist views of language mobilized as criticisms of those claims, we can recognize the outlines of positions that would later be labeled postmodernism. In these self-consciously elaborated philosophical arguments, the study of language had cultivated the habit and then a tradition of imagining such disputes by means of ethnographic and aesthetic vocabularies rather than by means of a pure discourse of logic and function: natives and field linguists, race and culture, models and metaphor, art and language. This does not mean we should read American linguistic anthropology as the "true" source of postmodern criticism, nor does it mean we could not trace a plausible genealogy of recent radical philosophy that began instead with Nietzsche or even Frege or a genealogy of cultural history that began with Burckhardt and ran through the Annales school. Our story does illustrate, though, two broader and significant points: First, that the limited array of French and German texts and events that historians have subsumed under the phrase *linguistic turn* represented a comparatively tiny and belated subset of a much larger set of texts and events. And second, that the emergence of new ethnographic languages shaped analytic philosophy and history of science while also providing much of the vocabulary into which the various continental canons—from de Saussure's lectures to the linguistic revolutions of Paris '68—might be translated. Our new discursive habits display, however faintly, the marks of a colonial history.

FOUR Postmodernism and the People without History

When G.W.F. Hegel spun his epochal story of universal history, he left little doubt that "History" belonged to some people but not to others. It was not just that Europeans had taken up the torch of historical destiny. As he saw it, indigenous Americans and Africans lacked history altogether. Without writing, the concrete manifestation of collective consciousness, they remained "peoples without history," and in the greater tale of Spirit's evolution they would either disappear or assimilate to the rising West. Today, decolonization has made this bit of Hegel's tale both implausible and unappealing. Peoples "without history" have been subjugated, colonized, and exploited, but they have neither vanished from the story nor become European. Since the middle of the twentieth century, new works in cultural studies, comparative literature, ethnography, history of anthropology, and other fields have tried to make sense of the situation, and in that revised scholarly discourse cultures die, disappear, assimilate, acculturate, proliferate, reinvent themselves, and become nations in a confusing video collage. We wonder if we have lost the central thread of the narrative. What frontiers now stand between the peoples with and without history? How can we adjudicate tales in which the world's peoples become increasingly alike and stories in which they differ ever more violently?

The front cover of a 1988 book condenses these conflicts into a single image. It shows a black-and-white photograph of a dark-skinned man (the credits tell us he is an Igbo), his face covered with light cloth, and a false head perched on his own. The fake head is white, male, and wears a pith helmet. The masker holds a pad and pencil. He is, we understand, playing anthropologist, turning the imperial tables on Western academe by taking up the icons of history. Strangely, the designer has doubled the photograph, setting the figure back to back with his own mirror image. Inside the book—James Clifford's justly acclaimed *Predicament of Culture* (1988)—readers find this schizophrenic doubling transposed into print: "There is no master narrative that can reconcile the tragic and comic plots of global cultural history," Clifford tells us. "Indeed, modern ethnographic histories are perhaps condemned to oscillate between two metanarratives: one of homogenization, the other of emergence; one of loss, the other of invention." Usually, both are relevant, "each denying to the other a privileged, Hegelian vision." This is a tale for a postmodern season, one that seems to refuse the metaphysical closures of Hegel's universal history in favor of oscillating conflicts and ironic inversions. Indeed, Clifford's work of the 1980s appeared to thematize several of the defining features of the emergent scholarship known as New Historicism or New Cultural History.[1]

The idea that we have escaped universal history threatens to become an article of academic faith. While Clifford's association of Hegel, metanarrative, and political mastery is common enough in recent literature, we should treat these themes with care. The desire to escape universal history or narrative mastery is not new. Pragmatists, positivists, and behaviorists all derided Hegel's "speculative" philosophy of history long before post-structuralism began showing up in American journals. After

Jean-François Lyotard defined postmodernism as "incredulity toward metanarratives," academics had a new vocabulary for a familiar position. None of us, it seems, wants to be a narrative master of squishy metaphysics and totalitarian politics. Whether careful policing of our storytelling habits will keep us from that fate is another question. A genealogy of "master narrative" reveals some strange affinities. From Lévi-Strauss to Lyotard, from Clifford to Fukuyama, we remain haunted by history, returning ever and again to the big story even as we anxiously affirm our clean break with the evils of narrative mastery. We have foresworn Hegelian hubris and created new forms for narrating postcolonial histories of culture change, and these developments are laudable. But the continuing quest for formal principles differentiating "master" and "local," "historical" and "nonhistorical," modes of discourse threatens to burden our new tales with the bad, old metaphysics we claim to have escaped. We have replaced Hegel's peoples with and without history by scientific and savage minds, hot and cold societies, and master and local narratives, but that deep antinomy remains, surfacing unbidden at inopportune moments and wreaking havoc on our attempts to understand the global world in which we live.

Although accounts of the rise of New Historicism and New Cultural History generally stress the role played by Clifford Geertz's essays, no one seeking to account for the ways that Western academics today contrast historical and nonhistorical modes of discourse and experience can safely avoid Claude Lévi-Strauss. His writings, and especially his 1962 work, *The Savage Mind,* with its attacks on Jean-Paul Sartre and Marxist historicism, assisted in the displacement of existentialism by structuralism. They also served as critical events in academia's redefinition of historicity. If we are to understand the current debates over narrative mastery, we need to return to Lévi-Strauss's critique of capital-H History and colonialism, for his writings helped to make possible such texts as *The Predicament of Culture.* The French anthropologist has cast a bright shadow across virtually all ethnographic productions undertaken in recent America, and his ruminations over the global frontier narrative still surface in unlikely texts far from their original source. Lévi-Strauss sought to transfigure the received Hegelian and Marxist narratives of the evolution of historical consciousness while remaining sensitive to the global contexts of culture change. In place of peoples with and without history, he divided the world into hot and cold societies, scientific and savage minds. Those Lévi-Straussian antinomies, together with his suspicion of history as both a method and a subject, structured much subsequent writing about postcolonial history.

Nostalgia for the vanishing primitive drove Lévi-Strauss's great confessional essay, *Tristes Tropiques* (1955). In a masterwork of travel writing, autobiography, and ethnographic criticism, he limned the significance of deteriorating memory, worried about the duplicity of the past with its substitution of idealized images for grim reality, and drew an unhappy comparison of the world as it had existed in his youth with the cold-war globe overrun by the homogenizing and destructive effects of colonial capitalism. Of the pluralistic world of his youth, little remained but "contaminated memories." As a novice ethnographer, fresh from an abandoned career in philosophy, he had ventured into the backcountry of Brazil to search out a proverbial lost tribe, the Nambikwara, who reputedly lived apart from the press of modernity. What possible meaning could their American lives have for the young scholar? Lévi-Strauss hinted the meeting had world historical significance.[2]

The encounter of French ethnographer and American informant reenacted older dramas. Reconstructing for his readers the "highly charged atmosphere" of period research on American prehistory, Lévi-Strauss raised the possibility of a cultural connection between the Neolithic revolution in Europe, the event in which we find the origins of history, and the cultures of the New World.

> Is it not conceivable that this major event in the history of mankind ... may have aroused a kind of excitement among the less advanced communities of Asia and America? ... Once, we refused to allow pre-Columbian America an historical dimension, simply because post-Columbian America had none. We now perhaps have to correct a second mistake, which consists in assuming that America remained cut off from the world as a whole for twenty thousand years.... Everything would seem to suggest rather that the deep silence on the Atlantic side was offset by a buzz of activity all along the Pacific coast.

Post-Columbian America and its native inhabitants had no historical dimension, but this did not necessarily mean that their distant precursors also existed in the "deep silence" of peoples without history. The stakes were great: research might uncover hidden traces of continuity between primitive tribes like the Nambikwara and the great literate civilizations of the Aztec and the Maya, linkages evincing a pre-Columbian world of historical dimensions, affiliated, either by homology or actual transoceanic contact, with the historical cultures of Europe.[3]

Encamped in the Brazilian backcountry, Lévi-Strauss ruminated on the meanings of the imperial exchange. What differentiated European self from American other? One night, he distributed sheets of paper and pencils as gifts and was intrigued to watch the chief, in emulation of the ethnographer's own note-taking, lord it over his kinsmen by pretending to read from a text of "pre-literate" scribbling. From the event Lévi-Strauss drew a moral. Writing, he said, is an "artificial memory." Of the many criteria used to distinguish "barbarism and civilization," it is "tempting" to retain the division of literacy: "peoples with and without writing." But the division is not so clear; some Neolithic groups built civil life without developing literacy. The only phenomenon reliably associated with writing is the "creation of cities and empires." From this the structuralist derived his hypothesis: "The primary function of written communication is to facilitate slavery."[4] Writing is not only the precondition of the artificial memory we call history, it is also the instrument of human enslavement. The imposition of literate Western reason on the mythic innocence of orality lies at the very heart of the historic loss of cultural difference, the great modern tragedy.

In *Tristes Tropiques*, Lévi-Strauss recalled having been socialized into an educational system that immersed aspiring philosophers in a suffocating, pseudo-Hegelian language of ascending dialectic. Little wonder that the young intellectual found liberation in the clean lines of positivism and the structuralist figures of radical discontinuity. And so he associated the ahistorical vocabularies of linguistic structuralism with the political interests of his colonized subjects. He returned again and again to Hegel's division of the world into peoples with and without history. Lévi-Strauss offered at least three ways to circumvent or subvert the equation and its celebration of European empire. First, one might posit a pre-Columbian historicity for Native America; perhaps, he mused in *Tristes Tropiques,* one could find traces of historical consciousness in the wilds of South America contemporaneous with Europe's Neolithic revolution. A second possibility located the origins of historical consciousness in the mythic thought of natives. But this threatened to reactivate the old stories of the rise of historical consciousness as a march of progress. The third option inverted Hegel and encoded history as evil: it was *good* to be without history. Lévi-Strauss's texts emplotted history-as-events as the march of imperial oppression facilitated by literacy and science. They depicted history-as-method as one option among others. As he noted in *The Savage Mind* (1962), "History may lead to anything, provided you get out of it." Getting out of history became a critical obsession for intellectuals after structuralism, and many followed Lévi-Strauss in *not* positing a fourth option: history might be dramatically transfigured by new voices.[5]

For Lévi-Strauss, the conflict between native and European, orality and literacy, nonhistory and history, echoed the thematic of nature and culture that he saw as a deep structure of language and cognition, and in *The Savage Mind* he expanded on the cognitive and discursive frontiers separating savage and modern cultures. Mythic and scientific thought were not evolutionary stages but parallel and equally valuable ways of thinking. Myths, rooted in orality and memory, subordinated change to a deeper timeless order and relied on analogy, classification, and metaphor; science, including historical knowledge, sought explanation of change and relied on conceptions of temporal continuity and metonymy. The book concluded with a critique of Sartre's existential Marxism by denying that history had any unique central subject, such as "humanity" or "existence." History consisted solely of method: "Even history which claims to be universal is still only a juxtaposition of a few local histories." The structuralist had prepared the ground for its subsequent occupation by postmodernism. From his tragic march of literate reason and opposition of local histories to universal History, later theorists drew the postmodern critique. Universal history is made of "clouds of stories," said Lyotard, some years later: "It is a mass of billions of local histories [*historiettes*]." Indeed, Lévi-Strauss's work on "savage" discourse cleared the ground for Lyotard's influential analysis of narrative mastery, and his enthusiasm for an authentically savage "other" glimmers through Lyotard's privileging of *local* over *master narrative* or *metanarrative*.[6]

Lyotard can hardly be described as a Lévi-Straussian, but his popular coinages, *master* and *local* narrative, reinscribed Levi-Strauss's antinomies of science and savagism. What few critics have noted is that Lyotard's definitions of local and master narrative changed dramatically over the years; indeed, his earliest accounts of narrative mastery are not compatible with his later ones. Over the course of a decade, Lyotard shifted from pragmatic descriptions of narrative mastery as a matter of situation to descriptions of master narratives as functions of form. As his analysis developed, he spun out an ever more tenuous rationale for distinguishing local and metanarratives, and he turned to a racial other, Native American tribal communities, to justify his belief in different narrative kinds. His new vocabulary resonated so strongly with the contemporary critique of traditional metaphysics that it fairly colonized critical discourse. In the end, though, the figure of narrative mastery proved sufficiently plastic that another "postmodern" thinker, Richard Rorty, could turn it back against Lyotard.

In a 1971 essay, "Le 23 Mars," Lyotard called for a Nietzschean "antihistory" and radicalized the structuralist accounts of historical narrative as a mode of mystification. Story and history, Lyotard declared, impose continuity and closure on the gaps and silences of reality. He associated narrative with myth, fairytale, teleology, and metaphysics and implicitly contrasted its reactionary effects with the liberating sophistication of critical analysis. This description looked much like that elaborated by Hayden White in the United States in the late seventies and early eighties, another thinker who found much to admire in Lévi-Strauss's injunctions against history. But Lyotard did not entrench this position, and by the late seventies he was undertaking a critical recuperation of narrative that distinguished master narratives from local narratives. The criticism of big stories was part of a project in the validation of oppositional tales, the little stories or histories told by "others."[7]

Lyotard's first lengthy critique of narrative mastery appeared in the imaginary dialogue of *Instructions Païennes* (1977). In it, he aligned himself with the narrators and narratives of dissent slipping out of Peking, Budapest, and the Gulag, and he indicted *"le grand récit marxiste"* and the "masters of metanarrative," namely, the intellectuals narrating the grand history of "work" that served the communist will to power. Against big stories or metanarratives, he set *"les petites histoires,"* little stories or local narratives. To the query "why petites?" he responded, "Because they are short, because they are not the tired old grand history, and because they are difficult to insert within it." Note, thus far we are speaking of pragmatics, at least as Lyotard understood it. The metanarratives of communism are "official," "the grand institutionalized narrative apparatus," "canonical narratives," the "legitimations of theorists," those stories "which are supposed to rule." (*Maître,* of course, is a keyword, and on one page, Lyotard joined it with *story: "maître-récit."*) Meta or master narratives are simply those that are canonized by party and state. Local narratives are those that are not. Perhaps the clearest insight into what might count as a metanarrative came when Lyotard described its alter ego, local narrative. He associated local narratives with their typical narrators: "abortionists, prisoners, appellants, prostitutes, students, peasants." But he also labeled Kant's *Third Critique* a local narrative because "it is not a metanarrative" but is "itself a work of art." So little, or local, narratives are also characterized by being works of artistry and imagination. But there was more to come, as Lyotard further extended his debt to Nietzsche.[8]

His interlocutor asked him to explain how he would avoid vulgar relativism, once he had discarded all the metanarratives and their claims to truth. What did Lyotard want? Lyotard responded, "Paganism." In place of communist and liberal dogma, he offered paganism, which is both "impious" and "just." While paganism had its religion, it was not truly "pious," for its gods were notoriously fallible. Pagans prayed to the gods, but "they speak to obtain certain effects, not to utter the truth, reveal disclosures, or confess their culpability." And this absence of omniscience, sin, and absolution characterizes pagan narrative as well. According to Lyotard, "The pagans do not ask themselves if stories conform to their object; they know that reference is organized in words and that the gods are not their guarantors, because their speech is no more veridical than that of humans." So we may, by negation, add still more characteristics to metanarrative: it claims omniscience, it claims to refer to an external object, and it claims to be a veridical representation of that object. Lyotard's own tale refused such totalizing claims. "My story," he said, "like all stories, refers to other stories."[9]

Still, even his tale, like the many alternative stories in circulation, could not claim a pure, oppositional status. While *les petites histoires* resisted narrative mastery, as Lyotard conceded to his interrogator, "the master of our stories is not a pagan god, it is capital." Stories proliferate under capital and circulate in apparent indifference, save for one particular tale that *"l'argent"* privileges again and again: "the canonical story which privileges the autonomous activity of the narrator and which subordinates to that single name those of narratee and narrated." Here Lyotard introduced the pragmatics of naming as a key to understanding narrative mastery. Naming illuminates the contradiction of historical consciousness under capitalism; the story must *deny* that it is a story; it must "forget" its own narrativity in order to maintain the fiction of the autonomous self. But narrative is not created through free acts of authorial will: "Stories are not the products of a subjective faculty of narration which has set them going. Stories tell themselves, they are in motion as a matter of principle, and their narrators are only one of their conductive valences." In the event, Lyotard counseled openness to changing stories and denied that justice could be found in a "formula" or canonized in law.[10]

We may abstract a thematized understanding of narrative from *Instructions païennes:* Metanarrative is institutionalized, canonical, and legitimizing. It is in a position of intellectual mastery. It ignores the obvious pagan truism that stories refer to other stories. Instead it pretends to represent an external object and then pretends *not* to be a narrative. Local narrative, in contrast, is told by the subaltern. It is never omniscient but always aware of its own narrative debts. It cannot easily be "inserted" into a master narrative. It is artistic and imaginative. Appearing as it did in the middle seventies, Lyotard's account was original and suggestive, although some might squirm at his description of Kantian aesthetics as a paradigm of narrative modesty. Unfortunately, he did not rest content with this sociohistorical account of narrative politics.

Lyotard's *La Condition postmoderne: Rapport sur le savoir* (1979), which appeared in English in 1984 as *The Postmodern Condition,* set out his best-known definition of metanarrative and moved away from the situated readings of *Instructions païennes* toward a more codified description.

> Science has always been in conflict with narratives.... But to the extent that science does not restrict itself to stating useful regularities and seeks the truth, it is obliged to legitimate the rules of its own game. It then produces a discourse of legitimation with respect to its own status, a discourse called philosophy. I will use the term *modern* to designate any science that legitimates itself with reference to a metadiscourse of this kind making an explicit appeal to some grand narrative, such as the dialectics of Spirit, the hermeneutics of meaning, the emancipation of the rational or working subject, or the creation of wealth.... Simplifying to the extreme, I define *postmodern* as incredulity toward master narratives.

The modern had produced diversity of experience, knowledge, and languages, but it no longer commanded the power of belief to join them into a meaningful whole. The liberal faith that open communication would produce social consensus did "violence to the heterogeneity of language games." Different cultures, different visions, could be contained or persuaded only within what Lyotard saw as a totalitarian system of education and information. "Consensus" meant that difference, dissent, faced one of two choices: assimilation into the dominant language game or else complete exclusion from the circle of rational humanity.[11]

Lyotard spun a story of the postmodern as an historical epoch. Science, as it developed in the West, had carved out an identity for itself by differentiating its own mode of discourse from narrative. "The scientist," said Lyotard, "questions the validity of narrative statements and concludes that they are never subject to argumentation or proof." So viewed, narratives belonged to a different mentality: "savage, primitive, underdeveloped, backward, alienated, composed of opinions, customs, authority, prejudice, ignorance, ideology. Narratives are fables, myths, legends, fit only for women and children." This distinction underwrote "the entire history of cultural imperialism from the dawn of Western civilization." The marginalization of story and oratory legitimated and facilitated the imperial conquest of non-Western peoples. But even science could not sustain its claims to authority without narrating an account of its own place in the world. Those stories, modeled on Judeo-Christian theologies of history and honed to a fine secular edge in the nineteenth century, became the master narratives of Hegelian Spirit, Marxist emancipation, and technical progress. But they contained internal contradictions and produced alternate accounts and critiques. Pressed by the twentieth century's diversity, they fractured beyond repair. Today, in postmodernity, "the grand narrative has lost its credibility," and "most people have lost the nostalgia for the lost narrative."[12]

Lyotard also cast the postmodern as a style and a politics. The postmodern is characterized by a widening array of incommensurable language games, such as local and master narratives, each with its own players, rules, and ends. The account deepened the divide between local and master narrative, and Lyotard forsook his old exemplary subalterns (abortionists, prostitutes, prisoners in the Gulag) in favor of a racial "other," a Native South American community, the Cashinahua. Their "local stories" always contain as their referent or subject the tribe itself. The names of many tribal cultures translate as "the people" or "the humans." All others fall outside that charmed circle. By Lyotard's account, such texts as Pueblo creation tales tell of the origins of the Pueblo alone; the stories never weave the Pueblo *and* their neighbors into a single plot. Judeo-Christian theology of history, Hegelian or Marxist universal history, and evolutionary biology all do. The difference is crucial. Where *Instructions païennes* offered mainly functional or pragmatic descriptions of metanarratives (master narratives were those that occupied positions of dominance), *The Postmodern Condition* outlined a logic of narrative mastery, an analytic algorithm that could routinely differentiate local from master narratives on the basis of formal structure.[13]

In *The Differend* (1983), Lyotard further refined the distinction and again invoked the Cashinahua. Of their stories, he claimed: "The bond woven around 'Cashinahua' names by these narratives procures an identity that is solely 'Cashinahua.'" To take them up into another narrative is to erase their original identity: "The little stories received and bestowed names. The great story of history has its end in the extinction of names (particularisms). At the end of the great story, there will simply be humanity." Hence the postmodern as politics: to denounce metanarratives and applaud the proliferation of local narratives is to resist totalitarian universal history and political oppression. Lyotard had moved from *Instructions païennes*'s pragmatic reading of narrative mastery, which employed Aleksandr Solzhenitsyn's *Gulag Archipelago* (1973) as the preeminent example of local narrative, to the more routinized method of *The Differend* and examples drawn from non-European cultures to illustrate universal principles of narrative form. In *The Differend,* Lyotard could not use *Gulag Archipelago* to illustrate local narrative, for Solzhenitsyn so often appealed to "humanity" or "universal human ideals" to denounce the crimes of Soviet communism. In two short years, it seems, Solzenitsyn's work had metamorphosed from a subaltern story into yet another instance of the totalizing humanist metanarrative. But Lyotard's new example, the tales told by the Cashinahua, while it certainly did not reify humanism, ran into other troubles.[14]

Lyotard's claim that the origin tales of groups like the Cashinahua name only "one name" is highly problematic. He admitted at the time that even these tales might have a "cosmopolitical import," but insisted that the problem was "linkage"—what will join Cashinahua stories with a "universal history"? Only a master narrative, associated with a European or Euro-American genre of discourse, can create a universal frame of reference for such tales. Since many, if not most, tribal communities do tell stories that discuss the place and status of "others," much depends on Lyotard's often elusive discussion of naming. In *The Differend* he used Saul Kripke's analytical classic, *Naming and Necessity* (1980), to support his new generic distinction between local and master narratives. Names (proper nouns) are, in Kripke's phrase, "rigid designators." They are not capable of infinite extension. Only one object can be the referent of a proper name. In this way, names differ from all other potential subjects. As Lyotard saw it, the difference between a "History of the Cashinahua" or a "History of the Pueblo" and the "History of

Humanity" is profound; one writes the latter only by subsuming the former and effectively erasing their names. Universal history destroys the local, the particular, the singular, in favor of an abstract collective.[15]

Despite its appealing simplicity, the account does not hold up under critical scrutiny. First, many tribal communities develop narrative mechanisms for recognizing outsiders and even for assimilating them into the community. Marriage with nontribal members was hardly unknown in pre-Columbian Native America. (In the Pueblo Creation tale, says Laguna storyteller Leslie Silko, "there is even a section of the story which is a prophecy—which describes the origin of the European race, the African, and also remembers the Asian origins.")[16] Second, and more problematic for Lyotard's argument, we may doubt whether *Cashinahua* or *Hopi* or other comparable "names" truly qualify as Kripkean rigid designators. As Lyotard and a host of ethnolinguists have told us, the names of many tribal communities translate simply as "the People" or "the Human Beings." So far as the Cashinahua are concerned, the *history of the Cashinahua* and the *history of humanity* are interchangeable phrases; there is no difference between them. Both are universal history, and Lyotard's designation of such stories as local or centered on rigid designators reflects a retrospective, ironic intervention (the Cashinahua may have believed that they alone were truly human, but we moderns know better; humanity is a much vaster category). *Cashinahua* and *Hopi* are rigid designators *only within* a horizon of universal history; only after we have extended the range of "humanity" beyond their frontiers may we say they speak only "one name."[17]

In a 1985 special issue of *Critique,* Lyotard engaged in an exchange with Richard Rorty that cast a bit more light on the topic. The philosophers squared off over the politics of language and the legacy of Wittgenstein. The sharpest conflict came in a disagreement about the distinctions to be drawn between language games. Lyotard's "Missive sur l'histoire universelles et les différences culturelles" (basically abstracted from *Le Différend*) described genres of discourse as so radically different that they could never be meaningfully intertranslated without extreme violence. Rorty, in "Cosmopolitanism without Emancipation," countered that the idea of languages as closed, rule-ordered systems was just heuristics, and that natural languages (unlike a game of chess or a computer program) were never so self-contained that they could not be interwoven. But here the exchange faltered, and one of the sticking points, though perhaps neither speaker realized it at the time, was Lyotard's idea of metanarrative. In an earlier essay, "Habermas and Lyotard on Postmodernity," Rorty had endorsed Lyotard's "incredulity toward metanarratives." We no longer need transcendental or final grounds for our beliefs. Social consensus, persuasion, and pragmatic criticism are not only all that we have, and all that we are ever going to get; they are all we need. Rorty characterized Habermas's search for a transcendent logic of discourse as a metanarrative. In place of this, he suggested, we simply need to keep spinning "first order narratives" about particular places and groups that will help us imagine a more cosmopolitan future in which all the world might conceivably enjoy the benefits of social democracy.[18]

Rorty and Lyotard's agreement on the evils of metanarrative concealed a deeper conflict, for the two did not mean the same thing by *metanarrative*. Rorty took metanarrative to be the sort of philosophical discourse that grounds its claims in an unchanging universal logic of spirit, nature, or language. Renounce this sort of dogmatic and futile philosophizing, and we are more likely to enjoy a cosmopolitan future. For Lyotard, though, it was "cosmopolitanism" that threatened narrative mastery. The inclusion of multiple names inside a single story erases local names and culture differences. By Lyotard's lights, Rorty, for all his postmodern pragmatism, was still telling a metanarrative about the progressive emancipation of humanity from metaphysics and particular cultures. Ironically, if we define *metanarrative* as Rorty did, as insistence upon timeless rules of reason or language, then Lyotard's own explorations of language qualify, for his account of differends and agonistics clearly aims for something higher—more traditionally philosophical—than the mere social-historical criticism that Rorty sees as the only realistic task for philosophy. (Indeed, Rorty had elsewhere identified Kripkean theories of reference as one of analytic philosophy's last monuments of metaphysics, what he pejoratively called "realist epistemology.")[19] *Metanarrative* was for both Lyotard and Rorty a word of opprobrium, a bad language game that each saw the other playing. But the conflict illuminates the deeper divisions in their postures toward the philosophical traditions of the "West." For Rorty, the remnants of the metaphysical and supra-historical aspects of that tradition made it harder to incorporate new, opposing voices and perspectives. For Lyotard, this very inclusiveness was suspect: no cosmopolitanism without mastery.

In such works as James Clifford's *Predicament of Culture* we can see the emergence of a new story line for narrating global histories, one that employs a double plot to render the antinomies of the postcolonial world. Lyotard's conception of "master narrative" has found a place in the new stories, but that place is an uncertain one. Notoriously, his *Postmodern Condition* struck sparks off another famous text, Fredric Jameson's *Political Unconscious* (1981), and the clash illuminates the shift in narrative politics. For Jameson, the postmodern proliferation of histories disguised the incorporation of all plots into the single Marxist or "Left Hegelian" tale of the struggle between necessity and freedom tending toward a classless tomorrow. For Lyotard, Western capitalism's progressive obliteration of local narratives and cultures will and must be opposed by the radical differentiation of histories. Some reader was bound to split the difference, and Stephen Greenblatt synthesized Jameson and Lyotard in his much-read essay "Towards a Poetics of Culture" (1986). The general question Jameson and Lyotard meant to address simply did not have a single satisfactory answer. Neither Marxism nor postmodernism alone, as theoretical enterprises, could account for the contradictory effects of late capitalism. As Greenblatt saw it, capitalism had generated discursive regimes in which "the drive towards differentiation and the drive towards monological organization operate simultaneously, or at least oscillate so rapidly as to create the impression of simultaneity." The construction prefigured Clifford's *Predicament of Culture* and its oscillating double plot: the history of European colonialism and native cultures, in the United States and elsewhere, demands dual narratives in which the tragic loss of cultural difference and the comic creation of new ways of being native "oscillate," each denying the other philosopher Hegelian mastery.[20]

Clifford and Greenblatt's metaphor, "oscillate," did indeed, as Clifford said, strike a very un-Hegelian tone. It suggests a rapid mechanical movement back and forth between essentially distinct forms rather than the more fluid moments of dialectic. The figure calls to mind Hegel's "bad infinity": the static repetition, aimlessly into eternity, of two separate and mutually hostile alternatives, black against white, the two never creating any of the multifarious shades and patterns that even so stark a contrast as black and white could achieve. Since *The Predicament of Culture* described cultures as defined by their opposition to some imagined other, refashioning themselves in Technicolored shadings with each new context, we should be surprised by its mechanical description of narrative form. Clifford posited a much greater plasticity for culture than for narrative, thus displacing the problems of autonomy and assimilation to the level of literature: cultures may not always assimilate one to another, but stories (and storytellers?) do. None of his described tribal communities were anywhere near so starkly individuated and eternally self-identical as his opposed modes of emplotment. The crux is the insistence that a story is *either* tragedy or comedy, but never both, at least not at the same time. Like Greenblatt, Clifford believed that an oscillating double plot could engage the fluidity of culture change without succumbing to narrative mastery.[21]

A specific intertextual reference and a brief digression can illuminate Clifford's "oscillation" of history, for the tone and topoi of *The Predicament of Culture* recall Jacques Derrida's critique of Lévi-Straussian anthropology. In *Of Grammatology* (1967), Derrida placed Lévi-Strauss's noble savagism within a history of "writing." Derrida meant to dismantle the ancient conception of speech and writing as fundamentally opposed ways of being. But he also commented briefly on *Tristes Tropiques*' emplotment of the rise of the literate, historical West as a tragedy of enslavement: "What is going to be called *enslavement* can equally legitimately be called *liberation*. And it is at the moment that this oscillation is *stopped* on the signification of enslavement that the discourse is frozen into a determined ideology that we would judge disturbing if such were our first preoccupation here." In affirming his subjects' "lack" of writing, even while suggesting that this absence gifted them with a certain Edenic grace, Lévi-Strauss had recreated a metaphysical tradition of ascribing radical but intelligible alterity to another. But tragedy, the ascription of violated innocence to the observed natives, was not, as he believed, firmly centered on a single equation, in this case, the erasure of orality by writing. Its meaning depended on its implicit opposition to some other theme, some other telling, some other plot, some other figure. As Derrida saw it, Lévi-Strauss's inversion of the old Hegelian equations (writing, orality, primitive, modern, myth, science) was "classically ahistorical" and potentially totalitarian. Derrida followed the path into regions we cannot survey here, but the resonance with Clifford and Greenblatt's oscillating stories deserves comment.[22]

The Predicament of Culture appeared to put the Derridean critique to work in a new narrative that avoided simple celebrations or lamentations of the rise of the West, but appearances are deceptive. Clifford feared that narration of culture change might stop on one metanarrative or the other, and so to Lévi-Strauss's tragedy of loss he attached the comedy of cultural invention. The endless alternation of the two stories seemed to avoid dogmatic narrative closure. But the resulting story differs from Derrida's formulation in subtle but significant ways. For the philosopher, both liberation and enslavement flickered through Lévi-Strauss's tragedy, despite the ethnographer's best efforts to stick to a single story. Clifford, in assigning specific plots to enslavement and liberation, simply went Lévi-Strauss one better. Tragedy and comedy are not the true alternatives. The alternative is a *different* combination of plot and figure. Clifford's narrative of tragic loss and comic invention of cultural difference is shadowed by a telling in which cultural loss is emplotted as comedy and invention as tragedy, an assimilationist story that narrates the incorporation of natives into white society as a happy march of progress and describes local cultural resistance as tragic fragmentation: Europeans brought history, science, and civil reason to the ends of the earth. Some natives joined happily into this comically integrated society. Others, unfortunately, resisted, and today they tragically press factionalizing and ultimately undemocratic claims for tribalism, quotas, and separatism. That story of comic assimilation and tragic fragmentation remains a popular one from polemics against multiculturalism to Francis Fukuyama's *End of History and the Last Man* (1992). And while Clifford's politics pointed him toward a happier reading of cultural diversity, like Lévi-Strauss's tragedy of enslavement, it will, in his own figure, call forth its reactionary counternarrative, each denying the other a "privileged Hegelian vision."[23]

Indeed, the conflict between celebrations and elegies of culture change surfaced in *The Predicament of Culture.* The book's longest essay, "Identity in Mashpee," recounts the civil suit by the Mashpee Wampanoag Tribal Council for the legal right to an Indian identity and title to "tribal" lands. At issue was "whether the group calling itself the Mashpee was in fact an Indian tribe, and the same tribe that in the mid-nineteenth century had lost its lands through a series of contested legislative acts." The defendants claimed the Mashpee had assimilated and were no longer a tribe; the plaintiffs claimed that the Mashpee had maintained tribal identity despite years of homogenizing pressure. Narratives of assimilation and narratives of resistance fought it out under the watchful eye of the state. Clifford's interest, and ours, stems from the compelling experiences of those involved, but also from the trial's illumination of the painful collisions of divergent philosophies of history.[24]

Clifford cast the suit and its defense as two ways of imagining the past of the Mashpee and the United States: "The Mashpee were a borderline case.... Looked at one way, they were Indian; seen another way, they were not. Powerful *ways of looking* thus became inescapably problematic." Ultimately at issue was the nature of "American" and "Indian" identity. The structure of the essay implies a *Rashomon*-style relativism, with the same events retold through the eyes of different spectators, emplotted, like one of Hayden White's neutral historical series, as tragedy or comedy depending on one's aesthetic and political tastes. And Clifford's introduction, with its denial of Hegelian metanarrative, seems to point toward a Derridean subversion of centered knowledge. Yet the result thwarts expectation, for the essay draws some straightforward morals and even drifts close to the narrative patterns of *Tristes Tropiques.*[25]

The contrast of plaintiff and defendants, comedy and tragedy, invention and assimilation, at first exemplifies Clifford's oscillating stories.

"The case against the plaintiffs [the Mashpee] was based on a reading of Cape Cod history.... The story emerged of a small mixed community fighting for equality and citizenship while abandoning, by choice or coercion, most of its aboriginal heritage. But a different, also coherent story was constructed by the plaintiffs, drawing on the same documentary record. In this account the residents of Mashpee had managed to keep alive a core of Indian identity over three centuries against enormous odds." For Clifford, "the trial can be seen as a struggle between history and anthropology." History, characterized by an expert witness for the defense, Francis Hutchins (actually trained as a political scientist), relied on written documents to produce a "seamless monologue." Anthropology, led by an expert witness for the plaintiffs, James Axtell (actually a historian), relied on oral interviews and produced a babble of "contending voices." History won out, and the jury returned a verdict that effectively refused to recognize the Mashpee as a legal "tribe."[26]

Despite the alternation of tragedy and comedy in the expert testimony, only one mode dominates Clifford's narration of the trial, and that is the Lévi-Straussian tragedy of history's obliteration of culture difference. "The law," observed Clifford, "reflects a logic of literacy, of the historical archive rather than changing collective memory.... The Mashpee trial was a contest between oral and literate forms of knowledge." On this note, Lévi-Strauss and the writing lesson derived from the story of the Nambikwara creep into Clifford's plot: "Indian life in Mashpee—something that was largely a set of 'oral' relations, formed and reformed, remembered in new circumstances—had to be cast in permanent, 'textual' form." Textualizing (historicizing) oral experience brutalizes its subtle shapes. The metanarratives of history efface local orality, collective memory, and plural voices. Writing facilitates enslavement, erases, as Lyotard would say, the names of the different. Few readers will be left wondering where Clifford's sympathies lie, for "Identity in Mashpee" projects a clear moral: we ought to reform our ways of seeing, reading, and remembering so as to create a world of freer, more expressive collective and individual identities. Orality, local narrative, collective memory, and ethnography—all associated with peoples of color—come out of the story looking very good. History, excluded from these figures and associated with the whitened one-thing-after-another facticity of simple chronology, looks very bad indeed.[27]

"Identity in Mashpee" emplots history's narrative enslavement of "others," and as Derrida warned in his reading of *Tristes Tropiques,* the story of enslavement depends on its alternative tale of liberation. Clifford clearly hoped that the tragedy of the historicization of Mashpee identity and their consequent courtroom "setback" would oscillate into a story of heroic cultural invention. Perhaps the Mashpee could still find "new ways of being Indian." But the defendants who denied the "Indianness" of the Mashpee had not depicted the disappearance of tribal culture as a tragedy. Instead, they emplotted the assimilation of the natives as a happy, progressive movement of a local group into the broader circle of modern life, a shift from exclusive ethnic identity to inclusive American identity. In the summation, the counsel for the defense described the Mashpee's acculturation as a "'slow but steady progress' toward 'full participation' in American society." "Oscillating" in the courtroom with Clifford's tragedy of homogenization and comedy of differentiation were an assimilationist comedy and a warning that the recognition of Mashpee identity would tragically balkanize the United States. *The Predicament of Culture* keeps this counterhistory hidden in the shadows. Of *Tristes Tropiques,* Clifford noted that it captured a great truth, but "it is too neat, and it assumes a questionable Eurocentric position at the 'end' of a unified human history, gathering up, memorializing the world's local historicities." This critique applies, with less force, perhaps, to "Identity in Mashpee."[28]

The formal distinction between "meta" and "local" narrative comes apart in "Identity in Mashpee." Trying to avoid Lévi-Straussian noble savagism, Clifford struggled to refuse narrative mastery.

> The Mashpee were trapped by the stories that could be told about them.... Tribal life had to be emplotted, told as a coherent narrative. In fact, only a few basic stories are told, over, and over, about Native Americans and other "tribal" peoples. These societies are always dying or surviving, assimilating or resisting.... But the familiar paths of tribal death, survival, assimilation, or resistance do not catch the specific ambivalences of life in places like Mashpee over four centu-

> ries of defeat, renewal, political negotiation, and cultural innovation. Moreover most societies that suddenly "enter the modern world" have already been in touch with it for centuries.... Indians in Mashpee lived and acted *between* cultures in a series of ad hoc engagements.

The courtroom's demands for narratives of continuous authentic identity clash with the discontinuous subjects of real life. Narrative closure distorts our pluralistic world. For Clifford, the problems with the stories told about Mashpee are problems of form: the law demands metanarratives of homogeneity, when local narratives would be more realistic.[29]

Clifford's local narratives, though, differed from those of Lyotard. Despite similarities of vocabulary, Clifford and Lyotard told very different stories about the relation of the West to the rest and the mechanisms of enslavement. The tensions between *The Postmodern Condition* and *The Predicament of Culture* lie partly in their different uses of *metanarrative*. For Lyotard, any narrative winding the names of different groups into a single story is a grand *récit*. For Clifford, any big story emplotting a naively unitary subject seems to be a master narrative. On Lyotard's account, Clifford's tale is a metanarrative; on Clifford's usage, Lyotard's imagined stories naming a "single name" might qualify for the insidious label. Lyotard sees the tragedy of enslavement in the erasure of single names; Clifford sees danger in the demand for a unified subject rigidly designated by a name like *Cashinahua* or *Mashpee*. Clifford employs Lyotard's vocabulary, but his usage undercuts Lyotard's position: the desire for authentically "local" histories contains more than a grain of modernist nostalgia, and *The Postmodern Condition*'s tale of universal history's destruction of names sounds suspiciously like Lévi-Strauss's tragedy of the vanishing native. "Identity in Mashpee" convincingly demonstrates the naïveté of a construction that makes the purity of "local names" the measure of narrative value: "Most societies that suddenly 'enter the modern world' have already been in touch with it for centuries." The Mashpee lost *because* they were expected to produce what Lyotard would see as an authentically "local" narrative of a subject whose single name has not been contaminated through imaginative incorporation of other identities. But neither the Mashpee nor most "tribal" peoples can, or should, construct stories of cultural purity untainted by the press of other subjects, whether American, European, African, or Asian. "Identity in Mashpee," with its multiple subjects and modern primitives, demonstrates the *impossibility* of avoiding "meta"-narrative, at least as defined in *The Differend.*

All of us, it seems, wish to be "local" subalterns rather than masters of the narrative universe, but it is difficult to imagine a more cosmopolitan book than *The Predicament of Culture.* Clifford's tale of alternating tragedy and comedy, homogenization and differentiation, may tell a better story than the simpler stories at war in the courtroom, but its merits do not lie in its postmodern escape from master narrative or in its triumph of anthropology over history. Disturbed that the Mashpee, and us with them, are "trapped" by bad stories, Clifford, a good historian, tried to tell a better one. From such acts come revision, but we need not appeal to some magic essence to demonize the stories we critique.[30]

We do need stories of greater subtlety than either-or, all-or-nothing tales of pure assimilation, absolute resistance, and unbroken continuity. But Derrida, Greenblatt, and Clifford's metaphor, "oscillation," reinforces such stories. It implies an ahistorical repetition of two distinct entities into an unchanging future, surely not the world Clifford wishes to open up. Like cultural identities, narratives—tragedy and comedy, "meta" and "local"—are not aesthetic monads. They define each other through interaction, shifting meaning and morals with each new juxtaposition, are taken up into one another en route to changing aims, and are reinvented with each new situation in processes not fairly captured by the mechanical images of alternating current. Their differences, like those of Clifford's cultures, will be anchored at our peril. "If the word 'history' did not carry with it the theme of a final repression of *différance,*" said Derrida in 1968, "we could say that differences alone could be 'historical' through and through and from the start." The philosopher wished to describe the play of language, the movement of meaning from one sign to another, as basically historical. The differentiation of tragedy and comedy, mastery and slavery, is not out of history, or a mechanical representation of a more subtle historical world, but history itself. But he could not say the word *history* without a disclaimer, because he feared that it still evoked Hegel's history as spirit. History as the "repression of *différance*" refers obliquely back to the peoples without history. It was, after all, Hegel's history and historical consciousness that the well-meaning Lévi-Strauss denied his natives.[31]

Clifford's narration of the trial over Mashpee identity as a collision between history (universal, written, static, and hegemonic) and anthropology (local, oral, fluid, and subaltern) tied into that venerable division of the world into peoples with and without history. In "Identity in Mashpee," the agon rested partly on the old differences drawn in scholarly and public discourse, from Hegel to modern expert witnesses. But the divisions no longer look so clear: a political scientist, Francis Hutchins, testified for "history"; a historian, James Axtell, testified for "anthropology"; and still another historian, Clifford, encoded history as one-thing-after-another and anthropology as an inventive engagement with multiple voices. He might as easily have described the trial as a clash between different conceptions of history, rather than between anthropology and history, but he did not, and his choice of narrative codes is telling. The kernel of the trial and of *The Predicament of Culture,* the antagonisms of history and counterhistory, history and culture, universal histories and local histories, literacy and orality—all those deepening borders between people with and without history—had been cultivated before Clifford ever went to graduate school, before Lyotard radicalized Lévi-Strauss, before the Mashpee filed their suit. As Michel Foucault warned, just when you think you have escaped Hegel, you turn the corner and there he is.

Whatever the depth of our postmodern incredulity toward master narratives, universal history has not disappeared. New varieties of world history now bid to replace Western civilization courses and texts.[32] Indeed, Clifford's story can be read as a subtle new universal history, which partly accounts for its power and its appeal. And the demonic twin of his oscillating tales, the old vision of a comically integrated universe of spirit, found a popular voice in Fukuyama's *End of History and the Last Man* (1992), a remarkably influential and popular return to the sort of philosophy of history that had intrigued U.S. readers in the salad days of the cold war.

Fukuyama claimed that Hegel (or at least Alexandre Kojève's Hegel) was right about the end of history. History has a direction and a purpose, and once that purpose is realized, History will end, no matter how many local wars and battles continue on into the future. Thus, the spectacular collapse of the Soviet empire demonstrated the ultimate triumph of liberalism. While we still argue the relative merits of more libertarian versus more social democratic solutions to economic and social problems, virtually everyone now agrees on the virtues of democracy; the chief alternatives have vanished and we have reached the end of "the ideological evolution of mankind." *The End of History and the Last Man* was a typical postmodern "master narrative," but it showed some suggestive homologies of structure with the tales told by vocal critics of narrative mastery.[33]

Fukuyama, like Lyotard, acknowledged the importance of Kant in universal historiography, and a comparison of their readings is enlightening. In the last section of *The Differend,* "The Sign of History," Lyotard engaged Kant's brief essay "Idea for a Universal History from a Cosmopolitan Point of View" (1784). Kant had suggested that, out of the apparent chaos of nature, a Newton or a Bacon of history might abstract a lawful process of development toward a universal cosmopolitan condition. Lyotard found two different language games at work in Kant's hypothesis: "cognitive phrases" that recognize the "chaos of history," and "speculative phrases" that await "the progress of freedom." But a chasm yawns between these two genres. How will it be bridged? While we cannot empirically experience the future and thus verify our hope that history is progressing toward a cosmopolitan end, Kant thought we might locate a "historical sign" *(Geschichtszeichen)* in a modest but accessible event that can demonstrate or "point toward" a progressive moral tendency. He later found such a sign in the "mode of thinking" revealed in the "universal yet disinterested sympathy" for the French Revolution. The skeptical Lyotard, armed with two centuries of hindsight, had his own signs in mind. The "philosophies of history" that inspired the Romantics and the Victorians have given way before the names of "our history." "Auschwitz" has refuted Kant and Hegel; Budapest 1956 has refuted Marx; and "'May 1968' refutes the doctrine of parliamentary libertarianism." Fukuyama read the signs differently, but he shared Lyotard's desire to find a world-historical significance in such political watersheds.[34]

Other features of Fukuyama's text also resonated strangely with older voices, and one was his return to Kant's instrumentalist argument for the *efficacy* of universal history. If, said Kant, "one carries through this study, a guiding thread will be revealed. It can serve not only for clarifying the confused play of things human ... but for giving a consoling view of the future." If we smile at a pragmatic appeal from the author of the transcendental subject, it was no less surprising to hear it echoed by a conservative critic of relativism supported by the Rand Corporation: "Any Universal History," says Fukuyama, is an "enormous abstraction.... A Universal History is simply an intellectual tool." The phrase recalled Rorty's injunction that we keep on spinning edifying histories of moral uplift: "One does not have to be particularly cheerful or optimistic ... about the likelihood of a final victory of persuasion over force, to think that such a victory is the only plausible political goal we have managed to envisage—or to see ever more inclusive universal histories as useful instruments for the achievement of that goal." The end of faith in a fixed human nature is not, both Fukuyama and Rorty agreed, the end of liberalism, but its triumph.[35]

Indeed, by the end of the century, liberalism had come to stand on a pragmatic tolerance of difference. On Rorty's view, if pragmatists have an "Idea," it is "Tolerance." As Fukuyama put it, for democracy to work, eventually citizens have to imagine tolerance as *more* than a means to an end: "Tolerance in democratic societies becomes the defining virtue." And this historical sign pointed toward liberalism's strong suit, its preparedness for a cosmopolitan future. Like Greenblatt and Clifford, Fukuyama saw both an increasing assimilation of peoples into the spirit of liberal democracy contingently allied with capitalism and a growing diversity of local traditions. He, too, had adopted the double plot for universal history: "In the contemporary world, we see a curious double phenomenon: both the victory of the universal and homogenous state and the persistence of peoples. On the one hand, there is the ever-increasing homogenization of mankind being brought about by modern economics and technology, and by the spread of the idea of rational recognition as the only legitimate basis of government around the world. On the other hand, there is everywhere a resistance to that homogenization, and a reassertion, largely on a sub-political level, of cultural identities that ultimately reinforce existing barriers between people and nations." Like Clifford and Greenblatt, Fukuyama was ambivalent, but he predicted that competition between "different cultures," rather than "rival ideologies," will dominate international life in the future.[36]

The varied histories of Fukuyama, Rorty, Clifford, and Greenblatt evinced some surprising congruences of narrative structure. All wished to find global significance in local historicities. All claimed to evade "metaphysical" philosophical foundations. And all saw a world in which differentiation and homogenization went hand in hand, a vast, new double plot of culture history. Their writings mapped new postmodern universal histories and projected worlds in which *universal* was not a synonym for *homogenous*, and in which culture difference *as* culture difference remained real, viable, and even desirable, so long as it did not become exclusive nationalism.

The similarities did not, however, reduce to a bland consensus. If we return to the cover of *The Predicament of Culture* and think again about the Igbo man playing Western anthropologist, we can imagine the different readings that picture might evoke from our new universal historians. For Lévi-Strauss, the picture might tell a story of the vanishing primitive taking up the instruments of literacy and power in pathetic imitation of his political masters. Lyotard might read it as the embodiment of local narrative heroically shouting out the single name of the Igbo over the generalized din of the West. In Clifford's tale, the picture offers an ironic commentary on the shifting positions of observer and observed, its cultural cross-dressing an admirable warning against assumptions about ethnic autonomy. For Rorty, it might point toward the hope for intercultural dialogue and be a useful reminder that "our" knowledge is always contingent and negotiated. And for Fukuyama, the Igbo assumption of the icons of literate reason could signify the progress of spirit:

what used to be a Third World of peoples without history has become the new historical world, a changing border rimmed round the posthistorical West. The readings differ in instructive ways, but it would be a vain hope to believe that we could separate out some of them as metanarratives and describe others as local narratives. The tellings interweave, without collapsing.

The search for eternal principles separating the discursive modes of the West and the rest has reproduced the sort of metaphysics that so many of us wish to escape. And that quest for narrative certainty threatens to drag down a potentially constructive negotiation of what counts as plausible postcolonial history or histories. We would be better off recognizing that narrative mastery comes not from "meta" form but from social situation. And if we wish to salvage *master narrative* as a phrase, we should return to the pragmatic description in Lyotard's *Instructions païennes:* Master narratives are simply those that hold positions of dominance. The distinctions between local and metanarratives are contingent rather than axiomatic. Some groups have been more effective at institutionalizing their tales and imposing them on others. The imposition can be crude or subtle, openly contested, as in the Mashpee trial, or implicitly negotiated, as with ethnographic fieldwork. But there is no literary legerdemain behind the event, no hidden circuitry of masterful cognitive power to be unmasked and deactivated. We will not find a logical or aesthetic essence common to Solzhenitsyn's *Gulag Archipelago,* the courtroom testimony of accused prostitutes, or the creation tales of the Pueblo. If these are local narratives, it is by virtue of positions that are always changing and historically specific. No special way of telling can guarantee that today's local narrative will not become tomorrow's narrative master. Virtually overnight, the chanting of subaltern protest may modulate into the crack of the historical whip.

While *meta* or *master narrative* may help to remind us that narratives can be powerful determinants of experience, in a post-Foucauldian academy we should be leery of the simple dualistic vision of power that the phrases imply. Many of us writing on decolonization and history wish to identify with the suffering and the oppressed, but we should not succumb to the temptation to dichotomize narrative forms into "bad" master texts and "good" local texts, and then try to ground that distinction in an ahistorical narrative logic. For the Igbo man standing in schizophrenic isolation on the cover of *The Predicament of Culture,* capitalism's tale of the march of science may well be an oppressive force to be resisted, altered, or transformed. For his spouse or lover, Igbo narrative might be a harsh and sometimes unhappy master. And the picture itself serves as a warning, for without contextual or intertextual points of reference, the image is either hopelessly plastic or impossibly opaque. Lacking a more detailed description of its situation, could we possibly *know* that the masker is a "native" and not a state-certified anthropologist participating (in time-honored scholarly fashion) in local life? In some situations, mastery is comparatively easy to define and denounce. In others, it is not. Unfortunately, no narrative gospel, no analytic algorithm, nor even the Kantian sublime, can cast an eternal light upon our path.

So what is to be done? Do we toss our hands in the air and declare "History" evil and despair of rendering postcolonial frontiers without engaging in intellectual terrorism? Such fatalism seems pointless as well as needless. We are living a golden age of global narratives in which universal history is not simply possible but also unavoidable. Instead of imagining historicity as something that Europe invented and then imposed upon, or bequeathed to, the benighted "others" of the earth, we might imagine European historicities as some among many, historicities in both conversation and conflict with a profusion of narrative traditions. Rather than elaborating ever more intricate principles for differentiating historical and nonhistorical cultures and texts, we need to consider what happens to historicity when we imagine all peoples, regardless of race, religion, or literacy, as historical, and to think of their narratives as different varieties of historical discourse rather than romantic alternatives to it. So long as we are willing to refigure history, that sort of inclusiveness need not efface "local" stories.[37] Indeed, it may be the only way of taking seriously the histories of others. It is one way of hearing the words of Native American poet Joy Harjo when she tells us, "I know there is something larger than the memory of a dispossessed people."[38]

FIVE On the Emergence of *Memory* in Historical Discourse

Welcome to the memory industry.[1] In the grand scheme of things, the memory industry ranges from the museum trade, to the legal battles over repressed memory, and to the market for academic books and articles that invoke *memory* as a keyword. Our scholarly fascination with things memorable is quite new. As Jeffrey K. Olick and Joyce Robbins have noted, "collective memory" emerged as an object of scholarly inquiry only in the early twentieth century, contemporaneous with the so-called crisis of historicism. Hugo von Hofsmannsthal used the phrase "collective memory" in 1902, and in 1925 Maurice Halbwachs, in *The Social Frameworks of Memory,* argued, against Henri Bergson and Sigmund Freud, that memory is a specifically social phenomenon. But outside of experimental psychology and clinical psychoanalysis, few academics paid much attention to memory until the great swell of popular interest in autobiographical literature, family genealogy, and museums that marked the seventies.[2]

The scholarly boom began in the 1980s with two literary events: Yosef Yerushalmi's *Zakhor: Jewish History and Jewish Memory* (1982) and Pierre Nora's "Between Memory and History," the introduction to an anthology, *Les lieux de mémoire* (1984). Each of these texts identified memory as a primitive or sacred form opposed to modern historical consciousness. For Yerushalmi, the Jews were the archetypal people of memory who had adopted history only recently and then only in part, for "modern Jewish historiography can never replace an eroded group memory." For Nora, memory was an archaic mode of being that had been devastated by rationalization: "We speak so much of memory because there is so little of it left." Despite or perhaps because of their elegiac tone and accounts of memory as antihistorical discourse, these works found an amazing popularity and were quickly joined by others. In 1989 the translation of Nora's influential essay in a special issue of the journal *Representations,* and the founding of *History and Memory,* based in Tel Aviv and Los Angeles, showed the crystallization of a self-conscious memory discourse. A decade later, the scholarly literature brimmed with such titles as "Sites of Memory" or "Cultural Memory" or "The Politics of Memory."[3]

The emergence of *memory* as a keyword marks a dramatic change in linguistic practice. We might be tempted to imagine the increasing use of *memory* as the natural result of an increased scholarly interest in the ways that popular and folk cultures construct history and the past. Such a reading would be too hasty. For years, specialists have dealt with such well-known phenomena as oral history, autobiography, and commemorative rituals without ever pasting them together into something called "memory." Where we once spoke of "folk history" or "popular history" or "oral history" or "public history" or even "myth," we now employ "memory" as a metahistorical category that subsumes all these various terms. Indeed, one of the salient features of our new memory talk is the tendency to make fairly sweeping philosophical claims for memory, or even to imagine memory discourse as part of what is vaguely hailed as the rise of theory in departments of literature, history, and anthropology.

Recent works on memory often tie the rise of the word to the waves of theory that had washed over American human sciences by the 1980s. In its most popular (if simplistic) understandings, theory talk—variously figured through high "structuralism," "post-structuralism," "postmodernism," "deconstruction," *posthistoire,* and a host of other often confused labels—was imagined as a devastating critique of the totalizing aspects of historical discourse. And yet by the end of the eighties, we were awash in new historicisms that took *memory* as a keyword. These seemingly antithetical trends, the discourse of memory and the antihistoricist vocabularies of postmodernity, converged in the New Cultural History as historians began borrowing from semiotics, and scholars in traditionally formalist fields—literature, art, and anthropology—began venturing into historicism.[4] I am not much interested in trying to define *New Cultural History,* let alone *postmodernism*. Many of the scholars popularly associated with postmodernism do not even use the word. Nor am I interested, here, in trying to separate out the ways certain post-structural texts may radicalize rather than escape historicism. But I am very interested in the common sense that memory is the new critical conjunction of history and theory, or as Alon Confino and Allan Megill put it, that *memory* has become the leading term in our new cultural history.[5]

Memory is replacing old favorites—*nature, culture, language*—as the word most commonly paired with *history,* and that shift is remaking historical imagination. It is not as if *History* or *history* or *historicity* or *historical discourse* denoted unproblematic realms of experience that now face an alien memorial invasion.[6] *History,* like other key words, finds its meanings in large part through its counterconcepts and synonyms, and so the emergence of *memory* promises to rework *history*'s boundaries. Those borders should attract our interest, for much current historiography pits memory against history, even though few authors openly claim to be engaged in building a world in which memory can serve as an alternative to history. Indeed, the declaration that history and memory are not really opposites has become one of the clichés of our new memory discourse. In preface after preface, authors declare that it would be simplistic to imagine memory and history as antitheses, and then proceed to use the words in antithetical ways in their monographs. Such disclaimers have little effect on how the words work. Where history is concerned, memory increasingly functions as antonym rather than synonym, as contrary rather than complement, and as replacement rather than supplement.[7]

We need to reconsider the relationship between historical imagination and the new memorial consciousness, and we may begin by mapping the contours of the new structures of *memory.* The appearances of the word are so numerous, and its apparent meanings so legion, that it would take the work of a lifetime to begin disentangling them. Here I wish to do something different, namely, explore what these multifarious uses share. And I am interested in the word as a word, not in the various referents (from acts of recollection to funerary practices) at which it is aimed.

How does a term popularized as an antihistorical concept become an identifying feature of new historicisms? How does a word associated with the sacred become part of a critique of metaphysics? And what are the effects of our new linguistic practice?

A brief semantic history of *memory* shows a revolution in progress. A full reckoning is far beyond my range here, since the new memory discourse circles the globe, and a thorough account would require a gift for speaking in tongues. But a glance at English language histories of memory reveals some surprises. Our new memory is both very new and very old, for it marries hip new linguistic practices with some of the oldest senses of memory in a union of divine presence and material object.

Although current usage conventionally joins *history and memory* in a single phrase, that proximity creates distance. We may get a sense of that distance even in the vernacular employment of the words as synonyms, an old rhetorical practice that has grown infinitely more popular since the 1980s. Instead of simply saying *history* (perhaps for the thousandth time in the lecture or the monograph), we may substitute *public memory* or *collective memory* with no theoretical aim other than improving our prose by varying word choice. That sort of substitution commonly figures a tonal shift, however. We sometimes use *memory* as a synonym for *history* to soften our prose, to humanize it and make it more accessible. *Memory* simply sounds less distant, and perhaps for that reason it often helps draw general readers into a sense of the relevance of history for their own lives.[8]

Memory appeals to us partly because it projects an immediacy we feel has been lost from *history*. At a time when other such categories—man, history, spirit—have lost much of their shine, memory is ideally suited for elevation. One of the reasons that memory promises auratic returns is that its traditional association with religious contexts and meanings is so much older and heavier than the comparatively recent effort of the early professional historians to define *memorial practice* as a vestigial prehistory. When historians began professionalizing in the nineteenth century, they commonly identified memories as a dubious source for the verification of historical facts. Written documents seemed less amenable to distortion and thus preferable to memories. We can also imagine their suspicions of memory as part of a painful effort by academics to separate history as a secular practice from a background of cultural religiosity. But as Nietzsche contended, that separation was never complete, and the return of memory discourse suggests that at least some of us have lost interest in maintaining the separation.

In academic and popular discourse alike, *memory* and its associated keywords continue to invoke a range of theological concepts as well as vague connotations of spirituality and authenticity. Authors writing in secular academic contexts necessarily trade upon these associations but seldom make them explicit. Part of that trade stands upon the place of remembrance in Judeo-Christian tradition—*Zakhor* (remember), in the Old Testament, and "Do this in remembrance of me," in the New. And it is a commonplace that memorial practice anchors religious rituals in a wide variety of communities of belief. We could bracket memory's theological connotations, though, and not nearly be done with essentialism. Explicit religiosity aside, from elite to popular culture, memory serves as a critical site for the generation and inflection of affective bonds—Remember the Alamo; "Remember me when the candlelight is gleaming"; "You must remember this, a kiss is just a kiss"; *I Remember Mama*. The "mystic chords of memory" are, as Abraham Lincoln recognized, essentially mystic, their notes swelling to the touch of the "angels of our nature."[9] If *history* is objective in the coldest, hardest sense of the word, *memory* is subjective in the warmest, most inviting senses of that word. In contrast with *history, memory* fairly vibrates with the fullness of Being. We all know these associations, and yet we like to pretend they have no effect upon our new uses of *memory*.

Much recent work in the human sciences contrasts the rigor of its use of *memory* with the squishy meanings of *memory* in everyday use. In *Watergate in American Memory* (1992), sociologist Michael Schudson observes that most people understand memory as "a property of individual minds." To those not trained as social scientists, memory appears to be a psychic event associated with a specific person. But the public has gotten memory wrong, and the "social-scientific tribe" has gotten it right, says Schudson. Not only is memory "essentially social," but it is also located in "rules, laws, standardized procedures, and records[,] . . . books, holidays, statues, souvenirs." Memory may also "characterize groups" by revealing a "debt to the past" and expressing "moral continuity."[10] Memory is not a property of individual minds but a diverse and shifting collection of material artifacts and social practices.

We should pause briefly to examine Schudson's definition, for it is a fair picture of academic practice. To begin with, we should note that the definition not only goes well beyond "general usage," but it also reaches far past the truism that the social environment shapes how and what we remember, which is an idea that most folks outside the social-scientific tribe would probably accept. Memory here becomes "structural," provided we use that word with sufficient flexibility to invoke both the notion of "social structure" typical of recent social history and the notion of systems of difference common in the high structuralism descended from Saussurean linguistics. As Schudson notes, in current academic usage memory bridges a wide array of physical objects on the one hand, and the psychic acts of individuals on the other. The definition makes memory a structural rather than individual phenomenon, and it makes a seemingly endless array of physical objects part of memory. A monograph on the history of tombstones may advertise itself as a history of memory; a statue of Lenin is not just a mnemonic device to help individuals remember but is memory itself. Such an expansion of *memory* is indeed foreign to general usage. And while Schudson's account makes it seem a natural part of social science discourse, that broadly structural sense of memory was unthinkable until very recently.

A glance at reference works for the social sciences shows that the "tribal" roots of structural memory are shallow. Social science handbooks published in the first half of the twentieth century defined *memory* in the same squishy ways as did ordinary folk, as a "conscious recurrence" of some aspect of the past, but also listed the changing usage in experimental psychology beginning with Herman Ebbinghaus. Increasingly, these sources began to subordinate *memory* to other terms: *remembering, learning, forgetting,* and *retention.* The publication of Frederick Bartlett's 1932 study, *Remembering,* marked a turning point. *Memory* grew increasingly marginal, and in 1964 *A Dictionary of the Social Sciences* claimed that the word verged on extinction: "It is one of those substantive terms which have come to be used less frequently in modern psychology. Today it is more usual to speak of remembering or retention, with the sub-types of recall or recognition."[11]

Memory's association with old-fashioned varieties of psychologism had placed it on the endangered species list. The 1968 edition of *International Encyclopedia of the Social Sciences* declined to define *memory* at all, despite the luxurious stretch of the encyclopedia's contents over seven volumes. Nor did cognates and related terms—*remembering, retention*—make even a token appearance. Instead, the source referred the curious to entries for *forgetting* and *learning*. By 1976 the story had grown grimmer yet, and Raymond Williams's classic study *Keywords* found space for *history, myth,* and *ideology* but ignored *memory* altogether. Yet in 1993 Michael Schudson could speak of the structural usage of memory as if it were a natural feature of the landscape. Little more than two decades separate *memory*'s virtual disappearance and triumphal return.[12]

The new structural memory is part of a dramatic semantic shift, and we may broaden our sense of its novelty by consulting the *OED*. That source tells us that Schudson's account of general usage is on the money, for definition 1a reads: "The faculty by which things are remembered; the capacity for retaining, perpetuating, or reviving the thought of things past." Material objects appear in 1b, but only as supplements to memory: "mnemonics; a system of mnemonic devices." One must scan far down the list to find anything resembling our current usage: definitions 7 through 10 include "a commemoration," "a memorial writing," "an object serving as a memorial; a memento," and "a memorial tomb, shrine, chapel or the like; a monument." These meanings begin to sound more contemporary. But the *OED* lists them as obsolete. The most recent example dates from 1730, and the rest date from earlier periods, as in the 1624 example from Bedell: "It is a memorie and representation of the true Sacrifice . . . made on the Altar of the Crosse."[13]

The convergence of archaic and contemporary meanings suggests a narrative in which memory found its early meaning in the union of material objects and divine presence, a meaning that was displaced by the rise of the modern self and the secularization and privatization of memory. That is, roughly, the story told in most recent accounts of memorial practice. But what do we make of the return of these archaic forms in the academic avant-garde? The most popular genealogies of our current memory discourse begin in the nineteenth century and piece together a lineage descending through Freud and Halbwachs and into our current texts. The new memory is commonly rendered as a growing awareness of the constructedness of subjectivity or even described as a deconstruction of the modern self. Recent books by Richard Terdiman, Ian Hacking, and Matt Matsuda take this general tack; but as semantic histories, these works are virtually Whiggish.[14]

A closer look at Matsuda's wonderful book *The Memory of the Modern* (1996) suggests how such works naturalize our current usage. Matsuda argues that memory discourse emerged from fin de siècle Europe as one of the characteristic concerns of modernism as a response to the acceleration of history. Of Matsuda's nine chapters, only three focus on topics (neuroscience, mnemonics, and Henri Bergson's theories of memory) that discourse of the period described in terms of "memory." In the other chapters—on film, dance, politics—Matsuda projects our current structural uses of memory onto his subjects. Few of the sources of the period that appear in these chapters use the actual term or its cognates. And even the chapters treating the usage of memory during this period show a creative flair. Bergson would never have said, as Matsuda does, that "archives remember," nor can we imagine a fin de siècle neuroscientist saying that the endless repetition of "mnemonic traces" has displaced "history as a positive or liberatory narrative," or contending that "the fragmentary, disputatious, self-reflexive nature of such a past makes a series of 'memories'—ever imperfect, imprecise, and charged with personal questions—the appropriate means for rendering the 'history' of the present."[15]

Matsuda's gloss employs a very recent language studded with keywords of postmodernity, but we cannot blame that fact on some perfidious French influence, for similar anachronisms appear in more conventional histories of ideas. Patrick H. Hutton's *History as an Art of Memory* (1993) narrates the evolution of memorial consciousness. Memory, says Hutton, consists of two moments, repetition and recollection. Repetition involves the "presence of the past," while recollection involves present representations of the past. The world has evolved (or devolved) from a place dominated by the presence of pure memory in premodern oral cultures to the ironic historical representations of postmodernity. Hutton traces memory from Giambattista Vico to Michel Foucault but, like Matsuda, regularly projects "memory" onto texts that seldom employ the term. *Memory* does not appear as a keyword until Freud and Halbwachs, and even then, Hutton admits, historians largely ignored the Halbwachsian notion of "collective memory." Not until the 1960s could the great Philippe Ariès employ Halbwachsian theory as a framework for a historical monograph, *L'homme devant la mort,* which Hutton reads as the first of our new works on history and memory. But even Ariès's study of death, mourning, and memorial practices did not employ the discourse of "history and memory" as we know it now and as Hutton himself uses the term. *Memory* did not appear in the book's index, and readers searching for *Halbwachs* will scan the book in vain.[16]

The most self-conscious attempt to connect the archaic sense of memory with our new structural equations appeared in 1993, in Amos Funkenstein's *Perceptions of Jewish History.* For Funkenstein, German historicism linked old and new, and he quoted Hegel's *Philosophy of History:* "History combines in our language the objective as well as the subjective side. . . . It means both *res gestae* (the things that happened) and *historia rerum gestarum* (the narration of things that happened)." In Funkenstein's gloss, "Collective awareness presumes collective memory." Funkenstein cautioned that we must use *collective memory* carefully, since "only individuals are capable of remembering," but concludes that collective memory has important uses, reminding us that all remembering occurs within social contexts of environment and discourse. The implication is that Nora and Yerushalmi had been mistaken in opposing memory and history—the old sense of memory as material object and divine presence had been taken up in Hegel's historicism, and so *historical consciousness* married history and memory.[17]

Perceptions of Jewish History provides us with perhaps the most lucid and succinct account of memory as a system of differences. In it, Funkenstein employed an analogy to show a continuous dualistic structure linking archaic usage of memory with Hegelian historicism and our current usage as represented by Ferdinand de Saussure's famous distinction between *langue* and *parole:* "Collective memory . . . , like 'language,' can be characterized as a system of signs, symbols, and practices: memorial dates, names of places, monuments and victory arches, museums and texts, customs and manners, stereotype images (incorporated, for instance, in manners of expression), and even language itself (in de Saussure's terms). The individual's memory—that is, the act of remembering—is the instantiation of these symbols, analogous to 'speech'; no act of remembering is like any other." Here we find one of the most rigorous formulations of the new structural memory, one altogether foreign to Hegel and even Halbwachs. And the placement of this equation in *Perceptions of Jewish History* guarantees its narrative impact, for it appears just after Funkenstein's gloss of Hegel and just before a claim that memory in the "infancy" of Hebrew and many other languages showed the same dualistic structure: memory as a mental act and *memory* as a synonym for *name* or *letter,* as in Yahweh's injunction "This is my name forever, and this is my memorial unto all generations" (Exod. 17:14). Again we have an essential continuity of premodern and postmodern uses of memory. Structuralism allows us to imagine the old sacred meanings in more accessible, modern terms, and the old, sacred meanings breathe life into our new structural consciousness.[18]

Funkenstein had drifted closer to Yerushalmi and Nora than he had intended, by way of a rather free appropriation of Hegel. Funkenstein's reading appears to turn upon an elision of the differences between *Erinnerung* and *Gedaechtnis.* Each word may be translated as "memory," and it is true that *Erinnerung* is important for Hegel's dialectic. But in that context, *Erinnerung* is more often translated as "interiorization." If we trace Funkenstein's quotation from *Philosophy of History,* we find it in the midst of that section of the lectures wherein Hegel distinguished the "people without history" from the historical development of Spirit; and it is worth nothing that *memory* (as either *Gedaechtnis* or *Erinnerung*) does not appear in the passage. *Memory* does appear just after the passage, but only in opposition to *history* and *consciousness;* here memory belongs specifically to those peoples, mostly in Africa, Asia, and the Americas, who have not yet attained the self-consciousness essential to historicity: "Family memorials and patriarchal traditions have an interest only within the family or tribe itself," and although the images of distinct deeds may be retained "within Mnemosyne," such "activities of memory" and the events they commemorate "remain buried in a voiceless past." Hegel's *Erinnerung* is supposed to be the middle term that will historicize archaic and postmodern memory; instead, divine presence and structural memory converge upon the people without history.[19]

We should pause for a moment of methodological reflection, for I do not wish to suggest that we convict Matsuda, Hutton, and Funkenstein of presentism and consign their books to oblivion. They have engaged in a valuable variety of intellectual history, one that revitalizes old texts by redescribing them in language that is relevant to us and telling edifying stories about important precursors to our current projects. We should not, however, confuse their projects with the sort of conceptual history we find in Philip Gleason's account of the rise of *identity* or Reinhart Koselleck's works on *modernity* and *history*.[20] And the tendency to conjoin preindustrial and postindustrial uses of memory offers us a guide to the currency of memory, for our new memorial consciousness synthesizes memory's traditional, essentialist connotations with explicit appeals to postmodern vocabularies.

Memory seems an unlikely site of engagement with the antihumanist discourses associated with postmodernity. Few terms are more tightly bound up with subjectivity; few are better positioned to take the place of the "soul" in shoring up humanist tradition. In the words of Michael Roth, "In modernity memory is the key to personal and collective identity[,] . . . the core of the psychological self." That sense of *memory* emerges clearly in the recurring associated terms that follow *memory* in introductions to historical monographs on history and memory. Roth's passage is suggestive: *identity, core, self,* and *subjectivity* have become virtually unavoidable tropes; thus we hear that "memory is the core of identity" or that "memory defines the core self" or that it is our *amour propre* or even that memory work is a "science of the soul."[21]

The identification of memory with the psychological self has become so strong that, despite the constant invocation of "public memory" or "cultural memory," it is difficult to find a sustained scholarly argument for the old-fashioned notion of "collective memory" as a set of recollections attributable to some overarching group mind that could recall past events in the (admittedly poorly understood) ways we believe that individuals recall past events. We speak often of *collective memory* but seem not to mean what Maurice Halbwachs meant by that term. As Amos Funkenstein notes, Halbwachs often engaged in a "hypostatization of memory," in which collective memory seemed but a modernist synonym for the bad old Romantic notions of the "spirit" or the "inner character" of a race or a nation.[22]

Some of the more careful scholars make prefatory disclaimers to ward off charges that they might be indulging in mystical transpositions of individual psychological phenomena onto imaginary collectivities. For instance, in his important work on Holocaust memorials, *The Texture of Memory* (1993), James Young explained his reluctance to "apply individual psychoneurotic jargon to the memory of national groups" by pointing out that "individuals cannot share another's memory any more than they can share another's cortex." Who could object to this reasonable proposition? And yet most historical studies of memory highlight the social or cultural aspects of memory or memorial practice to the point of projecting "psychoneurotic jargon" onto the memory of various national or (more often) ethnoracial groups. Strangely, although the new memory studies frequently invoke the ways in which memory is socially constructed, Freudian vocabularies are far more common than Halbwachsian or even Lacanian ones.[23]

The most common strategy for justifying the analogical leap from individual memories to Memory—social, cultural, collective, public, or whatever—is to identify memory as a collection of practices or material artifacts. This is the new structural memory, a memory that threatens to become Memory with a capital M, and although Funkenstein's account is unusual in its sophistication, the general sense has grown so popular that Michael Schudson could describe it as the generic social-science understanding of the term. The items adduced as memory are potentially endless, but certain tropes appear time and again. The most obvious are archives and public monuments from statues to museums, but another, more picturesque body of objects qualifies as well, and any cultural practice or artifact that Hegel might have excluded from History seems to qualify as Memory. Ideally, the memory will be a dramatically imperfect piece of material culture, and such fragments are best if imbued with pathos. Such memorial tropes have emerged as one of the common features of our new cultural history, where, in monograph after monograph, readers confront the abject object: photographs are torn, mementos faded, toys broken.

When defined in these terms, memory begins to look like a Foucauldian field of discourse, thoroughly material, empirical, and suitable for historical study. Individual memory thus becomes Memory and the subject of any number of potential generalizations. Freed from the constraints of individual psychic states, memory becomes a subject in its own right, free to range back and forth across time, and even the most rigorous scholar is free to speak of the memory of events that happened hundreds of years distant or to speak of the memory of an ethnic, religious, or racial group. The prosaic emancipation is tremendous, for an author can move freely from memories as individual psychic events to memories as a shared group consciousness to memories as a collection of material artifacts and employ the same psychoanalytic vocabularies throughout. The new "materialization" of memory thus elevates memory, giving it the status of a historical agent, and we enter a new age in which archives remember and statues forget.

We need not stray far to find an example of the hypostatization of memory. Despite its tough-minded empirical disclaimers and suspicion of the old-fashioned tropes of national memory, Young's *Texture of Memory* makes memory an active agent if not a hero: "memory never stands still"; and "the motives of memory are never pure"; and "memory" even "remembers." The apparent inconsistency is not a lamentable lapse in scholarly rigor—as a study of memorial practice, Young's monograph deserves the praise it has received—but a defining feature of much of the new memory scholarship, as in Matt Matsuda's construction: "archives remember." Scholars who might smile at corny Victorian constructions (try to imagine a hip young cultural historian writing, "History's motives are never pure") unselfconsciously repeat those clichés with a new subject, and less careful authors use *memory* to decorate their monographs with great splashes of anthropomorphic purple.[24]

While a few such examples would seem innocent enough, some recent work goes to, and sometimes over, the edge of explicit religiosity. At the moment, there are two popular discursive modes of memory as reenchantment. The first involves weak appropriations of Freudian language to valorize sentimental autobiography. In the past few decades, such terms as *mourning* and *working through* have demonstrated a dangerous tendency to attach themselves to New Age discourses, and for each monograph attempting a careful, rigorous engagement with psychoanalytic tradition, we suffer a host of self-help histories. A 1999 issue of *Time* touted the therapeutic power of memoir in both popular and scholarly discourse and guided readers to such texts as *Writing as a Way of Healing*.[25]

A second mode of memory as reenchantment represents itself as an engagement with postmodernism and appeals to the ineffable—the excess, the unsayable, the blank darkness, the sublime, or some other Absolute whose mysteries can be grasped only by those initiates armed with the secret code. In its most avant-garde roles, memory conjoins the post-structuralist tropes of *apocalypse* and *fragment,* manifested in our apparently insatiable appetite for pasting Walter Benjamin's more mystical aphorisms ("*Jetztzeit,*" "weak Messianic") directly into ostensibly secular accounts of memory work. As James Berger has noted in a review of trauma theory and its fascination with "discourse of the unrepresentable," certain postmodern rhetorics of catastrophe have begun to blur into "a traumatic-sacred-sublime alterity."[26]

These two modes, the therapeutic and the avant-garde, often run together. Consider, for instance, Michael M. J. Fischer's influential essay "Ethnicity and the Post-Modern Arts of Memory" (1984), in which memory links certain postcolonial strands of postmodernism and Freudianism. For Fischer, memory unites two disparate investments: on the one hand, Jean-Francois Lyotard's conception of postmodernism as the skeptical moment of modernism, and on the other, a commitment to ethnicity as the emergence of "one's essential being." Ethnicity lies buried beneath the surface of memory, an "'id-like' force" "welling up out of the mysterious depths" or, alternatively, in an allusion to the Lurianic Kabbalah, "re-collections of disseminated identities and of the divine sparks from the breaking of vessels." For Fischer, memory's aptitude for expressing primordial and anticolonial ethnic identities makes it a paradigmatically "postmodern art" that can answer ethnographer Stephen Tyler's call for the academic production of "occult documents."[27]

As Fischer's prose suggests, memory's claims to radical alterity may edge into the stereotypic identification of the savage and the sacred. That tendency is sometimes explicit, as in Pierre Nora's belief that "so-called archaic or primitive societies" provide the "model" for memory's installation of "remembrance within the sacred." More often, memory's subaltern status turns upon its affinity to the Hegelian notion of people without history. One strain in Nora's reception has been the conclusion that Nora was largely correct in his account of the differences between memory and history, but incorrect in his belief that true memory had disappeared. Memory still survives as an authentic mode of discourse among people of color, and so constitutes a line of defense against what Ashis Nandy describes as the "satanism" of historical consciousness. In Werner Sollors's more measured words, "What is called 'memory' (and Nora's *lieux de mémoire*) may become a form of counterhistory that challenges the false generalizations in exclusionary 'History.'" The implication is that the emergence of memory as a category of academic discourse is a healthy result of decolonization.[28]

In such constructions, memory's notorious vagaries become its strengths, and the acknowledgment of what some historians have taken as evidence of memory's inferiority to "real" history emerges as therapeutic if not revolutionary potential. As Marita Sturken puts it, "It is precisely the instability of memory that allows for renewal and redemption." Memory is partial, allusive, fragmentary, and transient, and for precisely these reasons it is better suited to our chaotic times. Sturken's prizewinning *Tangled Memories: The Vietnam War, the AIDS Epidemic, and the Politics of Remembering* (1997) exemplifies much of the better scholarship on memorial practice, and it takes the memory-as-fragment trope to its logical end, namely, that memory is the mode of discourse typical of "the postmodern condition." The moments that produce it are those that, as with the Vietnam War and the AIDS crisis, "disrupt master narratives of American imperialism, technology, science, and masculinity." Memory thus differentiates itself from "traditional" and "formal historical discourse" that has been "sanctioned or valorized by institutional frameworks or publishing enterprises." Despite Sturken's careful disclaimers, history and memory break apart into an unstable chain of antinomies: history is modernism, the state, science, imperialism, androcentrism, a tool of oppression; memory is postmodernism, the "symbolically excluded," "the body," "a healing device and a tool for redemption." A series of inversions provide drama: slave defeats master, female topples male, and the local resists the universal. The language enlists *postmodernism* in the service of transcendence, emplotted as a narrative process of "trauma," "catharsis," and "redemption."[29]

Not all usage of memory cleaves neatly to Hegelian divides or invokes the occult, and an entire body of work on memory focuses upon such conventionally "historical" or "white" subjects as national holidays, war memorials, and other state-certified forms of public history. And yet the affiliation of authentic memory with "others," and the contrasting attribution of nostalgia, amnesia, or even worse, History, to the white male subjects of the state, may make its presence felt here as well. Michael Schudson has confessed that he received "vigorous warnings" about the conception of his *Watergate in American Memory,* including one from "a friend who said that as a Jew I should not write about collective memory without writing about Jewish collective memory."[30] Schudson's experience points us deeper into these debates, for although heroic narratives of emancipation through memory are common in the new memory work, other scholars worry about aligning memory with the rhetoric of healing and redemption.

For some scholars interested in memory as a metahistorical category, trauma is the key to authentic forms of memory, and memories shaped by trauma are the most likely to subvert totalizing varieties of historicism. If we follow this line of argument, we will find a different explanation for the emergence of *memory* as a keyword, one that imagines memory as the return of the repressed: academics speak incessantly of memory because our epoch has been uniquely structured by trauma. To understand how such an account might work, we need to turn to one of the most productive sites of memory work, the theoretical debates involving the Holocaust.

In the 1980s, the Holocaust emerged as a test case for critiques of historical discourse. The old appeals to historical objectivity had become hopelessly suspect, but the best-known criticisms threatened to descend directly into the abyss. Hayden White's notorious claim that there were no good evidentiary or epistemic grounds for emplotting an event as tragedy rather than comedy seemed especially suspect when applied to the Nazi murder of European Jews. And the revelations of Paul de Man's anti-Semitic wartime writings developed into a crisis in the academic reception of deconstruction. Memory appeared to answer these problems, either by consuming history whole or by weaving into it so as to provide an authentic linkage with the past while still preventing the totalizing narrative closure that many historians believed marred the work of their predecessors.[31]

Rather than attempting a survey of a rich field, we may sample three of the most rigorous explorations of the ways memory may come to history's aid: Saul Friedlander's *Memory, History, and the Extermination of the Jews of Europe* (1993); Michael Roth's *Ironist's Cage: Memory, Trauma, and the Construction of History* (1995); and Dominick LaCapra's *History and Memory after Auschwitz* (1998).[32] Despite some important differences, these texts share a critical vocabulary and several overarching themes. First, the sudden appearance of memory in academic and popular discourse is to be understood in metahistorical terms as a return of the repressed: memory is the belated response to the great trauma of modernity, the Holocaust. Second, trauma provides a criterion of authenticity for both the Real and its postmodern negation. Since memories not defined by trauma are likely to slide into nostalgia, the Holocaust, the ultimate traumatic decentering of history and subjectivity, holds a privileged philosophical place.

Freud has long been a familiar figure within culture criticism, but structural memory has opened a host of problems involving the application of psychoanalytic vocabularies to collectivities. Friedlander has acknowledged the difficulties and moved away from some of his earlier psychohistories of Nazi Germany. *Memory, History, and the Extermination of the Jews of Europe* deploys psychoanalysis primarily on a historiographic level on those contemporary individuals (especially Holocaust survivors and historians) who, in the past few decades, have tried to engage the legacy of the Holocaust. When Friedlander speaks of the reasons for academia's sudden fascination with memory, he seems to suggest that sometime in the sixties the repressed symptoms of trauma surfaced, and that the rest of us have been drawn into memory discourse via transference, even though most of those engaged in memory discourse were not themselves victims. Friedlander's most careful discussions come in readings of texts composed by Jews and German Christians old enough to have lived through and remember the events. He is ambiguous on the question of how far we may generalize trauma and transference beyond these specific instances.[33]

LaCapra is more ambitious. In his view, all historians are psychoanalysts of a sort, and all stand in a transferential relation to the past. Freud was wrong to think that his method applied to individual psyches and needed some analogical ladder to reach the social level. Psychoanalysis deconstructs the dichotomy of individual and collective, and so it is pointless to ask how clinical vocabularies developed for the analysis of individual psyches may apply to collectivities. Nor does LaCapra argue the point; he simply makes it his premise. If we follow his footnotes back into his 1989 work, *Soundings in Critical Theory,* we find him quoting Freud's suggestion that transference "is a universal phenomenon of the human mind, it decides the success of all medical influence, and in fact dominates the whole of each person's relations to his human environment." In LaCapra's view, "historiography is no exception to this bold generalization." The generalization is more than bold, and in *History and Memory after Auschwitz,* transference emerges as a foundational principle: everyone has a transferential relation to everything—or more to the point, selves and society are abstractions from transference.[34]

Transference allows LaCapra to offer two reasons for our "turn to memory." First, "traumatic events" in recent history (that is, the Holocaust and the "increased awareness of the prevalence of child abuse") have staged their belated return as memory discourse. Second, the "interest in *lieux de mémoire*" has also turned our attention toward memory. (Since LaCapra explains that memory sites are "generally sites of trauma," this second cause appears to be a variation of the first.) In other words, the answer is the premise: trauma and transference. *History and Memory after Auschwitz* effectively naturalizes the sudden appearance of structural memory in academic discourse. The problem is not why or how did *memory* emerge as a keyword in recent decades but how best to define authentic and theoretically rigorous types of memory. Curiously, LaCapra views this sort of critique as a form of deconstruction; in *History and Memory after Auschwitz, memory* and its keywords occupy the space held by *deconstruction* and *theory* in his earlier books. And the new vocabulary leads LaCapra to a provocative prescriptive suggestion, namely, that we should consider adding *ritual* to *aesthetic* and *scientific criteria* for the evaluation of historical scholarship.[35]

Memory's displacement of deconstruction circles around Friedlander and LaCapra's reckoning of the Holocaust as a "limit-event" that transgresses the bounds of historical discourse. That contention has an empirical aspect, namely, that the Final Solution is, in Friedlander's words, "the most radical case of genocide in human history." In support of this contention, he carefully invokes the staggering numbers of victims, the intensity of state investment, the industrialized sadism, and (though the fact remains unspoken) the location of the events in the modern West, the putative heart of History. It is a compelling empirical case, but there is an extraempirical claim here as well, for Friedlander also imagines the Holocaust as "the" limit-event and thus as somehow definitive of eventfulness.

Although the concept of limit-event is key to the reckoning of memory as a potential means of evading totalizing or "normalizing" forms of historical discourse, neither Friedlander nor LaCapra explicates the concept at length. LaCapra describes the Holocaust[36] as "a" limit-event, intimating that there may be others, but he does not name any, nor does he explicate the concept other than to gloss Friedlander. And at precisely these points, Friedlander retreats to quotation: Jean Baudrillard on hallucination, Benjamin on the "weak Messianic," and Lyotard on incommensurability.[37] In the last essay of his book, "Trauma and Transference," Friedlander concludes that, since the Holocaust is paradigmatically postmodern in its inaccessibility to historical representation, "working through" will mean to "keep watch over absent meaning." The quote comes from Maurice Blanchot's *Writing of the Disaster* (1980), and in that text the injunction is frankly mystical: "*The unknown name, alien to naming: The holocaust, the* absolute *event of history* . . ." *Limit-event,* then, is not a term that aims strictly at empirical or even conceptual investments. Friedlander does not mean to repeat the sort of sacralization of the Holocaust common in popular discourse, but the biblical proscriptions upon images of God, and the unknowability of Yahweh's true name, threaten to return in postmodern form with the Holocaust at the center of a murky negative theology.[38]

Although Michael Roth's *Ironist's Cage* does not make a case for the Holocaust as a paradigmatic postmodern event, it too claims that memory can rescue history from the ironists while still deconstructing the master narratives that underwrote Fascism and Stalinism. Roth's Freud plays "memory" to Hegel's "History." Where Hegel imagined history as a theodicy, where one achieved freedom by interiorizing and transcending trauma, Freud deployed memory to emancipate oneself by "acknowledging the scars of one's history." Memory thus aligns itself with the postmodernists against Hegel, but instead of denying history, it transforms it into the "quintessential talking cure."[39]

As the language suggests, the old keywords of psychoanalysis have given way to a new preferred lexicon: *trauma, transference, melancholia, mourning,* and *working through* recur time and again. We do not hear much about Oedipus or the primal scene (although the female genitalia do reveal themselves through occasional allusions to the uncanny) or Freud's "second system." The preferred terms come from those sections of the tradition most closely identified with Freud's vision of psychoanalysis as an empirical science and a medical treatment of ill individuals. But Freud's therapeutic discourse was also his most redemptive; and stressing the therapeutic, Freud loads some of the weakest seams in psychoanalysis, for *talking cure* moves away from Freudian tradition as cultural hermeneutics toward psychiatry as a medical science, and clinical efficacy is not a place where psychoanalysis has covered itself with glory. And these new preferred clinical terms appear in close proximity to words with strong theological resonance: *witnessing, testimony, piety, ritual,* and so on.[40]

The discursive shift deserves more attention than we can give it here, but we may observe that the new memory work displaces the old hermeneutics of suspicion with a therapeutic discourse whose quasi-religious gestures link it with memory's deep semantic past. Where LaCapra and Friedlander invoke the ineffable, *The Ironist's Cage* resurrects the archaic notion of memory as the union of divine presence and material object. In the book's final essay, "*Shoah* as Shiva," Roth suggests that viewing Claude Lanzmann's film is a "ritual" and an "act of piety." *Piety* is not a rhetorical flourish. Roth imagines *piety* as a new keyword of philosophy of history that will answer the vexed questions of historical representation: "Piety is the turning of oneself so as to be in relation to the past, to experience oneself as coming after. . . . This is the attempt at fidelity to (not correspondence with) the past." In his introduction, Roth says that in an age of irony, piety will be a "weak dimension," but things work out differently over the course of the book, for *piety* is almost literally Roth's last word. (His final word is *Jewishness*.)[41]

Piety entails more than a secular reverence for the sufferings of victims and survivors, for it implies a corollary devotion to the discourse of memory, and that fact has implications for my argument. We may begin to sense those implications by noting that LaCapra, Friedlander, and Roth are joined as much by common exclusions as shared interests. For instance, each mentions only to dismiss the legal debacles that brought "repressed memories" of satanic child abuse into American courtrooms and publicized the unflattering views of Freudianism common to experimental psychologists. Michael Roth claims that the resulting "backlash against memory" sounds like the "denial of bad news rather than thoughtful criticism," and suggests that "false memory syndrome" and "political correctness" "may only be nasty full-time employment programs for journalists." The suggestion belies the role of Christian fundamentalists in promoting criminal trials based on "recovered" memories, but his complaint is less an argument than a manifesto.[42]

Where Roth dismisses potential critics, LaCapra describes inquiry into the rise of memory discourse as pathological. In his first chapter, hard on the heels of a chronicle of "historians" who deny that the Holocaust ever happened, he argues that an "important tendency" in recent historiography is "to dwell, at times obsessively, . . . on the danger of an obsession with, or fixation on, memory." Although LaCapra cites only Eric Conan and Henry Rousso, an informal talk by Charles Maier, and an unpublished lecture by Peter Novick, he describes the tendency as a "meta-obsession" and concludes that "these critiques run the risk of both pathologizing a necessary concern with memory and normalizing limit-events that must continue to raise questions for collective memory and identity." It is a remarkable moment: the recent explosion of journals, museums, films, art works, and monographs on memory suggest at most a "preoccupation," but two French books, one essay, and an unpublished paper evince a pathological obsession and threaten to "normalize" the Nazi murder of the Jews. The defensiveness suggests the stakes, but it also suggests that the intense distillation of memorial vocabularies risks hermeticism. There are good reasons for not submitting survivors' memories of the Holocaust to the sorts of suspicion we devote to the speeches of Ronald Reagan, but the demonization of potential critics effectively underwrites speculative claims by implying that any critique—such as this one—is politically tainted.[43]

The idea that the emergence of Memory as a metahistorical concept in the eighties and nineties represents the return of the repressed is ultimately a speculative premise rather than a historical or critical argument. It is one thing to say that we should use the concepts of trauma and mourning when listening to survivors of Auschwitz. It is still another to apply clinical psychoanalysis to those contemporary European Jews who, like Saul Friedlander, were forced into hiding or exile, or lost friends and family, or even survived the horrors of the death camps. But it is a dubious method of accounting for the rise of memory talk among American Jews, especially for the baby boomers prominent in recent discussions. And it is hopeless as an empirical explanation for the valorization of Memory in the discourse of white Protestants and various other ethnic groups, a phenomenon in which Holocaust commemoration is inextricably embedded.

We have, then, several alternative narratives of the origins of our new memory discourse. The first, following Pierre Nora, holds that we are obsessed with memory because we have destroyed it with historical consciousness. A second holds that memory is a new category of experience that grew out of the modernist crisis of the self in the nineteenth century and then gradually evolved into our current usage. A third sketches a tale in which Hegelian historicism took up premodern forms of memory that we have since modified through structural vocabularies. A fourth implies that memory is a mode of discourse natural to people without history, and so its emergence is a salutary feature of decolonization. And a fifth claims that memory talk is a belated response to the wounds of modernity. None of these stories seems fully credible.

A different way of reckoning with the rise of memory discourse is to place it within the cultural context of the postsixties United States and attribute it to identity politics. Charles Maier has warned of the "surfeit of memory" and the politics of victimization. In his view, memory appeals to us because it lends itself to the articulation of ethnoracial nationalisms that turn away from the cosmopolitan discourses of history. Allan Megill has gone further and offered a falsifiable proposition: if identity grows problematic, then memory will become more important. But as semantic history, that proposition is not very helpful. Identity is part of memory discourse; as Philip Gleason recounted back in 1980, *identity* was virtually unknown in the social sciences and humanities prior to the 1950s. Erik Erikson's work publicized the term, and it took off in the seventies, little more than a decade ahead of *memory*. The two words are typically yoked together; to mention the one is to mention the other. Richard Handler, at a conference on history and memory, warned that the enthusiasm for *identity*—the key word of bourgeois subjectivity—undercut the claims of memory work to deconstruct the Western self. Since Handler's cautions seem to have gone unheeded, I doubt that retelling the story here will do much good, but I reference it as evidence of the circularity that marks so much of what we flatter ourselves is postmodern reflexiveness.[44] I will go so far as to agree with this aspect of Maier's concern: we should be worried about the tendency to employ memory as the mode of discourse natural to the people without history.

If we limit ourselves to academia, another way of thinking of the rise of memory talk in the eighties is as a response to the challenges posed by post-structuralism. Viewed from a certain deconstructionist perspective, Memory looks like a reaction-formation. Faced with the threat of linguistic anarchism, the academy has asserted its conservatism by assimilating a few empty slogans and offering up a "new" cultural history effectively purged of real intellectual radicalism. Here one might cite the litany of dangers of Memory: the reification of bourgeois subjectivity in the name of postmodernism; the revival of primordialism in the name of postcolonialism; the psychoanalytic slide from the hermeneutics of suspicion to therapeutic discourse; the privatization of history as global experiences splinter into isolate chunks of ethnoracial substance; and the celebration of a new ritualism under the cover of historical skepticism.[45] I have some sympathy for such an account; certainly, one of the reasons for memory's sudden rise is that it promises to let us have our essentialism and deconstruct it, too. Even when advertised as a system of difference, memory gives us a signified whose signifiers appear to be so weighty, so tragic—so monumental—that they will never float free. But can we credibly imagine a "pure" postmodernism untainted by mystical tendencies? Can we even imagine a coherent narrative of postmodernism as a cultural movement? If the skeptical moments of Jacques Derrida belong to postmodernism, so do the mystical enthusiasms of Blanchot.

A fuller account of memory talk will require a detailed reckoning of the interweaving of popular and technical vocabularies, since our scholarly usage is so tightly bound up with the everyday. Memory serves so many different scholarly interests, and is applied to so many phenomena, that an inclusive history of its origins would indeed approach the universal. But having begun with the wider interpretive horizons of popular culture, I should conclude with them as well, for it is our position within broader publics that makes this genealogy of interest. Here, I am less interested in origins and more in effects. Were academic discourse as hermetically sealed as we like to believe, the benefits of memory talk might outweigh the risks. If it were a simple matter of a handful of progressive and predominantly secular academics reclaiming "piety" as an epistemic concept, we might, if only through appeals to strategic essentialism, make a case for sacralizing portions of the past out of respect for the worldviews and experiences of colonized peoples, or victims of child abuse, or the survivors of the Holocaust. But that is hardly the case, and the insistent association of memory with semireligious language not only undercuts the claims of memory to critique metaphysics, but it also opens troubling vistas.

Aura, Jetztzeit, Messianic, trauma, mourning, sublime, apocalypse, fragment, identity, redemption, healing, catharsis, cure, witnessing, testimony, ritual, piety, soul: this is not the vocabulary of a secular, critical practice. That such a vocabulary should emerge from the most theoretically engaged texts, and that it should advertise itself as a critique of metaphysics, is all the more remarkable. Were we to attend closely to the more numerous studies in which scholars simply appropriate such words without any careful discussion, the tendencies would appear far more pronounced. And we should remember that our scholarly language circulates within popular discourses saturated with religiosity. Many academics may live in enclaves of irony, but most Americans believe in angels. As I write this essay, the State of Kansas has just announced that it will eliminate all references to evolution in its standards for science education. Whatever its intentions, Memory will not deconstruct neoconservatism.

The clustering of quasi-religious terms around *memory* suggests some conclusions about the effects of our new keyword. I do not believe that our recycling of archaic usage is a simple matter of some primordial essence shimmering through a postmodern surface. Our use of memory as a supplement, or more frequently as a replacement, for history reflects both an increasing discontent with historical discourse and a desire to draw upon some of the oldest patterns of linguistic practice. Without that horizon of religious and Hegelian meanings, memory could not possibly do the work we wish it to do, namely, to reenchant our relation with the world and pour presence back into the past. It is no accident that our sudden fascination with memory goes hand in hand with postmodern reckonings of history as the marching black boot and of historical consciousness as an oppressive fiction. Memory can come to the fore in an age of historiographic crisis precisely because it figures as a therapeutic alternative to historical discourse.

SIX Remembrance and the Christian Right

"I was here last summer, the day the monument was pulled away. . . . I came and I saw the empty space, and it broke my heart." Betty Watts had come to Montgomery, Alabama, to watch as workers removed a two-and-a-half-ton granite replica of the Ten Commandments from the State Judicial Building. Roy Moore, chief justice of Alabama's Supreme Court, had installed the piece in the courthouse shortly after his election in 2000. Ordered to remove the monument, Moore refused. Instead, he filed suit, claiming that the Decalogue represented the foundation of moral law and the U.S. Constitution. A Gallup Poll found that 71 percent of Americans believed that Moore's Ten Commandments should remain in the courthouse. Conservative commentators from Rush Limbaugh to the Union of Orthodox Rabbis spoke out in support. Nevertheless, the State Supreme Court removed Moore from his post; the U.S. Supreme Court refused to hear his appeal; and dozens of true believers cried, prayed, and chanted as the moving truck pulled away from Montgomery.[1]

The day the *Montgomery Advertiser* interviewed Betty Watts, the monument was loaded onto flatbed trucks for a nationwide tour. Beginning outside the Dayton, Tennessee, courthouse, where a 1925 jury had convicted high school teacher John Scopes of illegally teaching the theory of evolution, the monument made its way through hundreds of stops and thousands of viewings. Appeals at an end, Moore and his lawyer, Herbert Titus, drafted and began lobbying for a new congressional bill, to establish the Constitution Restoration Act of 2004, a broadly worded document declaring that no federal court had jurisdiction in cases involving public officials who invoked divine authority in the course of their official duties. In 2005, Moore's memoir, *So Help Me God,* recreated his struggle to recover the nation's "Christian heritage" from judicial "tyranny." The monument, the media, the commemorative tour, the legal wrangling, and even Moore's memoir, along with the narrative language of trauma, repression, recovery, and a religious minority struggling to retain its collective memory against the incursions of a secular, modern state, should look familiar to students of recent historiography: we are in the presence of *memory.*

Historians have grown so accustomed to memory talk that a stock genealogy has become part of the doxa of the discipline. In 1982, Yosef Yerushalmi published *Zakhor;* a few years later, Pierre Nora made *Les lieux de mémoire* a hot commodity. In 1989 the journal *Representations* devoted a special issue to the topic, one that we now remember as cementing the bond between memory talk and New Cultural History. Seldom has a word come so far, so fast. As recently as the 1970s, the term verged on extinction in English-language academic discourse: absent from monograph titles, ignored by scholar encyclopedias and technical dictionaries, and too obscure for Raymond Williams's *Keywords.* Two decades later, *memory* was perhaps the hippest keyword in the humanities and a staple of more prosaic spaces as well, from television talk shows to the Library of Congress Web site American Memory. With Pope John Paul II ill in the spring of 2005, publishers cranked out thousands of copies of his autobiography, *Memory and Identity.* One suspects that his Holiness would have been heartened to realize that, even in the decadent halls of the university, thinkers on the cutting edge of historiography had begun experimenting with vocabularies from largely religious sources.[2]

In the late twentieth century, "history and memory" emerged as a subfield within cultural history, and in North America it emerged partly by clearing out a distinct linguistic space. Even a quick tour through that literature suggests a historiography reacting against earlier academic moments, namely, cold-war scientism from analytic philosophy to New Social History, or the corrosive skepticism of certain forms of literary deconstruction. In the 1960s, historiographers preferred *hypothesis, test, generalization, correlation, regression,* and other shiny linguistic instruments of postwar social science. In the seventies, the cognoscenti turned to a very different vocabulary, featuring *deconstruction, absence, narrativity, trope, semiotic,* and other terms of hermeneutic suspicion. By the end of the eighties, *memory* reigned supreme. Especially in American history, the new enthusiasm for a warmer language frequently accompanied a populist reclamation of the voices of the oppressed. In tone and style, well-intentioned progressive historians attempted to legitimize folkish "ways of history-making" against the imperious skepticism of scholarly elites.[3] Here, *Memory* worked its magic against a presumably secular public sphere, allowing religious and racial minorities, especially, to find their way in a disenchanted modern wilderness.

Yet even the quickest glance at any television newscast should suggest that modernity looks a lot less modern these days. From Hindu nationalisms and Islamic fundamentalisms to the triumphs of the Christian Right, the twenty-first century little resembles the administered rationality of Weberian tradition. Although portions of Europe remain fairly secular, the world's largest industrial nation is, if anything, more religious than it was in the eighteenth century. Most surveys suggest that nearly 90 percent of Americans believe in a Christian God. Diverse around the edges, that belief is so heavily Protestant that even Catholicism can take on a remarkably Lutheran flavor. Since the 1980s a variety of public opinion polls have suggested that most Americans consider themselves regular churchgoers, believe in angels, and think that public schools should teach fundamentalist versions of the Christian origin story as a sound alternative to biological science. An overwhelming majority of voters tell pollsters that they would never support an atheist for public office. *The Late, Great Planet Earth,* by the right-wing evangelical Hal Lindsey, was far and away the most widely read piece of literature in the 1970s; more recently, various installments of a millenarian fiction series, *Left Behind,* have trounced all challengers on best-seller lists. Christian music, self-help literature, medical therapies, magazines, and media empires regularly outsell "secular" alternatives.[4] More to the point, the languages of "secular" and "religious" discourse have grown together. Memory talk, with its resurrection of a term largely abandoned by midcentury intellectuals, and its parades of religious loan words, is a case in point.

In the United States, academic enthusiasms for "memory" emerged in tandem with a variety of conservative Christian commemorative discourses. Just as secular academics asserted the centrality of trauma to historical imagination, so did the Christian Right; just as secular academics pressed the importance of popular and folk forms of commemorative tradition, so did the Christian Right; and just as secular academics developed two broad streams of memory studies—those focused on trauma and repression, and those devoted to commemorative practice—so did the Christian Right.[5] We cannot even gesture at a complete survey of the relations between memory talk and Judeo-Christian tradition. As Yerushalmi has pointed out, *zakhor* appears 264 times in the Hebrew Bible. *Remember, memory,* and *memorial* recur throughout the Old and New Testaments; the cover of my King James Bible (liberated from a Motel 6 some time ago), one of the roughly fifty Bibles placed per minute by the Gideons, reads "In Loving Memory." Here, I wish simply to focus on three aspects of recent semantic and political history: first, the adoption of a traumatic-memory vocabulary by Christian conservatives; second, the development of a new postmillennial theology of history that encouraged revisionist approaches to the past; and finally, the rise of a politically engaged Christian commemorative movement.

In 1977 the Canadian psychotherapist Lawrence Pazder published a memoir of one of his patients, *Michelle Remembers.* The book seemed to belong to an increasingly popular genre of nonfiction, autobiography of everyday people, part of a larger democratization of the memoir. Michelle's memoir had been preceded by a number of other books by survivors of child abuse. *The Three Faces of Eve* appeared in 1952, detailing the case of a woman with multiple, or dissociative, personality disorder, or simply *schizophrenia* in the usage of the period. And in 1973 *Sybil* narrated the abusive childhood of a woman who had apparently survived by dissociating and splitting off a variety of different personalities, which emerged in therapy sessions. What Michelle remembered, though, set her book apart. The narrative included lurid details of years of sexual abuse, satanic ritual, animal sacrifice, serial rape, baby killing, and a climactic final battle between the devil (complete with horns and tail) and the Virgin Mary. Michelle named her mother as her abuser. Moreover, Michelle had apparently repressed the memory of these events for something like twenty years. Only after sessions with her therapist (whom she later married) did the memories reemerge, from the couch to the printed page. *Michelle Remembers* went the way of *Sybil,* reissued in a paperback editions and widely read through Canada and the United States. But this book was the first to really discover Satan, and many of its narrative moments would recur, endlessly, in the following decade in a series of expanding claims of a secret satanic conspiracy for world domination. As one law enforcement official put it, "Before *Michelle Remembers,* there were no Satanic child prosecutions. Now the myth is everywhere." Pazder, credited with coining the phrase *ritual abuse*, claimed in 1990 to have personally consulted in more than one thousand such cases.[6]

Newly emergent memories of satanic ritual abuse provoked one of the biggest law enforcement stories of the next decade. The first and most notorious case appeared in Southern California in 1983. The parent of a young boy enrolled at the McMartin Preschool in Huntington Beach, California, claimed that her son had been sexually abused while in day care. After a police investigation, the district attorney's office declined to prosecute the case because of the lack of corroborating evidence. Frustrated, the chief of police circulated a letter to the parents of all the children enrolled at McMartin Preschool advising them of the dropped charges and warning them to be alert. Predictably, the letters set off a firestorm. Children began to remember an array of suspicious events. Within weeks, there were new, more serious accusations. Under the direction of an innovative model of therapeutic interviews, children detailed elaborate memories—apparently formerly repressed—of incredible abuse. The stories began with sexual molestation but quickly degenerated into phantasmagoria. The school staff were Satanists; children had witnessed animal sacrifice; a marine had sodomized a dog in the classroom; children had been transported to Palm Springs by hot air balloon for satanic events; a series of secret tunnels beneath the school facilitated cultic abuse. A doctor claimed to have found evidence of anal penetration in more than one hundred of the children. The police began digging.[7]

In the seven years it took for the McMartin trials to wind through the courts and the country, satanic abuse charges and prosecutions spread outward, from California to the United Kingdom, virtually every case initiated by the emergence of apparently long-repressed memories. The mass media promoted the stories by regularly airing interviews with "cult survivors," encouraging television guests to retrieve repressed memories, and presenting law enforcement and health care professionals to testify on the extent of ritual abuse. In 1988 Geraldo Rivera's *Devil Worship: Exposing Satan's Underground* became the most-watched television documentary of all time. America, indeed much of the world—Canada, Australia, New Zealand, Wales—had been infiltrated by a secret satanic conspiracy whose members raised women as breeders, engaged in serial human sacrifice, deployed elaborate mind-control techniques to encourage repression and amnesia, and aimed at world domination. Many Christians believed that, in some places, the devil already ruled.

That year, in Olympia, Washington, the two female children of Paul Ingram, a conservative Christian, chairman of the local Republican Party, and chief civil deputy of the Olympia Sheriff's Department, accused their father of satanic ritual abuse. The daughters, who apparently had dissociated under the years of trauma, began to piece together their memories in sessions with friends, the family's pastor, and a therapist. After the police investigation formally began, the two young women accused several members of the sheriff's department of involvement. More remarkably still, Paul Ingram, who denied any memory of abusive behavior, had begun to worry that he, too, was repressing. Eventually, he began to remember details of a massive cultic conspiracy with other members of the local law enforcement community. The Ingram revelations were stunning, especially as five years of systematic investigation of satanic abuse elsewhere had failed to turn up much in the way of corroborating physical evidence—no bodies, no scars, no dead animals, and until Ingram, no confessions. So investigators turned to outside authorities for assistance.[8]

By 1988 a satanic-abuse industry of therapists, psychiatrists, law enforcement professionals, and religious leaders offered seminars, books, lectures, and conferences on memory and Satan. Among other resources, the Ingram investigators viewed a videotaped seminar by Dr. D. Corydon Hammond, a professor at the University of Utah School of Medicine, whose scholarly research focused on dissociation and multiple personality disorder, and who described the new emergent memories as evidence of a global satanic plot. In a later session at a 1992 conference, Hammond detailed these startling claims: The program of cultic brainwashing had originated in the death camps of Nazi Germany, where Satanists ran medical experiments on inmates. After the war, Allen Dulles and the Central Intelligence Agency had recruited satanic Nazi doctors to run mind control experiments. The CIA program broadened into a global cultic network involving breeders, programmers, and links to NASA and the military. Programmers abused infants and children to make them dissociate, implanted control codes keyed by letters of the Greek alphabet that could later be used as triggers, and then covered the process with "screen" memories, perhaps even of alien abduction, to prevent therapeutic recovery of the originals. At the center of the conspiracy, according to Hammond, stood a Hasidic Jew named Greenbaum who collaborated with the Nazis, introduced them to the Kabbalah, and then immigrated to the United States, where he continued to practice under a new name. Further out, at the highest levels of the international conspiracy, Hammond's patients were telling him, lurked a leadership known as the Illuminati. The professor of medicine warned the conference crowd that he feared for his life, and that people who said that ritual abuse "isn't" real "are either naïve like people who didn't want to believe the Holocaust or—they're dirty."[9] Even in the academy, the boundary between psychology and psychosis had begun to dissolve.

As the resuscitation of ancient anti-Semitic and anti-Masonic conspiracy theories might suggest, the satanic ritual abuse scare ended with a whimper rather than a bang. Aside from Paul Ingram, few accused abusers would confess to worshipping Satan let alone to systematic child abuse. The police found no tunnels beneath McMartin Preschool, and after a second trial the defendants were acquitted. Academic skeptics, most famously Elizabeth Loftus of the University of Washington and Richard Ofshe of the University of California, denounced the methodology of prosecutorial expert testimony. Accused parents founded a tax-exempt organization, the False Memory Foundation, and began an aggressive campaign against what they called recovered memory therapy. A series of journalistic and scholarly texts analyzed the "satanic panic." Geraldo Rivera apologized for his documentary. And something close to civil war erupted at the American Psychological and Psychiatric Associations. In 1995 the American Psychological Association concluded that the courts were not the proper place to determine the veracity of emergent memories. The American Psychiatric Association revised its diagnostic manual to focus on "dissociative amnesia," partly reflecting the controversy over the mechanisms of remembering. The courts, too, began to rule against "repressed" or "recovered" memories, casting doubt on hundreds of prosecutions based on such evidence. Ironically, one result may be increased skepticism toward more reliable cases of dissociative memory disorders, including those that may be rooted in traumatic episodes of child abuse.[10]

From a historiographical standpoint, one of the curiosities of the series of events is its near absence from the contemporaneous discussions of memory, trauma, and repression by historians. Although the new "memory" talk emerged in academia during the same fifteen or so years in which satanic ritual abuse and recovered memory saturated the mass media, few historians or theorists of history and memory seemed to notice. Strangely, a few historians even denounced skeptics of such abuse as part of a conservative, politically correct backlash, presumably against Jews, or African Americans, or others wishing to press claims of a traumatic remembered past against the larger secular or WASP culture. Most though, simply ignored the phenomenon. Eventually, after the public collapse of satanic ritual abuse as a mass media phenomenon, a 1998 article by Marita Sturken helpfully situated those events in the larger context of the discovery of the seriousness of child and spousal abuse during that period, on the one hand, and the emergence of a feminist concern with "experience" as the ground for political claims, on the other. One might go further in this general direction and note the timing and locale of many of the satanic abuse accusations: roughly a decade after the rise of the working mother as a middle-class phenomenon, and centered on preschools, day care, and the American family. The stories fairly dripped with middle-class anxieties over family, gender, and sexuality.[11]

Here I wish to step back a bit and situate the rise of traumatic Satanism against the larger and gendered horizon of a predominantly Christian American popular culture. The first remarkable feature of the period is the assimilation of key elements of Freudian tradition to Christian frameworks. Freud had served generations of conservative and liberal theologians as a bogeyman, not simply for his reckonings of religious belief as an infantile materialization of the death instinct, but also for his account of the self as a "bubbling cauldron" of impulses and, especially for fundamentalists, for his explicit and sometimes sympathetic discussions of a wide range of sexual behaviors. In fin de siècle academia, the situation was different. There, the Freudian legacy had become so tightly bound up with scholarly and commemorative work on the Holocaust that arguments over "trauma," "repression," and "memory" could become battles over Jewishness. But the satanic ritual abuse episodes demonstrated that, in the larger culture, "memory" worked in different directions—recovered memories took specifically Christian forms, and the injunction to remember a strongly Christian flavor. Even the Holocaust surfaced as evidence of an anti-Christian plot. Nor did the debunking of the satanic panic break those linkages. If the satanic ritual abuse scares showed the popularization of an implicitly Freudian conception of memory in conservative Christian discourse, it also revealed dramatic changes in conservative Christian belief.

The search for repressed memories of satanic ritual abuse contributed to the consolidation of a networked Christian Right with the ability to shape the discourse of the secular mass media. The sheer scale of resources devoted to the international satanic conspiracy was staggering. The McMartin Preschool trial alone cost $13 million. Book sales, television viewing, advertisement revenues, and church donations increased the sheer quantity of capital flowing to, through, and around conservative Christian institutions and audiences. Without a shared strategic plan, Christian conservatives had not simply demonstrated the power to set the terms of debate for health care and law enforcement professionals but had also shown their growing representation within those fields. Those invested in the satanic abuse scare would move on to new issues, but in so doing, they expanded the tropes of repression and recovery into an allegory of history: much as the Satanists had stolen the memories of ritual abuse victims, anti-Christian forces conspired to repress the nation's Christian heritage. To understand the links between the Christian discourse surrounding repressed memory and the Ten Commandments spectacle of Judge Roy Moore, we need to backtrack and engage with the new Christian theologies of history that provided a narrative framework through which conservatives could make sense of their new world order.

On conservative Christian Web sites in the early twenty-first century, one of the most cited authorities on topics ranging from ritual abuse to *Dungeons and Dragons* was a 1976 study by theologian Gary North titled *None Dare Call It Witchcraft*. North's book demonstrated that the recovery of repressed memories did not limit itself to a focused concern with cultic weirdos, but rather opened out on an entire theology of history. In the view of North and his fellow believers, the demonic forces ravaging the American family and promoting Christian amnesia represented a larger global battle for historical domination. North opened his book with a string of anecdotes about spontaneous human combustion. Why did people appear to be bursting into flame? Furthermore, why had Ouija boards begun to appear at children's parties even in the Bible Belt? Why did so many scientists pursue research into parapsychology and other occult phenomena? According to North, it was because demonic forces were calling pre-Christian paganism up from the dead. Paganism was advancing across the United States, and secular humanism was helpless to stop it. Indeed, secular humanism was part of the problem. Citing Thomas Kuhn's famous 1962 work, *The Structure of Scientific Revolutions,* North argued that scientific rationality had essentially destroyed itself from within; and as paganism spread, so had pagan politics, culminating in a "demonic state" of centralized and collectivist power. Yet most evangelical and fundamentalist Christians drew back from the public sphere, praying for Christ to return and set things straight. Christians could no longer afford passivity. The answer," North declared, "is a systematic, well-financed decentralized program of Christian reconstruction. Every area of life must be called back from the rot of humanism and the acids of occultism."[12]

North's text provides one of the links between the so-called repressed memories of satanic abuse and a new theology of history and set of commemorative practices. To understand the position of North's text, though, requires a brief detour into obscure corners of American theological tradition. What, exactly, is Christian reconstruction? And what is its relation to memory? Here, we can follow North's footnotes, with their peculiar mix of respectable scholarly work and conspiracy theory pamphlets. Two names mentioned by North especially deserve attention: Cornelius Van Til and Rousas J. Rushdooney.

Cornelius Van Til was a conservative Dutch Presbyterian who studied at the Princeton Theological Seminary, a Presbyterian school of theology founded in the early nineteenth century and loosely affiliated with Princeton University. In the late 1920s, Van Til joined the faculty of the seminary, which was then divided, like the rest of American theology, into warring factions. On one side stood all the representatives of a "modern" or "liberal" theology that had made its peace with historicism, science, and the higher criticism. On the other side stood a coalition of fundamentalists, conservative evangelicals, and some of the more studied intellectuals who came to be known as neoorthodox theologians. The liberals saved Princeton Theological Seminary for modernity, mandating that the faculty affiliate with more liberal denominations. The seminary's professor of apologetics, J. Gresham Machen, an unreconstructed southern Calvinist, resigned to found a new school, Westminster Seminary, in Philadelphia and persuaded Van Til to join him.[13]

At Westminster, Van Til became best known for developing an apologetics well to the right of neoorthodoxy. Influenced by the political success of Abraham Kuyper—the Dutch theologian, politician, and author who, as prime minister, attempted to install Calvinist ethics as the foundation of civil governance in Holland—Van Til argued that true Christians could not concede an inch of ground to secular society. Each believer faced a simple choice: "theonomy or autonomy." Either the world was centered on God, or it claimed, foolishly, to be autonomous. But even the so-called autonomous humanist or rationalist thinkers presupposed an essentially religious set of principles. Van Til's epistemological argument entailed practical consequences. Christians could not rest content with isolating themselves in the home and the church—ethics, politics, art, and education, all must be either reclaimed for Christ or relinquished to Satan. Although Westminster could scarcely command the attention accorded to places like Union Theological Seminary, where neoorthodox theologians Paul Tillich and Reinhold and Richard Niebuhr presided over a dramatic revision of mainline American theology, Van Til was on his way to cult status in 1959 when a book-length study of his thought appeared in print, titled *By What Standard?*[14]

The book's author, Rousas J. Rushdoony, was a recently ordained Presbyterian pastor from California. Rushdoony's parents had fled Armenia during the Turkish massacres. He had been born in New York City in 1916 and educated at the University of California, Berkeley, where he took classes in medieval history with the Jewish refugee Ernst Kantorowicz and completed a master's degree in education. After graduating, he studied with George Huntston Williams at the Pacific Institute of Religion, a liberal school affiliated with the University of California. Rushdoony served missions to San Francisco's Chinatown and a Shoshone Indian reservation, but never accepted the pluralism of the Berkeley curriculum. In the early sixties, he wrote columns for the agribusiness journal *California Farmer,* in which he denounced property tax, paper currency, and Cesar Chavez. In a 1963 book, *The Messianic Character of American Education,* Rushdoony condemned public education—and progressive theories of learning—as satanic. For several years he covered and consulted in an array of legal battles by Christian schools against various states and published a stream of monographs.[15]

In 1962 Rushdoony delivered a series of lectures on American history. *This Independent Republic: Studies in the Nature and Meaning of American History* argued the United States had never been a secular nation—its roots were "Christian and Augustinian," and the nation, from its colonial incarnation through the time when the Constitution was written, represented *"a Protestant feudal restoration."* In support of that startling claim, the book mixed creative readings of primary documents with selective citations of conservative scholars, from Carl Bridenbaugh to James Malin, and an aggressive interpretation of federalism. Counties, Rushdoony declared, were the "basic and determinative unit of American civil government." The notorious establishment clause of the First Amendment, which held that "Congress shall make no laws respecting an establishment of religion," simply prevented the federal government from usurping the religious prerogatives of the individual "Christian states." Rushdoony drew from this a moral:

> The revival and growth of the historic American settlement depends therefore on the Christian renewal of the citizenry and the renewal of the centrality of the local units of government. Not in Washington, but on the local level, the battle will be won or lost. The key resistance today is therefore to be found among those who battle for the integrity and independence from usurpation of country government, among those who establish and further Christian schools, among those, in short, who realize that the American answer to the problem of civil power was a Christian one, and anchored it firmly close to home.

The language of this passage—*home, Christian state, restoration,* and *renewal*—should sound familiar to anyone attentive to the poetics of recent American politics. Rushdoony's 1960s lectures and writings represented one of the earliest coherent theological statements of a key proposition for the new Christian Right, namely, that the United States was a Christian nation and not a constitutional democracy. Unlike many of the other period pamphleteers, from the Minutemen to the John Birch

Society, Rushdoony denied any American debts to classical liberalism or the Roman republic.[16]

In his 1969 book, *The Biblical Philosophy of History,* Rushdoony set American history in a global context. "History," he wrote, "is the battle of Christ versus antichrist." And, he claimed, this world historical battle had evolved through three stages. In the first, antiquity had established a pagan order with a pre-Christian religion, culture, and politics. In the second age, Christianity had vanquished paganism to establish a theonomous civilization. But with the rise of Neoplatonism, the Renaissance, and the Enlightenment, paganism had returned in new forms to bedevil the earth's third age. By reclaiming the Dark Ages from Enlightenment historiography, Rushdoony placed classical liberalism, libertarianism, and modern conservatism all in the anti-Christian camp. Reinhold Niebuhr, James Kirkpatrick, William Buckley, and Albert Schweitzer all displayed vicious pagan tendencies. And Rushdoony was working out a political solution to the pagan revival.[17]

In the middle 1960s, Rushdoony moved to Southern California and established the Chalcedon Foundation as a base for his preaching and publishing. Between 1968 and 1972 he delivered the lectures that became his most important book, *Institutes of Biblical Law* (1973), an eight-hundred-page legal guide for "reconstructing" the United States along Christian lines. The book began from a simple premise: The United States was a Christian nation whose legitimacy and law ultimately derived from God. Divine Law was revealed through the Bible, most importantly in the Ten Commandments, but also in a series of various proscriptions and injunctions scattered throughout the Old Testament. For Rushdoony, all the laws and crimes specified in the Old Testament remained binding on modern society unless specifically revoked by the New Testament. He methodically worked out "case law" from each of the Ten Commandments, supplemented by descriptions of biblical juridical practice.[18]

"Christian Reconstruction," Rushdoony's name for his project, promised a new civil order. Imprisonment would effectively end, since the only penalties for crime would be either restitution or corporal or capital punishment. Homosexuality, adultery, and blasphemy—including the teaching of secular doctrines—could be punished by death, a doctrine likely to guarantee the immediate execution of a plurality or even a majority of the citizens of the United States. To the book, he appended three essays on Christian economic law written by his son-in-law, Gary North. The *Institutes* elaborated Rushdoony and North's understanding of the implications of Van Til's conviction that Christians must claim "every inch" of life for biblical law. There was to be no waiting for the Judgment or miraculous intervention. As the pastor would later tell a conservative interviewer, "We are in the process of redivinizing the state."[19]

The language of Christian Reconstruction deserves a closer look. *Reconstruction* reworked post–Civil War historiography, a resonance that appealed to Rushdoony, a states' rights extremist, and a wide swath of his likeliest audience, white conservatives. Rushdoony was not a biological racialist—racism founded on modern biology simply represented another pagan revival as evinced by the anti-Christian politics of the Nazis. Culture and race were simply visible expressions of religion. But religious determinism did not make Rushdoony a racial liberal. *The Biblical Philosophy of History* condemned historians such as Kenneth Stampp for their "ahistorical" sympathy for civil rights. "The white man," said Rushdoony, "has behind him centuries of Christian culture and the discipline and selective breeding this faith requires." The meaning of *reconstruction* thus resonated with white southern folk-histories of union tyranny. If breeding, and more particularly, interbreeding, lurked beneath the religious surface, a variety of more sympathetic terms could amplify or even stand in for *reconstruction: renewal, restitution, restoration,* and *reform*. Despite his footnotes and references to contemporary scholarship, Rushdoony carefully aimed his prose at a general audience and preferred words that could double as secular concepts. "History is in part not only a long struggle for the minds, bodies and properties of men," he wrote in *This Independent Republic,* "but it is also a battle with respect to language."[20]

Although Rushdoony and Christian Reconstruction might make their strongest claim to influence through linguistic innovations, we cannot dismiss the Chalcedon Foundation as a cranky little corner on the right.

If the new theology amounted to a new paranoid style of American politics, it wielded power, nonetheless. From Rushdoony's role in the homeschooling movement to his connections with Valley Christian University—alma mater of talk-show host Morton Downey—and Chalcedon's involvement in the founding of the Rutherford Institute, a legal consulting group that provided the counsel for Paula Jones in her civil suit against President William Jefferson Clinton, Reconstruction stalked the major political battlegrounds of the late twentieth century. Conservative California philanthropist and political activist Howard Ahmanson Jr. would later describe Rushdoony as a "father figure," and during the McMartin Preschool trials Ahmanson told an interviewer, "My goal is the total integration of biblical law into our lives." *Time* magazine named the Chalcedon Foundation as a behind-the-scenes player in the second Bush White House, part of a phalanx of religious right organizations with regular access. But Christian Reconstruction would have more influence as the intellectual foundation for a new postmillennialism that sought to bring about Christian rule by earthly means.[21]

Where fundamentalists and conservative evangelicals of earlier generations had kept apart from the rough-and-tumble of secular institutions, partly out of fear of contact with sin and partly out of a premillennial conviction that Christ had to return prior to the establishment of a true Christian society, Christian Reconstruction spurred believers to mount an aggressive reclamation of everyday life, ranging from involvement in local school boards to policing to university curricula.[22] The implications for those involved with or following the satanic ritual abuse trials were clear enough, but in later years conservative Christians in fields ranging from law to pharmacy would apply their interpretations of Christian renewal to everything from jurisprudence to refusing to dispense birth control medication. Coins, currency, the local courthouse, and schoolrooms would all serve as memorials of Christian struggle.

In the 1980s, reconstruction reached a turning point. Gary North split with Rushdoony and left to establish his own brand of reconstructionist theology in the Institute for Christian Economics in Tyler, Texas. At

Westminster, one of Van Til's students, Greg Bahnsen, published *Theonomy: A Defense of Christian Ethics,* a study that divided the Westminster faculty and came to be reckoned as the most academically rigorous of reconstructionist studies. Moral Majority leader Jerry Falwell attacked Rushdoony for planning to execute homosexuals and drunkards. (Rushdoony indignantly replied that he had never endorsed the execution of *drunkards.*) Various Christian conservatives publicly distanced themselves from the most outrageous reconstructionist claims. The Christian Broadcast Network pushed out the first dean of its new law school, Herbert Titus, when it appeared that his presence might jeopardize the school's accreditation by the American Bar Association. (Titus had used Rushdoony's *Institutes of Biblical Law* in his courses.) But reconstructionist or theonomist organizations proliferated, and the Providence Foundation, Plymouth Foundation, and a host of other tax-exempt institutions sponsored an openly theocratic activism. Titus himself went on to serve as counsel in a range of conservative Christian suits against the federal government, including Judge Roy Moore's crusade against secularism, and in the writing of the Constitution Restoration Act.[23]

Tone and audience shifted as reconstructionist language and doctrine entered the policy arena. For those less concerned with doctrinal detail, a vaguer, but for that reason more popular, variety of activism came to be known as dominion theology. Dominionism took its name from Genesis, which charged Adam with establishing dominion over the earth. Dominionists largely ignored the hair-splitting conflicts among the Bahnsen, North, and Chalcedon camps. Instead, televangelists like D. James Kennedy and Pat Robertson diluted reconstructionism into a solution that could tempt Catholics as well as Calvinists. Although Rushdoony, North, and Bahnsen drifted into increasingly obscure sectarian fights, Christian Reconstruction, theonomy, and dominion theology provided the intellectual underpinnings and cultural networks for ecumenical religious assaults on secular institutions. Several crucial notions survived the dilution and popularization of Christian Reconstruction: that America was a Christian nation and not a constitutional democracy; that elitist, anti-Christian bigotry had repressed the public memory of the nation's Christian heritage; and that believers must fight to reclaim public life for Christ. The new theologies cultivated a commemorative practice that put a fine political edge on older and more mainline Christian traditions.

The efforts of Rushdoony—to create a vocabulary recognizable to the faithful but grounded in language familiar and appealing to a wide range of Americans—prevented the movement's descent into solipsism. We may well doubt that a majority of Christian conservatives could have used the word *theonomy* correctly in a sentence, and few openly demanded the stoning of adulterers or embraced predestination, but *Christian nation, spiritual heritage, Christian heritage, Judeo-Christian heritage, renewal, Godly reform,* and a host of related terms came to define "Christian memory," just as Ten Commandments monuments, lapel pins, and lawn signs proliferated across the country. Indeed, the most effective mobilizations were precisely those that avoided the more contentious elements of the Rushdoony heritage in favor of the other signs of Christian Reconstruction. Perhaps the most visible was the popularization of commemorative traditions that encouraged Americans to read public spaces as monuments of a Christian past obscured by the paganism, deism, and secular humanism of an anti-Christian academy.

The Christian Broadcast Network served as a major forum for the commemoration of the "Christian nation." Pat Robertson's CBN reached millions of American households weekly and linked to millions more through its Webcasts, radio programming, print publications, university, and homeschooling curricula. As part of a twenty-first-century Fourth of July special, *Remembering Our Christian Heritage,* CBN sent correspondents out into the field to uncover the biblical iconography of public architecture. Uncovering an aging statue of the prophet Daniel behind the Organization of American States Building in Washington, D.C., correspondent Carrie Devorah told viewers, "He's made from concrete and as you can see he's falling apart, but I have faith in Daniel." Down the street, at the Daughters of the American Revolution Building, Devorah paused over an inscription from Proverbs: "Remove not the ancient landmark which thy fathers have set." CBN's camera crew only recreated what a variety of Christian organizations were already doing for paying customers: Christian heritage tours brought busloads of faithful tourists to Washington, D.C., to follow guides around the monuments and halls in search of a "Christian memory." For a bit of scholarly heft, CBN brought in the president of a "Christian heritage group," David Barton, who pointed out that four paintings in the rotunda of the U.S. Capitol displayed "two prayer meetings, a Bible study and a baptism."[24]

Barton reappeared on Robertson's *700 Club* program as an expert on "the spiritual legacy of America." Barton—one of the directors of the Providence Foundation, a reconstructionist group, and the president of WallBuilders, an institution promoting the recovery of Christian heritage—presented a cheery, charismatic persona in his role as Christian historian and commemorative tour guide. "The question is asked," Robertson began, "was America founded as a Christian nation? We have said yes, yes, yes. But you have the proof." "There is a lot of proof," claimed Barton, and he spent much of the next fifteen minutes pulling out quotes from Founding Fathers, Christian mottos of early state legislatures, and a copy of the "first family Bible ever done in America." Barton also made a practical pitch, lamenting that only 15 million of the 60 million evangelicals had voted in the 2000 elections: "So if we want to see judges change we have to turn out this November and elect god-fearing guys to the Senate."[25]

Barton first appeared on the national stage in 1989, with the publication of a book titled *The Myth of the Separation of Church and State.* Barton's text essentially recreated Rushdoony's *This Independent Republic* for a more popular audience, compiling a thick chronicle of decontextualized and thinly sourced quotations from moments of American history in which virtually any use of *God, Christ, Bible,* or *pray* might appear. Barton eschewed Rushdoony's more careful intellectual narrative in favor of a text and videotape made for easy use in schoolrooms, elections, letters to the editor, presidential addresses, and other public spaces. Barton was momentarily embarrassed by the revelation that nearly a dozen of his chosen quotes could not be authenticated. Undaunted, he issued a revised edition, *Original Intent,* and a more professional video that found a wider audience. With the founding of WallBuilders, a tax-exempt organization offering publications, videos, Christian heritage tours, and seminars, Barton followed the lead of countless other right-wing activists in creating an institutional alternative to scholarly historiography. Not surprisingly, Barton surfaced as an expert witness for the defense of Judge Roy Brown in his battle against the State of Alabama and the United States. Although the WallBuilders Web site linked to a variety of reconstructionist sites, the organization and Barton himself refrained from public statements about the practical implications of theonomy, instead concentrating upon legitimizing the proposition that American was a Christian nation.[26]

Barton's place on the political scene was clarified by his selection as vice chairman of the Republican Party in President George W. Bush's home state, Texas. The Texas GOP attracted national attention when it adopted as a plank of its platform the proposition that American was a Christian nation whose legal authority derived from God. In 2004 Barton worked for the Republican National Committee. The White House, coordinating closely with religious conservatives, hoped both to cut into the Catholic vote, especially in southwestern and midwestern states, and to increase evangelical turnout. The plan depended on the labor of local "grassroots" organizations, especially church denominations and activists linked by mass media Christian outlets, for mobilizing and managing electoral dynamics. One of the strengths of church networks, though, was also a weakness: as tax-exempt organizations, churches were not allowed to endorse political candidates. But a muscular Christian legal movement persuaded the Internal Revenue Service to liberalize its interpretation of the proscription. Barton toured churches throughout the country, recounting the "Christian beliefs" of the founding fathers, exhorting religious leaders to embrace antigay ballot initiatives as a means of boosting conservative Christian voting, and "clarifying" the IRS rules. As one informed pastor put it, "I can't endorse a certain candidate, but as a Christian I can say, 'Here are the issues that are compatible with biblical teachings.'" In November of 2004, voters reelected George W. Bush in a campaign that was widely read as a triumph of a strategy that had aimed at energizing the conservative Christian base. The key state, Ohio, appeared to have been swung by an unexpectedly high evangelical turnout and defections from traditionally Democratic Catholic neighborhoods.[27]

Analysts will spend years sweating the precinct details, but Christian conservatives moved quickly to claim responsibility for the victory and to demand remuneration. "Judges are the issue," said one activist, "not an issue or one of the important issues, but THE issue." With seats to fill on the federal courts, and a bitterly divided Senate, each judicial appointment turned upon the careful parsing of each sentence ever scripted by the nominees. Senate Majority Leader Bill Frist, an evangelical Christian and a potential presidential candidate in the 2008 elections, worked to prevent a Democratic filibuster of the most conservative hopefuls. One Sunday in April 2005, he spoke at a public rally in which speakers lobbied for the Constitution Restoration Act and called for the impeachment (and worse) of federal judges. Frist's office had invited all one hundred of the nation's senators to tour the Capitol the following Monday with an expert guide who could offer "a fresh perspective on our nation's religious heritage." After severe criticism from Democrats, Frist's office reduced the party to simply the senator, his wife, and some of his aides. Inside the Capitol's rotunda, tour guide David Barton stepped into character and gestured toward the paintings: "You got two prayer meetings, a Bible study and a baptism."[28]

The emergence of a muscular and radical postmillennialism was only one small part of the creation of a new Christian Right in the postwar United States. And discourse on memory was only one small part of the development of the new theologies and practice. If we were to write a more nearly comprehensive account, we would have to attend much more closely to demographic shifts; to mainline as well as reconstructionist theology; to the institutional fabric of Christian schools, universities, and think tanks; and to the democratization of radical fundamentalism, which leaped from the backwoods to the boardroom in little more than a generation. But for Christian conservatives, as for academics, the discourse of memory pulled together the private and frequently therapeutic vocabularies of postwar selfhood with the civic rituals of a nominally secular state. *Memory* provided a language uniquely suited to opening secular public spaces to Judeo-Christian religious tradition.

This may not be the memory studies that *you* know and love. But our tale is not another sordid story of a progressive vocabulary or movement hijacked or co-opted by conservatives. The only aspect of memory talk that Christian conservatives may have derived from academia was the implicit Freudianism of trauma, repression, and recovery. But what is borrowed here seems to have come from popular culture—movies, novels, memoirs—and perhaps the growing self-help and recovery movements of the twentieth century, more than from any self-conscious turn to psychoanalytic theory. Christian conservatives in the United States and elsewhere did not need Pierre Nora to define a site of memory; for them, *lieux de mémoire* remain milieux *de mémoire*, places of divine presence. Rather than a story of a progressive poetics corrupted, our tale is more nearly the opposite: In the 1980s and 1990s, academics in retreat from scientism and nihilism blundered into a linguistic space shaped predominantly by religious thought and culture. But the cultural isolation of historiographic discussions of "memory" helped to insure that academics would imagine memory talk as a subaltern protest against the oppressive regimes of modernity, from Nazism to imperialism. Unfortunately, Christian conservatives share that imagination, seeing themselves as a besieged minority risking martyrdom to recover America's Christian heritage. Despite good academic intentions, memory talk in the academy of the late twentieth century was more nearly a symptom than an analysis of the resacralization of public life in the United States.

Pierre Nora, in one of his well-crafted but inscrutable phrases, has claimed, "Whoever says 'memory,' says 'Shoah.'"[29] That may be true. Certainly in academia, and in polite and most especially secular company, the relation of *memory* and *Holocaust* can be remarkably strong. But at most times and places in the twenty-first-century United States, and at many times and places in Australia, New Zealand, Canada and the United Kingdom, and in other times and places where the wings of empire have carried the English language, whoever says *memory* says *Christ*.

I am not calling for some imaginary act of linguistic purification. Since we use ordinary language, we are always subject to ordinary usage, even when we seek to set ourselves apart. Memory and its related terms have massed so much power that it is not as if we could pretend that this moment has never existed. In 2001, Jay Winter concluded a survey of the field by saying, "We are bound to go on using the term, *memory*."[30] I would quibble only with the prepositional phrasing—we are more nearly bound *by* it. But like all bonded people, we should at least dream of liberation. As I understand the relevant passage of *The Phenomenology of Spirit,* the bondsman or -woman is supposed to emerge from subjection with a more acute historical consciousness than the master. As a historian, I remain sufficiently Hegelian to hope that a skeptical critique here can have some effect. Or to put it in Hegel's own chapter and verse: "The fear of the Lord is the beginning of wisdom."

Afterword

HISTORY AND THEORY IN OUR TIME

In 1959, after Hans Meyerhoff had assembled the collection of authors for his teaching anthology, *The Philosophy of History in Our Time,* he—or perhaps some clever designer at the publisher's office, Doubleday Anchor—chose the appropriate image for the cover: a reproduction of Pablo Picasso's *Guernica* (1937), on loan to New York City's Museum of Modern Art. Picasso's work did reference a genuine historical event, the bombing of a small Basque village by the Luftwaffe. "Art for Our Time," after all, was the museum's notorious tagline. And Picasso himself was as much a North American celebrity as any other artist. By midcentury, the Spanish painter had become an icon of modernism, and his cubist rendition of the Spanish civil war struck all the proper notes for an authentically modernist moment: violence, mechanization, minority communities, fascism, communism, the collapse of historical meaning, the end of naturalism, and the rise of the artistic avant-garde as a warrior class. In retrospect, we might point out still another aspect of the Spanish civil war that resonated with Meyerhoff's motifs, namely, Francisco Franco's ability to play upon Catholic images and institutions.

For Meyerhoff, the story of philosophy of history in our time was the story of the emergence of new antihistorical forces as a result of historicism's inability to build a durable philosophical foundation for either a scientific or a romantic historiography. The nineteenth century's valiant attempt to understand the world as a historical place had ultimately failed, leaving the twentieth century awash in antihistorical tendencies. Some of these rebellions were entirely new, especially in the sciences and social sciences, where the search for predictive formula and neutral observation sentences had killed off the narrative tense of the historical past. But portions of the new century looked surprisingly, and ominously, old. *The Philosophy of History in Our Time* began with Wilhelm Dilthey but ended with the theological writings of Reinhold Niebuhr and Karl Jaspers. As Meyerhoff saw it, "the brilliant conquest of the most distant frontiers of historical knowledge also coincides with an increasing awareness of the meaninglessness of history. This awakening, in turn, has produced a strange loss of historical appetite. There is a deep craving for an escape from the nightmare of history into a mode of existence beyond history: art, mythology, religion, or apathy." As a result, he concluded, Christian interpretations of history "have reasserted themselves strongly after a lapse of a few hundred years."[1]

An émigré from Hitler's Germany, Meyerhoff may have been especially impressed by American religiosity, as many educated Europeans were, but he also wrote out of an awareness of the close relation between German theology and German historicism. The original crisis of historicism had been a theological as well as a historical crisis, and the dramatic reconstruction of theological writing on time, history, and eschatology that had emerged from those upheavals had returned as a direct challenge to the authority of professional secular historiography. Most of Meyerhoff's contemporaries in philosophy of history did not share his concern with the revival of religious interpretations of history, and none of the other major textbooks or anthologies of the period sampled theological writing or even identified Christianity as part of the broader horizon of current historical interpretation. By the late seventies, twenty years after publication, Meyerhoff's comments on religion appeared to belong to another time entirely. At least some historiographers, most famously Hayden White, had embraced the antihistorical tendencies of high modernism in an attempt to reground historical discourse as art. And many of the most strident critics of such an aesthetic refiguration of history continued to cling to the idealized models of midcentury social science. Structuralism and post-structuralism had denounced even secular humanism as so much priestcraft. The other antihistorical forces that worried Meyerhoff—art, apathy, and science—appeared to have united to drive out theology. Despite the apocalyptic tone of some literary theory, history seemed to have put God talk behind it.

Things are a bit different now. From the prospect of the early twenty-first century, in which the clash of new fundamentalisms threaten to eclipse the old ideological conflicts between fascism and communism, Meyerhoff's sense of the situation appears timely, if not prophetic. The scholarly turn toward words and tones associated with religious or at least postsecular discourse would have seemed impossible just a few decades ago. Yet in hindsight, we can say that the conditions of possibility for that change were already in place by the early years of the sixties. The critical vocabularies associated with French radicalism in 1968—whether we call them postmodernist, post-structuralist, deconstructionist, or by some other elusive label—were important but not causal in any narrow sense. As Raymond Aron once quipped, the search for causes in history is really about guilt. Who is to blame? It is indeed ironic that discourses known for criticizing historiography as a form of metaphysics could become associated with languages far murkier than those of logical positivism, but the occasionally nihilistic or even mystical trajectories that developed in academia could scarcely be described as a result of some French academic bohemians unleashing the dark forces of the American id. Americans could manage that feat on their own.

The politics of linguistic change have become the dark and bloody ground of historical discourse. One of the dangers of *From History to Theory* is that it might simply be assimilated to the theory wars. Fights over the meaning and legacy of 1968, and especially its French incarnations, still draw blood. Two recent accounts fairly represent two of the evolving positions in the early twenty-first century, each quite different from the one I have developed in this story. The first, represented by authors like Richard Wolin, states that American intellectuals were led astray by a French counter-Enlightenment posing as theory. A second account, especially visible in the widely read work of François Cusset, argues that "theory" was co-opted by consumer capitalism and diverted into identity politics.

Richard Wolin's work, especially *The Seduction of Unreason* (2004), has argued that the literary and philosophical discourses that materialized as "theory" in the North American academy had organic roots in dark places. In his account, Heideggerian hermeneutics, French structuralism and post-structuralism all descended from Joseph de Maistre, the counter-Enlightenment, and Catholic reaction. Wolin's controversial claims rest partly upon dubious genealogies, but also upon the notorious episodes of Paul de Man, Maurice Blanchot, and Heidegger himself, each of whom has been revealed to have participated to varying degrees in anti-Semitic agitation or even, in the Heidegger case, in the Nazi Party. And lurking in the background was the Sokal debacle, in which physicist Alan Sokal, outraged by the anti-Enlightenment tone of recent science studies, placed a Trojan horse, fashioned out of glued-together nonsensical jargon and hip phrases, with a respected theory journal and then revealed the hoax in the national media.[2]

Setting aside the question of the plausibility of Wolin's account of European intellectual history, I do not see the story of historical discourse in North America following anything like that trajectory: Our narrative is not one in which besotted Americans foolishly imported viral strains of irrationality. The deracinated collections of words, phrases, and stories that arrived in the United States from across the Atlantic did not serve as the advance guard of a counterrevolution. Nor did the rise of memory discourse derive from, or originate in, a planned collective decision to turn back the clock.[3] And although there have been a few attempts to systematically create a vocabulary for history and theory that could be shared by both historians and theologians,[4] the postsecular academic vocabularies that emerged late in the century probably succeeded precisely because they were not driven by a clear theological intent. Unlike in the case of enthusiasm for neoorthodox theology on 1950s college campuses, we cannot fairly reduce the quasi sacrality of the fin de siècle to a new failure of nerve. Within the university, the drift toward a language of reenchantment was unplanned, unconscious, and incomplete. The question, then, is not, What bad reading habits turned so many historians and theorists of history into counter-Enlightenment ideologues, but rather, What conditions made possible the reenchantment of historical discourse? As it turns out, that development was in part a contingency of a variety of earlier linguistic events, some of them quite far afield.

These linguistic changes were not always purposeful, but they were patterned. And they are not the changes one might have expected of a modern age: the rise and fall of historiography, a term whose eclecticism suited the craft orientation of historical practice of the period; the failure of highly scientistic models of historical discourse; the linkage of language and linguistic terms with racial difference and images of ethnographic encounter; the structuralist and postmodernist battle to replace the colonial metaphysics of universal history with new literary forms; the reappearance of a term abandoned earlier in the century, *memory*, with long strings of religious loan words in tow; and the emergence of new eschatological and theocratic discourses in popular culture and politics. Most of these shifts occurred relatively quickly, in the space of a few decades, and although, in the case of specific instances of usage, we might map some keyword preferences onto a vulgar sociology, we would be hard pressed to reduce these general trends in specifically academic language to any particular individual or group of individuals, aside from breaking down tendencies according to disciplinary affiliation or the expected disproportionate representation of research institutions.

The plainest place to imagine linguistic shifts in terms of particular actors is our single example from outside of the academy, the use of memory in popular eschatologies. Here we can more safely identify some degree of self-conscious direction to linguistic change, as new groupings of Christian ultraconservatives leveraged developments in popular culture to achieve concrete political goals. If we were to extend the study of keywords and vocabularies in the direction of social history, we could doubtless expand on the differences in the circulation of the analytic languages of the human sciences on the one hand, and the discourse of, say, professional marketing copy or partisan talking points on the other. Certainly we would benefit from more work that mixed the high intellectual history associated with linguistic analysis with genuinely rigorous social and economic history, especially given the accelerating development of the mass media in politics, consumer culture, and religion. The interaction of academic and popular discourses deserves more attention than I can give it here, but one reading of the story would go like this: In the North American university, an aggressive scientism helped a traditionally white Protestant historiography to strip away some of its more provincial traditions, thus allowing the rise of a more secular academic discourse, but one that was also better equipped to engage cultural and racial difference. Then, the failure of the scientistic program, and the apparent nihilism of its most radical, secular alternatives, enabled new forms of religious or postsecular language that offered to reenchant the world and further decolonize academic discourses.

Here this story can speak to some of Wolin's critics, as well. One recurring critique of the fate of structuralist and post-structuralist theory in American academia has been that the university's peculiar form of consumer capitalism reduced what had been a radical post-Marxist form of critique to an assortment of niche fashions. Once safely branded for departments of English or ethnic studies, theory became a rationale for identity politics or worse. François Cusset's famous account *French Theory* (2000) blamed the commodification of linguistic radicalism on the isolation, provincialism, and entrepreneurial organization of the American university system. Packaging was the key: a heterogeneous collection of authors and texts emerged in the American intellectual market as "theory" (or the "linguistic turn") and rapidly found an audience, first in elite institutions in the service of a fairly traditional literary canon, but then, spectacularly, in ethnic and cultural studies, where Foucault & Company "ended up authorizing a more fine-grained segmentation of the marketplace, an extension of capital into spheres of affinity and the clandestine intimacy of invisible differences."[5] On this reckoning, a theoretical intervention that sought to deconstruct historical consciousness and dissolve the subject actually became an instrument for legitimating new racialized or gendered or queer subjects. But the close association of linguistic analysis and cultural and racial difference clearly preceded the rise of the ethnic, gender, and cultural studies programs that Cusset believes derailed deconstruction.

When the vocabularies associated with French theory—textuality, narrativity, sign, discourse—arrived in North America, they entered a linguistic terrain already prepared by decades of ethnographic work. That midcentury conversation among linguists, ethnographers, and analytic philosophers was one of the high points of our narrative, and one that historians should work harder to recuperate and expand. The very different ways that a structural approach to language worked out in North America and Europe meant that, here, the study of language helped to erode biologically grounded accounts of racial difference and replace them with more democratic and even radical senses of culture before the century had reached its halfway mark. It is difficult to imagine what the reception of Derrida or Lyotard might have looked like absent those earlier moments. Indeed, one of the ironic but happy results of the surge of theoretical interest in departments of history in the 1970s and 1980s was the way that it helped to promote ethnographic vocabularies and rhetorical practices long associated with Boasian anthropology. Subsequent attempts at a more ethnographic variety of history, from the writings of historians like James Clifford to the philosophical essays of Richard Rorty, may occasionally have risked a return to the Hegelian varieties of universal history we hope to escape, but I cannot see that moment as any less hopeful for all of that. Historians working to talk about peripheral places and peoples face a daunting array of obstacles, but theory is not chief among them. For Cusset, the reduction of deconstruction to ethnoracial self-assertion is the tragedy of theory in North America. From my perspective, folks engaged in the history of peripheral places and peoples do not need more authentic or radical semiotics. They need more money.

With *theory,* we have come to our last word. But it is an opening more than an ending. My story cannot provide anything like a comprehensive accounting of what theory was, let alone what it might have been or could become. *History and theory* displaced *philosophy of history* and *historiography* because the older terms had not reproduced themselves in reliable ways, at least for professional scholarship. The inability of *philosophy of history* to create a strong position in departments of philosophy, and the comparable problems of *historiography* in departments of history, opened up space for alternatives. The very marginality of *historiography* and *philosophy of history* helped to create *theory*, first as a transitional zone in which historical discourse might transform into a social science; and then, more forcefully, as a place that some historians imagined as a site of resistance to colonialism or late capitalism or the power of the state.

For history and philosophy of history, *theory* by the 1980s had acquired a fuzzy halo of associations—*language, linguistic turn, culture, aesthetics*—but beyond that, the word could signify anything: simple reflection on historical practice; close reading of historiographic texts; continental varieties of philosophy; or even ambitious and occult revisions of universal history. Theory could present as radical secularization or a program of reenchantment. Here, Cusset's story helps to account for some of the ways theory could materialize as a black box. Deconstruction, especially, showed that putatively value-neutral administrative language could reify bad, old racial, gender, and sexual codes. But *theory* had no institutional tradition, and that fact was at once its promise and its problem. That theory could be everywhere and nowhere appealed to those who imagined it as a new radical politics that could transform the sclerotic traditions of the academy. But theory's transient condition also made it less easily subject to the sort of criticism and peer review that obtained in departments of philosophy, and it thus helped to create the conditions of possibility for such debacles as the Sokal incident. In any event, the recurring pairing of *history* and *theory* helped to generate situations in which the second term could alternately serve as fetish or demon. Those were never the only possibilities for the meaning of *theory*, and maybe not even the most important ones, but they remain active on campus. In our current North American moment, history and theory has its own journal, but no job lines.

From History to Theory, then, is neither a story about the transcendence of a conservative craft tradition by a more reflective historiography, nor a narrative of declension from a historiographic Eden into a postapocalyptic landscape ruled by roving foreign bands of linguistic nihilists. My aim in these essays has been both historicist and deconstructionist, if we can still make those words do intellectual work. Most of the terms I have traced here have appeared, at one time or another, as contrary or complementary to that basic word *history*. Since we define *history* through contrast and exclusion as often as through enumeration or catalogue or other forms of positive exposition, our genealogy amounts to something like a history of history's edges. Since language has stood near the center of so many methodological debates of the last century, *language* and its related terms have played a larger role than they might have had we focused on Victorian topics. And the desire of many of these vocabularies to transcend or negate or simply ignore history is neither accidental nor an artifact, but fairly reflects some of the most compelling intellectual developments of the period we have sampled.

The desire to escape history has been one of the recurring motifs of the twentieth century. For some, the escape from historical discourse promised an escape from the traumatic events it narrated. For others, history remained a final resting place for all of the Victorian metaphysics that the hard sciences had already banished. For others, historical discourse appeared so compromised by complicity with the crimes of various states that only a full and complete emancipation seemed likely to bring about other sorts of revolutions. For others, history was so implicated in the construction of white bourgeois subjects that the decolonization of intellectual life demanded a new form of discourse about the past. *History*'s gravitation toward other words that appeared to counter its tendency to colonize the world—what could not be historicized?—has long generated formulas in which *history* aligned with oppositional signs: *God, nature, eternity, language, culture, art, theory, memory*.

My opening anecdote, Hans Meyerhoff's invocation of Basques and Baptists, may seem dated, but I cannot quite put it behind me. We occupy our current positions, for good and bad, because of the conversations and conflicts between history and its interlocutors. And the measure of our efforts will be the way that they do or do not help us to engage both our subjects of study and our contemporary obligations. Perhaps the most surprising feature of this brief study has been the way that academics developed an ostensibly postmetaphysical theoretical discourse while seemingly unaware that much of the same language was mobilizing powerful antidemocratic forces outside of the academy. Today, many North American historians argue that they can separate their own discourse from popular discourses, and that, once transposed into an academic setting, our words can shelter themselves from their common and recurring and occasionally dangerous popular meanings. I find those arguments unpersuasive, and I believe that continuing commitments to the imperfect secularizing programs that have carried us from logical positivism to the hermeneutics of suspicion remain our best bet for decolonizing and democratizing historical discourse. But the convergence of deconstruction, decolonization, and dominion theology at the end of the twentieth century will not recur eternally. There will be new words.

Notes

INTRODUCTION

1. H. Stuart Hughes's remarks on language, translation, and migration remain suggestive. See his classic study *The Sea Change: The Migration of Social Thought, 1930–1965* (New York: Harper and Row, 1975), esp. 27–29.

2. I am thinking especially of Matei Calinescu, *Five Faces of Modernity: Modernism, Avant-Garde, Decadence, Kitsch, Postmodernism* (Bloomington: Indiana University Press, 1977); and Perry Anderson, *The Origins of Postmodernity* (London: Verso, 1998).

3. A. L. Kroeber and Clyde Kluckholn, *Culture: A Critical Review of Concepts and Definitions* (1952; reprint, New York: Vintage Books, 1963), remains the classic exposition for the nineteenth and early twentieth centuries.

4. Raymond Williams, *Keywords: A Vocabulary of Culture and Society* (Oxford: Oxford University Press, 1976); Williams, *Culture and Society, 1780–1950* (1957; reprint, New York: Columbia University Press, 1983); Quentin Skinner, "The Idea of a Cultural Lexicon," *Essays in Criticism* 29 (July 1979): 205–224. Compare two of the best-known semantic histories for the U.S. field, Daniel Rodgers,

Contested Truths: Keywords in American Politics since Independence (New York: Basic Books, 1987); and Philip Gleason, *Speaking of Diversity: Language and Ethnicity in Twentieth-Century America* (Baltimore: Johns Hopkins University Press, 1992). Martin Jay, *Cultural Semantics: Keywords of Our Time* (Amherst: University of Massachusetts Press, 1998), esp. 1–5, uses Raymond Williams's phrase *strong words*. For introductions to recent literature on the history of English, see Richard Hogg and David Denison, eds., *A History of the English Language* (Cambridge: Cambridge University Press, 2006); and Lynda Mugglestone, ed., *The Oxford History of English* (Oxford: Oxford University Press, 2006).

5. Lexicography has become a hot research topic, especially after the fighting over the "Old" and "New" philology in medieval studies of the last few decades (especially visible in *Speculum*). Histories of dictionaries and lexicography might begin with John Willinsky, *Empire of Words: The Reign of the OED* (Princeton, NJ: Princeton University Press, 1994); and Lynda Mugglestone, *Lost for Words: The Hidden History of the Oxford English Dictionary* (New Haven, CT: Yale University Press, 2005). Readers looking for a current historical lexicon could start with Alan Munslow, *The Routledge Companion to Historical Studies* (London: Routledge, 2000). At the moment, we appear to be on the verge of a dramatic technical revolution in the possible approaches to the field, a result of the creation of digitized searchable archives. See, for instance, the WordNet project at Princeton University and Oxford's Bank of English: www.wordnet.princeton.edu/ and www.titania.bham.ac.uk/docs/svenguide.html.

6. Michel Foucault, "Nietzsche, Genealogy, History," reprinted in Paul Rabinow, ed., *The Foucault Reader* (New York: Pantheon, 1984), 76–100.

7. For a quick glimpse at genealogy's legions, see Raymond Geuss, "Nietzsche and Genealogy," *European Journal of Philosophy* 2 (1994): 272–294.

8. See, for instance, Bernard Williams's engaging study *Truth and Truthfulness: An Essay in Genealogy* (Princeton, NJ: Princeton University Press, 2002).

9. Reinhart Koselleck, Otto Brunner, and Werner Conze, eds., *Geschichtliche Grundbegriffe: Historisches Lexikon zur politisch-sozialen Sprache in Deutschland* (Stuttgart: Klett-Cotta, 1967–1996). Some of Koselleck's work is available in translation: *Futures Past: On the Semantics of Historical Time*, English language edition, trans. Keith Tribe (1979; reprint, Boston: MIT Press, 1985); and *The Practice of Conceptual History: Timing History, Spacing Concepts*, trans. Todd Samuel Presner et al. (Palo Alto, CA: Stanford University Press, 2002). See also Melvin Richter, "*Begriffsgeschichte* in Theory and Practice: Reconstructing the History of Political Concepts and Languages," in Willem Melching and Wyger Velema, eds., *Main Trends in Cultural History: Ten Essays* (Amsterdam: Rodolpi, 1994), 121–149. But compare Hans-Ulrich Gumbrecht, *Dimension und Grenzen der Begriffsgeschichte* (Munich: Fink, 2006), and the contributions from different national perspectives in Iain Hampsher-Monk, Frank van Vree, and Karin Tilmans, eds., *History of*

Concepts: Comparative Perspectives (Amsterdam: Amsterdam University Press, 1998). Melvin Richter has tirelessly promoted the idea of a *Begriffsgeschichte* model suitable for export to English. See especially his *History of Political and Social Concepts: A Critical Introduction* (Oxford: Oxford University Press, 1995). Compare, though, Mark Bevir, *The Logic of the History of Ideas* (Cambridge: Cambridge University Press, 1999). In France, the journal *MOTS* has served as a vehicle for a somewhat different approach to semantic history.

10. Gottlob Frege, "On Concept and Function" (1892), in Peter Geach and Max Black, eds., *Translations from the Philosophical Writings of Gottlob Frege* (Oxford: Oxford University Press, 1952), 42; Martin Heidegger, *Basic Concepts*, English language edition, trans. Gary E. Aylesworth (1981; reprint, Bloomington: Indiana University Press, 1993).

11. Skinner, "Idea of a Cultural Lexicon," 206; Ludwig Wittgenstein, *Philosophical Investigations*, 3rd ed., trans. G. E. M. Anscombe (1953; reprint, New York: Macmillan, 1968), 71–72, 76.

12. W. V. Quine and J. S. Ullian, *The Web of Belief* (New York: Random House, 1970), 5; W. V. Quine, *Quiddities: An Intermittently Philosophical Dictionary* (Cambridge, MA: Harvard University Press, 1987), 87–89. Compare Anthony Flew, *A Dictionary of Philosophy*, rev. 2nd ed. (New York: St. Martin's Press, 1979), 69, with *Stanford Encyclopedia of Philosophy*, at http://plato.stanford.edu/entries/concepts/, accessed April 2009. Richard Rorty, *Philosophy and the Mirror of Nature* (Princeton, NJ: Princeton University Press, 1979), remains the important account.

13. I would prefer to approach in this pragmatic fashion the typology of historical concepts developed in Henri-Renée Marrou, *De la connaissance historique*, 2nd ed. (Paris: Éditions du Seuil, 1955), 146–168.

14. Gustav Bergmann, "Logical Positivism, Language, and the Reconstruction of Metaphysics" (1953), in *The Linguistic Turn: Recent Essays in Philosophical Method*, ed. Richard Rorty (Chicago: University of Chicago Press, 1967), 63.

15. Henry May, *The End of American Innocence: A Study of the First Years of Our Own Time, 1912–1917*, rev. ed. (1959; reprint, New York: Columbia University Press, 1994). This edition includes essays by May and one of his students, David Hollinger, that helpfully situate the book in the more recent literature. Lary May, *Screening Out the Past: The Birth of Hollywood and the Motion Picture Industry* (Oxford: Oxford University Press, 1983); David Hollinger, *Science, Jews, and Secular Culture: Studies in Mid-Twentieth-Century American Intellectual History* (Princeton, NJ: Princeton University Press, 1996).

16. I do not wish to dive into the scrum currently surrounding secularization theory. For a sampling of work on the concepts of secular, secularism and secularization, compare Larry Shiner, "The Concept of Secularization in Empirical Research," *Journal for the Scientific Study of Religion* 6 (Autumn 1967): 202–220; Karel Dobbelaere, "Trend Report: Secularization: A Multi-Dimensional Concept,"

Current Sociology 29 (1981): 3–153; and Wilfred M. McClay, "Two Concepts of Secularism," *Journal of Policy History* 13 (2001): 47–72.

ONE. THE RISE AND FALL OF *HISTORIOGRAPHY*

1. Hans Kellner, *Language and Historical Representation: Getting the Story Crooked* (Madison: University of Wisconsin Press, 1989), 265.

2. Carl Becker, "What Is Historiography?" (1938), reprinted in Phil L. Snyder, ed., *Detachment and the Writing of History: Essays and Letters of Carl L. Becker* (Ithaca, NY: Cornell University Press, 1958), 66.

3. For introductions to that literature, see David Pace, "The Amateur in the Operating Room: History and the Scholarship of Teaching and Learning," *American Historical Review* (109) at www.historycooperative.org/journals/ahr/109/4/pace.html, and Pace, "The Internationalization of History Teaching through the Scholarship of Teaching and Learning," *Arts and Humanities in Higher Education* 6 (2007): 329–335. For a selection of the recent literature, compare James Laspina, *The Visual Turn and the Transformation of the Textbook* (Mahwah, NJ: Lawrence Erlbaum, 1998); Sam Wineburg, *Historical Thinking and Other Unnatural Acts: Charting the Future of Teaching the Past* (Philadelphia: Temple University Press, 2001); and Peter Seixas, ed., *Theorizing Historical Consciousness* (Toronto: University of Toronto Press, 2004). For years I have regularly queried friends and colleagues about the training they received as undergraduates and graduates. At one point I attempted a more systematic tabulation of that sort of squishy data, but while it promised some fairly decorative diagrams, I was unable to convince myself that quantification was making this survey any more rigorous. Those conversations remain present here simply as background.

4. Variations proliferated from the late fifteenth century to roughly the middle of the nineteenth. *Historiograph* was used for *history* as late as 1732; *historiographal* for *historical* in an 1841 example; and *historiographer* for *historian* in 1832. *Historiographer* could also refer to an official historian appointed to a royal court, hence the 1881 reference to "historiographership." Peter Novick, *That Noble Dream: The "Objectivity Question" and the American Historical Profession* (Cambridge: Cambridge University Press, 1988), 8n6.

5. Herbert Butterfield, *Man on His Past: The Study of the History of Historical Scholarship* (1955; reprint, Cambridge: Cambridge University Press, 1969), 2, 5, 11. Classic German studies include Friedrich Meinecke's *Die Enstehung des Historismus* (1936) translated into English by J.E. Anderson and H.D. Schmidt as *Historism: The Rise of a New Historical Outlook* (London: Routledge, 1972); and

Ernst Troeltsch, *Der Historismus und seine Ueberwindung* (Aalen, Germany: Scientia Verlag, 1966). Compare Georg G. Iggers's more recent foreword to *Historiography: An Annotated Bibliography* (Santa Barbara, CA: ABC-Clio, 1987), 1:vii–x; Peter Hans Reill, *The German Enlightenment and the Rise of Historicism* (Berkeley: University of California Press, 1975); Iggers, *The German Conception of History: The National Tradition of Historical Thought from Herder to the Present*, rev. ed. (1968; reprint, Hanover, NH: University Press of New England, 1983); and the recent synoptic account by John Kent Wright, "History and Historicism," in Theodore M. Porter and Dorothy Ross, eds., *The Cambridge History of Science*, vol. 7, *The Modern Social Sciences* (Cambridge: Cambridge University Press, 2003). The story became so conventionalized that, in Anthony Grafton's words, "every schoolboy knows—or at least every German high school student once knew—what scientific history is and who invented it." See Grafton, *The Footnote: A Curious History* (Cambridge, MA: Harvard University Press, 1997), 34. For a recent survey, see Donald R. Kelley's books, *Fortunes of History: Historical Inquiry from Herder to Huizinga* (New Haven: Yale University Press, 2003) and *Frontiers of History: Historical Inquiry in the Twentieth Century* (New Haven: Yale University Press, 2006).

6. Frederick Jackson Turner, "The Significance of History" (1891), reprinted in Fulmer Mood, ed., *The Early Writings of Frederick Jackson Turner* (Madison: University of Wisconsin Press, 1938), 43–68; Lord Acton, "German Schools of History," *English Historical Review* 1 (January 1886): 7–42; Ernst Bernheim, *Lehrbuch der historischen Methode und der Geschichtsphilosophie* (Leipzig: Dunker und Humblot, 1889); Charles Victor Langlois and Charles Seignobos, *Introduction aux études historiques* (Paris: Librairie Hatchette, 1898); J.G. Droysen, *Grundriss der Historik* (1858–1882), reprinted in Peter Leyh, ed., *Historik: Historisch-kritische Ausgabe von Peter Leyh* (Stuttgart-Bad Cannstatt: Frommann-Holboog, 1977). See also Kerwin Lee Klein, *Frontiers of Historical Imagination: Narrating the European Conquest of Native America, 1890–1990* (Berkeley: University of California Press, 1997), 58–78. On German historicism in the United States, see especially Dorothy Ross, "American Historical Consciousness in the Nineteenth Century," *American Historical Review* 89 (December 1984): 909–928; and Jürgen Herbst, *The German Historical School in American Scholarship: A Study in the Transfer of Culture* (1965; reprint, Port Washington, NY: Kennikat, 1972).

7. Turner owned the 1883 edition of the *Grundrisse*, but later acquired the 1897 translation, which appears to have been his teaching text. Johann Gustav Droysen, *Outline of the Principles of History*, English language edition, trans. E. Benjamin Andrews (Boston: Ginn and Company, 1897). The best account of Droysen's engagement with philosophy of history remains Jörn Rüsen, *Begriffene Geschichte: Genesis und Begründung der Geschichtstheorie J. G. Droysens* (Paderborn, Ger.: Ferdinand Schöningh, 1969). But compare Hans-Georg Gadamer, *Truth*

and Method, English language edition, trans. Joel Weinsheimer and Donald G. Marshall (New York: Crossroad, 1992), 212–218; and Hayden White, *The Content of the Form: Narrative Discourse and Historical Representation* (Baltimore: Johns Hopkins University Press, 1987), 83–103. For a better sense of Droysen's position in German politics and academia, see Georg Iggers, *The German Conception of History* (Middletown, CT: Wesleyan University Press, 1968); and Robert Southard, *Droysen and the Prussian School of History* (Lexington: University of Kentucky Press, 1995).

8. The two best biographies are Allan G. Bogue, *Frederick Jackson Turner: Strange Roads Going Down* (Norman: University of Oklahoma Press, 1998); and Ray Allen Billington, *Frederick Jackson Turner: Historian, Scholar, Teacher* (Oxford: Oxford University Press, 1973). See also Klein, *Frontiers of Historical Imagination.*

9. Benedetto Croce, *History: Its Theory and Practice,* trans. Douglas Ainslie, English language edition (1916; reprint, New York: Harcourt, Brace, 1921); G.P. Gooch, *History and Historians in the Nineteenth Century,* 2nd ed. (1913; reprint, London: Longmans, 1952); James T. Shotwell, *An Introduction to the History of History* (New York: Columbia University Press, 1922); Harry Elmer Barnes, *A History of Historical Writing* (Norman: University of Oklahoma Press, 1937). A second edition was published by Dover in 1962.

10. James Westfall Thompson, *A History of Historical Writing* (New York: Macmillan, 1942); Social Science Research Council, bulletin 54, *Theory and Practice in Historical Study: A Report of the Committee on Historiography* (New York: SSRC, 1946); SSRC, *The Social Sciences in Historical Study* (New York: SSRC, 1954); SSRC, *Generalization in the Writing of History,* ed. Louis Gottschalk (New York: SSRC, 1962); John Higham, *History: Professional Scholarship in America* (1965; reprint, Baltimore: Johns Hopkins University Press, 1983), 141–142.

11. Higham, *History,* 139–142; Novick, *That Noble Dream,* esp. 361–411.

12. Fritz Stern, ed., *The Varieties of History* (Cleveland: Meridian, 1956); Hans Meyerhoff, ed., *Philosophy of History in Our Time* (New York: Doubleday Anchor, 1959); Patrick Gardiner, ed., *Theories of History* (New York: Free Press, 1959).

13. Fritz Stern, introduction to Stern, *Varieties of History,* 23–24; Jacques Barzun, "Cultural History as a Synthesis," in Stern, *Varieties of History,* 402.

14. Marc Bloch, *The Historian's Craft,* trans. Peter Putnam (New York: Vintage, 1953). On the editions of the work, see especially Massimo Mastrogregori, "Reconsidering Marc Bloch's interrupted manuscript: Two missing pages of *Apologie pour l'Histoire ou Metier d'Historien," European Legacy* 3, no. 4 (1998): 32–42. I have been unable to consult Mastrogregori's larger work, *Il manoscritto interroto di Marc Bloch: Apologia della storia o mestiere di storico* (Rome: Istituti editoriali e poligrafici internazionali, 1995). For Bloch's biography, see Carole Fink, *Marc Bloch: A Life in History* (Cambridge: Cambridge University Press, 1989); and

Olivier Dumoulin, *Marc Bloch. Références/Facettes*, ed. Nicolas Offenstadt (Paris: Presses de la Fondation Nationale des Sciences Politiques, 2000).

15. Dexter Perkins and John L. Snell, eds., *The Education of Historians in the United States* (New York: McGraw-Hill, 1962), 39, 77–78, 145, 228–229.

16. Wood Gray and others, *Historian's Handbook: A Key to the Study and Writing of History*, 2nd ed. (1956; reprint, Boston: Houghton Mifflin, 1964), iv, italics in the original; Norman F. Cantor and Richard I. Schneider, *How to Study History* (New York: Thomas Y. Crowell, 1967), 106–129.

17. Walter Rundell Jr., *In Pursuit of American History: Research and Training in the United States* (Norman: University of Oklahoma Press, 1970), 15, Cross quoted on p. 10. Rundell blamed the social studies movement, which was advocated by John Dewey and other midcentury reformers. One of the social studies advocates, Merle Curti, agreed with Rundell that methodological training was inadequate; Rundell did not note Curti's explication for the problem. The complaint has become perennial. See the more recent AHA report, Myron Marty et al., *Liberal Learning and the History Major* (Washington, DC: American Historical Association, 1990).

18. According to Cantor and Schneider, "It is because formal work in historiography often descends to foisting upon students the preconceived notions of the lecturer that many eminent and wise scholars are opposed to offering such a course in the curriculum of their departments" (*How to Study History*, 244).

19. Ernst Breisach, *Historiography* (Chicago: University of Chicago Press, 1983); E.H. Carr, *What Is History?* (New York: Random House, 1961). Other traditional favorites had included Marc Bloch, *The Historian's Craft* (New York: Alfred Knopf, 1953); Pieter Gieyl, *Debates with Historians* (New York: Philosophical Library, 1956); and J.H. Hexter, *The History Primer* (New York: Basic Books, 1971).

20. *History as a Career: To Undergraduates Choosing a Profession* (Washington, DC: American Historical Association, 1961); Novick, *That Noble Dream*, 574–576.

21. The departments surveyed came from the top twenty-five on the list compiled by *U.S. News and World Report*. Only Johns Hopkins University and Harvard University required historiography for an undergraduate major in history.

22. Robert Lowie, *Primitive Society* (New York: Boni and Liveright, 1920), 441.

23. Much writing was stimulated by attempts to render postmodernism or post-structuralism either accessible or unattractive to undergraduate and graduate students, and by the attempts to adapt straightforward methods texts to the Internet age, but the recent work is far too vast to list. For a sampling of teaching texts, compare William Kelleher Storey, *Writing History: A Guide for Students* (Oxford: Oxford University Press, 1996); Beverly Southgate, *History: What and*

Why? Ancient, Modern, and Postmodern Perspectives (London: Routledge, 1996); Michael Bentley, *Modern Historiography: An Introduction* (London: Routledge, 1999); John H. Arnold, *History: A Very Short Introduction* (Oxford: Oxford University Press, 2000); Martha Howell and Walter Prevenier, *From Reliable Sources: An Introduction to Historical Methods* (Ithaca, NY: Cornell University Press, 2001); and Jenny L. Presnell, *The Information-Literate Historian: A Guide to Research for History Students* (Oxford: Oxford University Press, 2007). Some of the best recent monographs return to the craft tradition and highlight evidentiary aspects of historical discourse, especially Grafton, *Footnote;* Richard J. Evans, *Lying About Hitler: History, Holocaust, and the David Irving Trial* (New York: Basic Books, 2001); and Carlo Ginzburg, *History, Rhetoric, and Proof* (Hanover, NH; Brandeis University Press/Historical Society of Israel, 1999). We should also at least note recent public controversies in the United States that involved questions of historical method: Gary B. Nash et al., *History on Trial: Culture Wars and the Teaching of the Past,* new ed. (1997; reprint, New York: Vintage, 2000); Edward T. Linenthal and Tom Englehardt, *History Wars: The "Enola Gay" and other Battles for the American Past* (New York: Metropolitan, 1996); Ron Robin, *Scandals and Scoundrels: Seven Cases That Shook the Academy* (Berkeley: University of California Press, 2004); Peter Charles Hoffer, *Past Imperfect: Fact, Fiction and Fraud in the Writing of American History* (New York: Publicaffairs, 2004); and Jon Wiener, *Historians in Trouble: Plagiarism, Fraud and Politics in the Ivory Tower* (New York: New Press, 2005).

TWO. FROM *PHILOSOPHY* TO *THEORY*

1. Ankersmit is something of a special case, a professor of intellectual history and historical theory at the University of Groningen, the Netherlands, where linguistic analysis never really displaced continental interest in history. The other, Danto, is at least as well known for his art criticism as for his 1965 book, *The Analytical Philosophy of History.*

2. Arthur C. Danto, "The Decline and Fall of the Analytical Philosophy of History," in Frank Ankersmit and Hans Kellner, *A New Philosophy of History* (Chicago: University of Chicago Press, 1995), 72; Ewa Domenska, *Encounters: Philosophy of History after Postmodernism* (Charlottesville: University Press of Virginia, 1998), 185.

3. The rankings were taken from Jack Gourman, *Gourman Report of Graduate Programs* (New York: Random House, 19970; at the University of Pittsburgh, Kenneth Manders and Gerald Massey listed "philosophy of history" as a research interest. See also Aviezer Tucker, "The Future of the Philosophy of Historiography," *History and Theory* 40 (February 2001): 37–45.

4. Michael S. Roth, introduction to Ralph S. Cohen and Roth, eds., *History and … Histories within the Human Sciences* (Charlottesville: Virginia University Press, 1995), 3; Carl G. Hempel, "The Function of General Laws in History," *Journal of Philosophy* 39 (January 1942): 35–48. The phrase *covering law model* was applied by William H. Dray in *Laws and Explanation in History* (London: Oxford University Press, 1957).

5. Thomas S. Kuhn, *The Structure of Scientific Revolutions* (Chicago: University of Chicago Press, 1962). Compare the different narrative in Louis O. Mink, "Philosophy and Theory of History," in Georg G. Iggers and Harold T Parker, eds., *International Handbook of Historical Studies* (Westport, CT: Greenwood, Press, 1979), 17–27.

6. Richard Rorty, ed., *The Linguistic Turn: Recent Essays in Philosophical Method,* ed. Edwin R.A. Seligman (Chicago: University of Chicago Press, 1967).

7. Henri Berr and Lucien Febvre, "History and Historiography," in *Encyclopedia of the Social Sciences* (New York: Macmillan, 1937), 357–389.

8. Bruce Kuklick, "Seven thinkers and how they grew: Descartes, Spinoza, Leibniz; Locke, Berkeley, Hume; Kant," in Richard Rorty et al., eds., *Philosophy in History* (Cambridge: Cambridge University Press, 1984), 125–139; Kuklick, *The Rise of American Philosophy* (New Haven, CT: Yale University Press, 1977); Kuklick, *Churchmen and Philosophers: From Jonathan Edwards to John Dewey* (New Haven, CT: Yale University Press, 1985); Georg Wilhelm Friedrich Hegel, *The Philosophy of History,* trans. J. Sibree (New York: Dover, 1956).

9. J.G. Droysen, *Outline of the Principles of History,* trans. E. Benjamin Andrews (Boston: Ginn and Company, 1897); Benedetto Croce, *History: Its Theory and Practice,* English language edition, trans. Douglas Ainslie (1916; reprint, New York: Russell and Russell, 1960), 81; Michael Oakshott, *Experience and Its Modes* (Cambridge: Cambridge University Press, 1933), 154; Raymond Aron, *Introduction to the Philosophy of History,* English language edition, trans. George J. Irwin (1938; reprint, London: George Weidenfield, 1961); Maurice Mandelbaum, *The Problem of Historical Knowledge: An Answer to Relativism* (1938; reprint, New York: Harper, 1967), 1, 305–306; R.G. Collingwood, *The Idea of History* (Oxford: Clarendon Press, 1946).

10. William H. Walsh, *Philosophy of History: An Introduction,* rev. ed. (1951; reprint, New York: Harper, 1960), 8, 13.

11. Morton G. White, "Toward an Analytic Philosophy of History," in M. Farber, ed., *Philosophic Thought in France and the U.S.A.* (Buffalo, NY: University of Buffalo Publications in Philosophy, 1950), 708, 710; Gustav Bergmann, "Logical Positivism, Language, and the Reconstruction of Metaphysics" (1953), in Rorty, *Linguistic Turn,* 63.

12. Walsh, *Philosophy of History*, 16–26; William H. Dray, *Philosophy of History* (Englewood Cliffs, NJ: Prentice-Hall, 1964); Alan Donagan and Barbara Donagan, eds., *Philosophy of History* (New York: Macmillan, 1965). See also J. E. Malpas, ed., *Historical Understanding and the History of Philosophy, Philosophical Papers of Alan Donagan*, vol. 1 (Chicago: Chicago University Press, 1994). The topic also found its way into standard reference works. See W. H. Dray, "Philosophy of History," in Paul Edwards, ed., *The Encyclopedia of Philosophy* (London: Macmillan, 1967), 3:247–254; and Patrick Gardiner, "The Philosophy of History," in David L. Sills, ed., *International Encyclopedia of the Social Sciences* (London: Macmillan and Free Press, 1968), 428–433. See the more recent Gordon Graham, "Philosophy of History," in Edward Craig, ed., *Routledge Encyclopedia of Philosophy* (London: Routledge, 1998), 3:453–459. There is no entry for "philosophy of history" in Ada Kuper and Jessica Kuper, eds., *The Social Science Encyclopedia* (London: Routledge, 1996).

13. Arnold J. Toynbee, *A Study of History (Abridgement of Volumes I–X)* (Oxford: Oxford University Press, 1946); Reinhold Niebuhr, *Faith and History: A Comparison of Christian and Modern Views of History* (New York: Charles Scribner's Sons, 1949); Roderick Seidenberg, *Posthistoric Man: An Inquiry* (Chapel Hill: University of North Carolina Press, 1950); Norman O. Brown, *Life Against Death: The Psychoanalytical Meaning of History* (London: Routledge and Kegan Paul, 1959); Karl Löwith, *Meaning in History* (Chicago: University of Chicago Press, 1949); Ibn Khaldun, *The Muqaddimah: An Introduction to History*, trans. Franz Rosenthal, 3 vols. (Princeton, NJ: Bollingen, 1958); C. J. Friedrich, introduction to Hegel, *Philosophy of History*, n.p.

14. Isaiah Berlin, *Historical Inevitability* (London: Oxford University Press, 1954); Daniel Bell, *The End of Ideology* (Glencoe, IL: Free Press, 1961); Karl C. Popper, *The Poverty of Historicism* (1957; reprint, New York: Harper Torchbooks, 1964).

15. Dray, *Philosophy of History*, 11; Arthur C. Danto, *The Analytical Philosophy of History* (New York: Columbia University Press, 1965). See the similar preface to Morton White's *Foundations of Historical Knowledge* (New York: Harper and Row, 1965). A decade later such concerns still haunted a conference in Israel as a remarkable convocation of thinkers—Isaiah Berlin, Stuart Hampshire, Max Black, Paul Ricoeur, Yirmiahu Yovel, Raymond Polin, Donald Davidson, Nathan Rotenstreich, and Charles Taylor—considered the question "Is a philosophy of history possible?" See Yovel, ed., *Philosophy of History and Action* (Dordrecht: D. Reidel, 1978), 219–240.

16. Jack W. Meiland, *Scepticism and Historical Knowledge* (New York: Random House, 1965); White, *Foundations of Historical Knowledge;* Peter Dickson, *Kissinger and the Meaning of History* (Cambridge: Cambridge University Press,

1978); Michael Ignatieff, *Isaiah Berlin: A Life* (New York: Henry Holt, 1998), 239–243.

17. Patrick Gardiner, ed., *Theories of History* (New York: Free Press, 1959); Donagan and Donagan, *Philosophy of History.* Two other anthologies sampled only twentieth-century work: Hans Meyerhoff, ed., *The Philosophy of History in Our Time* (Garden City, NY: Doubleday Anchor, 1959); and William H. Dray, ed., *Philosophical Analysis and History* (New York: Harper and Row, 1966). Ronald H. Nash, *Ideas of History* (New York: E. P. Dutton, 1969) offered readers two volumes: one with speculative and the other with critical selections.

18. Dray, *Philosophy of History;* Kuklick, "Seven thinkers and how they grew."

19. William P. Alston, *Philosophy of Language* (Englewood Cliffs, NJ: Prentice-Hall, 1964); John Hospers, *An Introduction to Philosophical Analysis,* 2nd ed. (1953; reprint, Englewood Cliffs, NJ: Prentice-Hall, 1967), 422.

20. Histories of logical positivism remain internalist and fairly partisan. Even the label remains problematic—Quine preferred *logical empiricism,* and Popper refused the label entirely. *Positivism* here seems the appropriate term because of the idiosyncratic way in which the new forms of analysis actually materialized in philosophy of history: In this subfield, Ayer, Hempel, Popper, and Nagel essentially *were* logical positivism. The most frequently invoked common elements would include a radical linguisticism derived from early Wittgenstein; a unificationist account of scientific method; and a verificationist account of scientific truth claims, which was later amended to include falsificationist accounts. For overviews of the field, see Paolo Parrini et al., *Logical Empiricism: Historical and Contemporary Perspectives* (Pittsburgh, PA: University of Pittsburgh Press, 2003); Michael Friedman, *Reconsidering Logical Positivism* (Cambridge: Cambridge University Press, 1999); J. Alberto Coffa, *The Semantic Tradition from Kant to Carnap: To the Vienna Station* (Cambridge: Cambridge University Press, 1991); Alan Richardson, *Carnap's Construction of the World: The Aufbau and the Emergence of Logical Empiricism* (Cambridge: Cambridge University Press, 1998); and Michael Dummett, *Origins of Analytical Philosophy* (Cambridge, MA: Harvard University Press, 1993). Richard Rorty's *Philosophy and the Mirror of Nature* (Princeton, NJ: Princeton University Press, 1979) looks increasingly idiosyncratic in retrospect, but remains important. Theodor Adorno et al., eds., *The Positivist Dispute in German Sociology,* English language edition, trans. Glyn Adey and David Frisby (1969; reprint, London: Heineman, 1976), rendered the various high points of the *Positivismusstreit* into English. Ernest Gellner's review of the translation, in the *British Journal for the Philosophy of Science* 34 (1983): 173–175, suggests the ways that the German exchanges could be assimilated to the very different Anglo debates.

21. A.J. Ayer, *Language, Truth and Logic* (London: Gollancz, 1936); Ayer, ed., *Logical Positivism* (Glencoe, IL: Free Press, 1959).

22. Some recent work has contended that many of the key players, notably Wittgenstein and Karl Popper, were Kantians at heart who were badly misunderstood by British and North American audiences. See especially Malachi Haim Hacohen, *Karl Popper—the Formative Years, 1902–1945: Politics and Philosophy in Interwar Vienna* (Cambridge: Cambridge University Press, 2000); and Allan Janik and Stephen Toulmin, *Wittgenstein's Vienna* (New York: Touchstone Press, 1972).

23. Ayer, *Language, Truth and Logic.* Compare the more recent treatment of this issue in Michael Dummett, *Truth and the Past* (New York: Columbia University Press, 2003).

24. Walsh's *Philosophy of History* did not so much as mention Hempel or any of the logical positivists; White and Cohen each mentioned Hempel but only in passing: White, "Toward an Analytic Philosophy of History," and Jonathan Cohen, "A Survey of Work in the Philosophy of History, 1946–1950," *Philosophical Quarterly* 2 (1950): 172–186. Patrick Gardiner's *Nature of Historical Explanation* (Oxford: Oxford University Press, 1952) helped to stimulate interest in the covering law model.

25. Morris R. Cohen, *The Meaning of Human History* (LaSalle, IL: Open Court Press, 1947); G. E. M. Anscombe, *Intention* (London: Basil Blackwell, 1957); W. V. O. Quine, *From a Logical Point of View* (Cambridge, MA: Harvard University Press, 1953); Peter Winch, *The Idea of a Social Science and Its Relation to Philosophy* (London: Routledge, 1958).

26. William H. Dray, "The Historical Explanation of Actions Reconsidered," in Sydney Hook, ed., *Philosophy and History: A Symposium* (New York: New York University Press, 1963), 132–133, emphasis in the original. The debate provided the launching point for Isaiah Berlin's famous 1953 lecture, "Historical Inevitability," reprinted in *Four Essays on Liberty* (Oxford: Oxford University Press, 1969), 41–117.

27. Hook, preface to Hook, *Philosophy and History,* ix; John Higham, *History: Professional Scholarship in America* (1965; reprint, Baltimore: Johns Hopkins University Press, 1983), 142. For a more engaged treatment by a period historian, see Perez Zagorin, "Historical Knowledge: A Review Article on the Philosophy of History," *Journal of Modern History* 31 (September 1959): 243–255.

28. George Macauley Trevelyan, *Clio, A Muse and Other Essays* (London: Longman, Greens, 1913), 140–176; C. P. Snow, *The Two Cultures* (Cambridge: Cambridge University Press, 1998), reprints Snow's various essays and includes a useful introduction by Stefan Collini. Peter Novick, *That Noble Dream: The "Objectivity Question" and the American Historical Profession* (Cambridge: Cambridge University Press, 1988), sketches the extended debate in North American historiography.

29. H. Stuart Hughes, "The Historian and the Social Scientist," *American Historical Review* 66 (1960): 20–46; Hughes, *History as Art and as Science:*

Twin Vistas on the Past (1964; reprint, Chicago: University of Chicago Press, 1975), 4.

30. Claude Lévi-Strauss, *The Savage Mind,* English language edition (1962; reprint, Chicago: University of Chicago Press, 1966), 262; Lévi-Strauss, *Structural Anthropology,* English language edition, trans. Claire Jacobson and Brooke G. Schoepf (1958; reprint, New York: Doubleday, 1967), 31; Hayden White, "The Burden of History" (1966), reprinted in *Tropics of Discourse: Essays in Cultural Criticism* (Baltimore: Johns Hopkins University Press, 1978), 1–66, emphasis in the original.

31. According to Richard Vann, a number of American and British publishers passed on the journal before Nadel finally found a publisher in the Netherlands. Richard T. Vann, "Turning Linguistic: History and Theory and *History and Theory,* 1960–1975," in Ankersmit and Kellner, *New Philosophy of History,* 43.

32. Compare Vann's summary of the journal's early editorial mission with the canon we have seen in the textbooks and teaching anthologies: "The great speculators, Vico and Hegel and later Marx, were (if treated analytically) in; Toynbee was taken seriously, if critically; but Spengler and Voegelin were out. More recent speculative constructions, like those of Lloyd DeMause on the history of childhood or Shulamith Firestone on the history of women, would not have been published, and were not even reviewed, on the grounds that no reader or reviewer could be found who could evaluate their claims. This was a polite way of saying that these were not falsifiable." Ibid.

33. See, for instance, John Toews, "Intellectual History after the Linguistic Turn: The Autonomy of Meaning and the Irreducibility of Experience," *American Historical Review* 92 (1987): 879–907; Domenska, *Philosophy of History after Postmodernism;* Kerwin Lee Klein, "What Was the Linguistic Turn?" *Clio* 30 (2000): 79–90.

THREE. GOING NATIVE

1. Dominick LaCapra, *Soundings in Critical Theory* (Ithaca, NY: Cornell University Press, 1989), 189, 192–193. Compare the milder formulations in LaCapra, *History and Its Limits: Human, Animal, Violence* (Ithaca, NY: Cornell University Press, 2009), 13–36, 214–215.

2. Lynn Hunt, "Introduction: History, Culture and Text," in Hunt, ed., *The New Cultural History* (Berkeley: University of California Press. 1989), 1–24; Lloyd S. Kramer, "Literature, Criticism, and Historical Imagination: The Literary Challenge of Hayden White and Dominick LaCapra," in Hunt, *New Cultural History,* 97–129.

3. Hunt, "Introduction: History, Culture, and Text," 16; Victoria E. Bonnell and Lynn Hunt's preface to Bonnell and Hunt, eds., *Beyond the Cultural Turn: New*

Directions in the Study of Society and Culture (Berkeley: University of California Press, 1999), ix; Bonnell and Hunt's introduction to Bonnell and Hunt, *Beyond the Cultural Turn,* 1–32; Hayden White, afterword to Bonnell and Hunt, *Beyond the Cultural Turn,* 320–321. Compare Allan Megill, "Coherence and Incoherence in Historical Studies: From the Annales School of the New Cultural History," *New Literary History* 35 (2004): 207–231.

4. Sande Cohen, *Passive Nihilism: Cultural Historiography and the Rhetorics of Scholarship* (New York: St. Martin's Press, 1998), esp. 1–30; but also Cohen's account of Carlo Ginzburg's work on pp. 127–160. On *aesthetic turn,* see especially Hans Kellner, "Introduction: Describing Redescriptions," in Frank Ankersmit and Kellner, eds., *A New Philosophy of History* (Chicago: University of Chicago Press, 1995), 1–18; and Ankersmit, "Statements, Texts and Pictures" and "Bibliographical Essay," in Ankersmit and Kellner, *New Philosophy of History,* 212–240 and 278–283. Eva Domenska, in *Encounters: Philosophy of History after Postmodernism* (Charlottesville: University of Virginia Press, 1998), deployed aesthetics as a theme to integrate her interviews of various historical theorists. See also Kerwin Lee Klein, "What Was the Linguistic Turn?" *Clio* 30 (2000): 79–90.

5. John Toews, "Intellectual History after the Linguistic Turn," *American Historical Review* 92 (1987): 879–908; Martin Jay, "Should Intellectual History Take a Linguistic Turn? Reflections on the Gadamer-Habermas Debate," in Dominick LaCapra and Stephen L. Kaplan, eds., *Modern European Intellectual Tradition: Reappraisals and New Perspectives* (Ithaca, NY: Cornell University Press, 1982); Richard Rorty, "Introduction: Metaphilosophical Difficulties of Linguistic Philosophy," in Rorty, ed., *The Linguistic Turn: Recent Essays in Philosophical Method* (Chicago: University of Chicago Press, 1967), 3; Gustav Bergmann, "Logical Positivism, Language, and the Reconstruction of Metaphysics" (1953), partially reprinted in Rorty, ed., *Linguistic Turn,* 63. Compare the more recent Elizabeth A. Clark, *History, Theory, Text: Historians and the Linguistic Turn* (Cambridge, MA: Harvard University Press, 2004); and Gabrielle M. Spiegel, "The Task of the Historian," *American Historical Review* 114 (2009): 1–15.

6. Clifford Geertz, *The Interpretation of Cultures: Selected Essays* (New York: Basic Books, 1973). Compare the different reckonings of Geertz and New Cultural History in Aletta Biersack, "Local Knowledge, Local History: Geertz and Beyond," in Hunt, *New Cultural History,* 72–96; and Richard Biernacki, "Method and Metaphor after the New Cultural History," in Bonnell and Hunt, *Beyond the Cultural Turn,* 62–93.

7. Michel Foucault, *The Order of Things,* English language edition (1967; reprint, New York: Random House, 1970); Jacques Derrida, *Of Grammatology,* English language edition, trans. Gayatri Spivak (Baltimore: Johns Hopkins University Press, 1967); Clifford Geertz, "Notes on the Balinese Cockfight," in Geertz,

Interpretation of Cultures, 452; Geertz, "Thick Description" in Geertz, *Interpretation of Cultures,* 5–7. Hunt and Bonnell single out this last quote, with the Weber allusion. See their introduction to *Beyond the Cultural Turn,* 3. The closest Geertz's footnotes come to a conventional French '68 "linguistic turn" figure is a single reference to *Freud and Philosophy* by theologian and philosopher Paul Ricoeur (English language edition [New Haven: Yale University Press, 1970]).

8. Susanne Langer, *Philosophy in a New Key: A Study in the Symbolism of Reason, Rite, and Art* (Cambridge, MA: Harvard University Press, 1942); Langer, "On a New Definition of 'Symbol,'" in *Philosophical Sketches* (Baltimore: Johns Hopkins University Press, 1962); Geertz, *Interpretation of Cultures,* 89.

9. Langer, "On a New Definition of 'Symbol,'" 56–57; cited in Geertz, *The Interpretation of Cultures.* Cassirer's *Philosophie der symbolischen Formen,* 3 vols. (Berlin: Bruno Cassirer, 1923–1929), did not appear in English until after the war, as *The Philosophy of Symbolic Forms,* trans. Ralph Mannheim, 3 vols. (New Haven, CT: Yale University Press, 1953–1957). Compare Geertz's bibliographic histories of this development in *Interpretation of Cultures,* 208nn19, 20, with his account in *Local Knowledge: Further Essays in Interpretive Anthropology* (New York: Basic Books, 1983). One of the ironies of this line of reference is that many young German philosophers already considered Cassirer antiquated, his theories supplanted by Martin Heidegger's hermeneutics. For a more rigorous but less influential period integration of Anglo analytic and German hermeneutic philosophy, see Paul Ricoeur, "The Model of the Text: Meaningful Action Considered as a Text," *Social Research* 38 (1971): 529–562.

10. Margaret Schlauch, *The Gift of Language* (1942; reprint, New York: Dover, 1955); Mario Pei, *The Story of Language,* rev. ed. (1949; reprint, New York: New American Library, 1965); Edward T. Hall, *The Silent Language* (New York: Doubleday, 1959); Robert A. Hall Jr., *Linguistics and Your Language,* rev. ed. (1948; reprint, New York: Doubleday, 1950); Noam Chomsky, *Syntactic Structures* (The Hague: Mouton, 1957).

11. Susanne Langer, *Feeling and Form: A New Theory of Art Developed from Philosophy in a New Key* (New York: Scribner's, 1953); Langer, *Introduction to Symbolic Logic* (Boston: Houghton Mifflin, 1937); Langer, *Mind: An Essay on Human Feeling,* 3 vols. (Baltimore: Johns Hopkins University Press, 1967–1984).

12. Langer, *Philosophy in a New Key,* 95–96; Edward Sapir, "Language" (1933), reprinted in David G. Mandelbaum, ed., *Culture, Language and Personality: Selected Essays* (Berkeley: University of California Press, 1961), 1–44.

13. Leonard Bloomfield, *Language* (New York: Holt, Rinehart, and Winston, 1933); Edward Sapir, *Language: An Introduction to the Study of Speech* (New York: Harcourt, Brace, 1921); Archibald A. Hill, "Linguistics since Bloomfield," *Quar-*

terly Journal of Speech 41 (October 1955): 253; W. Nelson Francis, "Revolution in Grammar," *Quarterly Journal of Speech* 40 (October 1954): 299.

14. See, for instance, Edward Sapir, "Linguistics as a Science" (1929), in Mandelbaum, *Culture, Language and Personality,* 65–66; or Eric P. Hamp, introduction to E.H. Sturtevant, *Linguistic Change: An Introduction to the Historical Study of Language* (1917; reprint, Chicago: University of Chicago Press, 1961), v–xii. Thus Harold B. Allen's popular anthology, *Applied English Linguistics,* 2nd ed. (1958; reprint, New York: Appleton-Century-Crofts, 1964), divided the field up into history of grammar, as represented by Karl W. Dykema, "Where Our Grammar Came From," 3–14; and linguistics, as narrated by James B. MacMillan, "Summary of Nineteenth-Century Historical and Comparative Linguistics," 31–35. As of July 2006, the LSA's website still endorsed this particular narrative. See Frederick J. Newmeyer, "The History of Linguistics," at http://lsadc.org/info/ling-fields-history.cfm, accessed April 2009. For the version as imagined from the standpoint of generative grammar, see Noam Chomsky, "The Current Scene in Linguistics: Present Directions" (1966), reprinted in David A. Reibel and Sanford A. Schane, eds., *Modern Studies in English: Readings in Transformational Grammar* (Englewood Cliffs, NJ: Prentice-Hall, 1969), 3–11. But compare Robert B. MacLeod's contrast of a Humboldtian tradition with a more *Naturwissenschaftliche* tradition, in his foreword to Joseph Church, *Language and the Discovery of Reality* (New York: Vintage, 1961), v–ix. After the breakdown of structural linguistics into various competing schools, and the emergence of transformational grammar, many textbooks began to present a more encompassing view of the history of linguistics, going back to either the Greeks or the Indian study of Sanskrit and imagining grammarians, rhetoricians, and philologists as linguists by another name. See, for instance, John Lyons, *Introduction to Theoretical Linguistics* (Cambridge: Cambridge University Press, 1968), 1–52.

15. Although the highly edited version of Ferdinand de Saussure's influential lectures did not appear in English translation until 1959—*Course in General Linguistics,* ed. Charles Bally and Albert Sechehaye, trans. Wade Baskin (1959; reprint, New York: McGraw-Hill, 1966)—Bloomfield, among others, had been strongly influenced by the original French language edition. Saussure himself placed the origin of modern linguistics not in the earlier Orientalist work of Jones and Bopp but in the rise of Romance language study in the period stretching from the 1830s to the 1870s. Regarding the contrast of the historical effects of European and American linguistics, Steven Conn, *History's Shadow: Native Americans and Historical Consciousness in the Nineteenth Century* (Chicago: University of Chicago Press, 2004), makes a similar point in regard to the divergence of archeology in Europe and North America.

16. Sapir, "Linguistics as a Science," 219; Martin Joos, "The Five Clocks," *International Journal of American Linguistics* 28 (April 1962): 7–62.

17. William Labov, *Language in the Inner City: Studies in the Black English Vernacular* (Philadelphia: University of Pennsylvania Press, 1972); Max Black, *Models and Metaphors: Studies in Language and Philosophy* (Ithaca, NY: Cornell University Press, 1962). For an overview of the expansion of studies in metaphor, see Paul Ricoeur, *The Rule of Metaphor: Multi-disciplinary Studies of the Creation of Meaning in Language,* English language edition (1975; reprint, Toronto: University of Toronto Press, 1977). On the British side, see especially Bronislaw Malinowski, *Coral Gardens and Their Magic,* vol. 2 (New York: American, 1935); John Firth, *Speech* (1930) and *The Tongues of Men* (1937), reprinted in Firth, *The Tongues of Men and Speech* (Oxford: Oxford University Press, 1964); D. Terence Landendoen, *The London School of Linguistics: A Study of the Linguistic Theories of B. Malinowski and J.R. Firth* (Cambridge, MA.: MIT Press, 1968); C.K. Ogden and I.A. Richards, *The Meaning of Meaning: A Study of the Influence of Language upon Thought and of the Science of Symbolism* (London: Kegan Paul, 1923); Richards, *Practical Criticism* (London: Kegan Paul, 1930); and Richard Hoggart, *The Uses of Literacy* (Hammondsworth, England: Penguin, 1958). Dennis Dworkin, *Cultural Marxism in Postwar Britain: History, the New Left, and the Origins of Cultural Studies* (Durham, NC: Duke University Press, 1997), offers a useful historical overview.

18. Sapir, "Linguistics as a Science," 69, 74.

19. Benjamin Lee Whorf's essays were collected in John B. Carroll, ed., *Language, Thought and Reality: Selected Writings of Benjamin Lee Whorf* (Cambridge, Mass.: MIT Press, 1956). Ludwig Wittgenstein, *The Blue and Brown Books: Preliminary Studies for the 'Philosophical Investigations'* (New York: Harper and Brothers, 1958). Wittgenstein's *Philosophical Investigations,* 3rd ed. (1953; reprint, New York: Macmillan, 1968), was written much later. One can grasp a sense of the remarkable differences between specifically American and British vocabularies for these discussions by comparing Anscombe's translations of Wittgenstein or virtually any of the work done in the period by English analytic philosophers from Ayer to Ryle.

20. Margaret Mead, *Coming of Age in Samoa* (1928; reprint, New York: Harper, 1971); Ruth Benedict, *Patterns of Culture* (New York: Alfred A. Knopf, 1934); Robert Redfield, *Tepoztlán, a Mexican Village: A Study in Folk Life* (Chicago: University of Chicago Press, 1930); W.V. Quine, *The Time of My Life: An Autobiography* (Cambridge, MA: MIT Press, 1985), 157. The role of *culture* in displacing *race* was first systematically set out in George Stocking, *Race, Culture and Evolution: Essays in the History of Anthropology* (Chicago: University of Chicago Press, 1968), and has since become one of the stock creation stories of twentieth-century anthropology in North America, endlessly revised, adjusted, and expanded with the passing of each academic season. See also Klein, *Frontiers of Historical Imagination,* esp. 129–211.

21. Quine, "Autobiography of W. V. Quine," in Donald Davidson and Jaakko Hintikka, eds., *Words and Objections: Essays on the Work of W. V. Quine* (Dordrecht: D. Reidel, 1969), 6; Quine, "Two Dogmas of Empiricism" (1951), reprinted in Quine, *From a Logical Point of View: 9 Logico-Philosophical Essays,* 2nd ed. (1953; reprint, Cambridge, Mass.: Harvard University Press, 1980), 44; Quine, *Word and Object* (Cambridge, MA: MIT Press, 1960). Joel Isaac's "W. V. Quine and the Origins of Analytic Philosophy in the United States, *Modern Intellectual History* 2 (2005): 205–234, is helpful for the earlier period.

22. Quine, *Word and Object,* 28. Quine had introduced the figure of the field linguist confronted with "a heathen tongue" as early as 1951 in his "The Problem of Meaning in Linguistics," in Quine, *From a Logical Point of View,* 47–64.

23. Quine, *Word and Object,* 27, 29.

24. Ibid., 52–53. The best overall account of Quine's work is Roger F. Gibson, *The Philosophy of W. V. Quine: An Expository Essay* (Tampa: University of South Florida Press, 1982). But see also Lewis Edwin Hahn and Paul Arthur Schilpp, eds., *The Philosophy of W. V. Quine* (LaSalle IL: Open Court, 1986), and Davidson and Hintikka, *Words and Objections.*

25. Quine, *Word and Object,* 77–78. See Roger F. Gibson, "Quine's Indeterminacy of Meaning Thesis," in Hahn and Schilpp, *Philosophy of W. V. Quine,* 139–154. Paul A. Roth, *Meaning and Method in the Social Sciences: A Case for Methodological Pluralism* (Ithaca, NY: Cornell University Press, 1987), remains a good explication of Quine's contribution and the larger debate. But see also John H. Zammito, *A Nice Derangement of Epistemes: Post-Positivist Philosophy of Science from Quine to Latour* (Chicago: University of Chicago Press, 2004).

26. Thomas Kuhn, *The Structure of Scientific Revolutions,* 3rd ed. (1962; reprint, Chicago: University of Chicago Press, 1996). For a sense of the period's reception of the book, see Imre Lakatos and Alan Musgrave, eds., *Criticism and the Growth of Knowledge* (Cambridge: Cambridge University Press, 1970); and Gary Gutting, ed., *Paradigms and Revolutions: Appraisals and Applications of Thomas Kuhn's Philosophy of Science* (Notre Dame: Notre Dame University Press, 1980). Compare Paul Hoyningen-Huene's more recent *Reconstructing Scientific Revolutions: Thomas Kuhn's Philosophy of Science,* trans. Alexander T. Levine (Chicago: University of Chicago Press, 1993); and Zammito, *Nice Derangement of Epistemes.*

27. Kuhn, *Structure of Scientific Revolutions,* 103, 111, 149–150, 204.

28. Sapir, "Linguistics as a Science," 223–224.

29. Quine, *Time of My Life,* 157; Donald Davidson, "On the Very Idea of a Conceptual Scheme" (1974), reprinted in *Inquiries into Truth and Interpretation,* 3rd. ed. (1984; reprint, Oxford: Clarendon Press, 2001), 183–198.

30. Davidson, "On the Very Idea of a Conceptual Scheme," 184. To keep the story manageable, and to retain the stress upon specifically American usage, I

have evaded the more Anglocentric parallel track of these arguments, frequently traced from late Wittgenstein through the writings of Peter Winch and others. Many of the other contributions to these debates, including Winch's deployment of Malinowski, have been collected in Mark Hollis and Steven Lukes, eds., *Rationality and Relativism* (Cambridge, MA: MIT Press, 1982); and Bernard Wilson, ed., *Rationality* (New York: Harper Torchbooks, 1970).

31. Davidson, "On the Very Idea of a Conceptual Scheme," 197–198.

32. Davidson, "A Nice Derangement of Epistemes," in Ernest Lepore, ed., *Truth and Interpretation: Perspectives on the Philosophy of Donald Davidson* (Oxford: Basil Blackwell, 1984), 446. Much of the subsequent debate has played out through the naturalization of epistemology in brain science and experimental psychology, where the various Chomskian and post-Chomskian strains of linguistics have remained important. See, for instance, two of the more provocative of recent works on language: Steven Pinker, *The Language Instinct: How the Mind Creates Language* (1994; reprint, New York: Harper, 2007); and Randy Allen Harris, *The Linguistics Wars* (Oxford: Oxford University Press, 1995).

33. See especially Rorty, "On Ethnocentrism: A Reply to Clifford Geertz" (1985), reprinted in Rorty, *Objectivity, Relativism and Truth: Philosophical Papers* (Cambridge: Cambridge University Press, 1991), 1:203–210. But see also Rorty's use of Davidson in *Contingency, Irony and Solidarity* (Cambridge: Cambridge University Press, 1989).

FOUR. POSTMODERNISM AND THE PEOPLE WITHOUT HISTORY

1. James Clifford, *The Predicament of Culture: Twentieth-Century Ethnography, Literature, and Art* (Cambridge, MA: Harvard University Press, 1988), 15, 17. See also Clifford and George Marcus, eds., *Writing Culture: The Poetics and Politics of Ethnography* (Berkeley: University of California Press, 1986); and Clifford, *Routes: Travel and Translation in the Late Twentieth Century* (Cambridge, MA: Harvard University Press, 1997).

2. Claude Lévi-Strauss, *Tristes Tropiques,* trans. John and Doreen Weightman (New York: Pocket Books, 1977), esp. pp. 27, 28, 33, 34, 39, 49. Among other critical readings, see Clifford, *Predicament of Culture,* esp. 236–246, and Clifford Geertz, *The Interpretation of Cultures: Selected Essays* (New York: Basic Books, 1973), 345–359. We still lack a comprehensive biography, but see Christopher Johnson, *Claude Lévi-Strauss: The Formative Years* (Cambridge: Cambridge University Press, 2003). The best intellectual history of structuralism is Francois Dosse

and Deborah Glassman, *History of Structuralism: The Rising Sign, 1945–1966,* vol. 1 (Minneapolis: University of Minnesota Press, 1998).

3. Lévi-Strauss, *Tristes Tropiques,* 52, 285, 286.

4. Ibid., 120, 275, 331, 333, 334, 336, 337, 338.

5. The claim that historicism was uniquely European and hopelessly colonial was a key trope of much self-consciously postmodernist writing, most famously Robert Young, *White Mythologies: Writing History and the West* (London: Routledge, 1990). The trope remains important for some recent literatures, most notably in the historiography of South Asia. See, for instance, the different formulations in Vinay Lal, *The History of History: Politics and Scholarship in Modern India* (Oxford: Oxford University Press, 2003); and Dipesh Chakrabarty, *Provincializing Europe: Postcolonial Thought and Historical Difference* (Princeton, NJ: Princeton University Press, 2000).

6. Claude Lévi-Strauss, *The Savage Mind* (Chicago: University of Chicago Press, 1966), esp. 1–34, 217–269. The quote is from p. 257; Lévi-Strauss, *Totemism,* trans. Rodney Needham (Boston: Beacon, 1963); Jean-François Lyotard, *Instructions païennes* (Paris: Éditions Galilée, 1977), 39.

7. Jean-François Lyotard, "Le 23 Mars" (1971), reprinted in *Dérive à Partir de Marx et Freud* (Paris: Union Générale des Éditions, 1973), 305–316. See Geoff Bennington, *Lyotard: Writing the Event* (Manchester, U.K.: Manchester University Press, 1988), for an introductory overview. Neither Hayden White nor Paul Ricoeur, two of the best-known theorists of narrative and history, speak of master or metanarrative.

8. Lyotard, *Instructions païennes,* 23, 25, 31, 34, 35. As an instance of pragmatics, Lyotard says that one finds the will to power in the "pragmatique" of official narratives. "Pragmatique," he explained, "c'est un mot pour désigner l'ensemble des rapports, très compliques, qu'il y a entre celui qui raconte et ce dont il parle, celui qui raconte et celui qui l'écoute, et ce dernier et l'histoire dont parle le premier" (p. 16).

9. Ibid., 18, 42, 45. See also his "De la force des faibles," *l'Arc* 64 (1976): 4–12.

10. Lyotard, *Instructions païennes,* 53, 56, 79, 86, 87. See the reading in Betty R. McGraw, "Jean-Francois Lyotard's Postmodernism: Feminism, History, and the Question of Justice," *Women's Studies* 20 (March 1992): 259–273.

11. Jean-François Lyotard, *La Condition postmoderne: Rapport sur savoir* (Paris: Éditions de Minuit, 1979); Lyotard, *The Postmodern Condition: A Report on Knowledge* (Minneapolis: University of Minnesota Press, 1984). The quote is from pp. xxiii, xxiv.

12. Lyotard, *Postmodern Condition,* 37, 41. See also David Carroll, "Narrative, Heterogeneity, and the Question of the Political: Bakhtin and Lyotard," in Murray Krieger, ed., *The Aims of Representation* (New York: Columbia University Press,

1987), 69–106; J.M. Bernstein, "Grand Narratives," in David Wood, ed., *On Paul Ricoeur: Narrative and Interpretation* (London, 1991), 102–123; and Timothy H. Engström, "The Postmodern Sublime? Philosophical Rehabilitations and Pragmatic Evasions," *boundary 2* 20 (Summer 1993): 190–204.

13. Lyotard, *Postmodern Condition,* 20, 21.

14. Ibid., 19–23, 60; Lyotard, *Le Différend* (Paris: Minuit, 1983); Lyotard, *The Differend: Phrases in Dispute,* trans. George Van Den Abbéele (Minneapolis: University of Minnesota Press, 1988), 151–181. The quote is from p. 155.

15. Lyotard, *Differend*, esp., 32–50, 151–155. Compare his account with that in Saul Kripke, *Naming and Necessity* (Cambridge, MA: Harvard University Press, 1980). I mean to leave aside the validity of Kripke's argument. Instead, we might ask whether a Kripkean account of naming is coherent with Lyotard's earlier definition of narrative forms, and will it do the work Lyotard wishes it to do? I believe the answer to both questions is "no."

16. Leslie Silko, "Language and Literature from a Pueblo Indian Perspective," in Leslie A. Fiedler and Houston A. Baker, eds., *English Literature: Opening Up the Canon* (Baltimore: Johns Hopkins University Press, 1979), 54.

17. To begin with, it is not clear that Kripke would endorse Lyotard's extension of *rigid designators* to collective singulars like *the Cashinahua* or *the Jews.* Kripke's examples are of human individuals, Richard Nixon or Moses. Lyotard ignores this difficulty entirely. Some readers might object that I am overlooking his description of the way the Cashinahua frame their stories, with each narrator naming himself. Unfortunately for Lyotard's argument, this is an example of the danger of drawing a universal moral from an anecdote, for this is not a paradigmatic narrative practice of tribal communities or oral texts. While many oral communities use ritualized frames for narrating sacred tales, the performance of "naming" here is hardly universal. Ironically, if anyone is erasing something, then Lyotard is doing it to the Cashinahua, reducing their specific discursive practice to an instance of a universe of "local" (read Lévi-Straussian "savage") narratives. The pragmatics of narrative in oral discourse is vastly complicated. For a sampling of different approaches, see Keith H. Basso, *Western Apache Language and Culture: Essays in Linguistic Anthropology* (Tucson: University of Arizona Press, 1990); Ronald Scollon and Suzanne Scollon, *Narrative, Literacy, and Face in Interethnic Communication* (Norwood, NJ: Ablex, 1981); Michael Harkin, "History, Narrative, and Temporality: Examples from the Northwest Coast," *Ethnohistory* 35 (Spring 1988): 99–130; and Kerwin L. Klein, "Frontier Tales: The Narrative Construction of Cultural Borders in Twentieth-Century California," *Comparative Studies in Society and History* 34 (July 1992): 464–490.

18. Lyotard, "Histoire universelles et les différences culturelles," *Critique* 41 (May 1985): 559–568; Richard Rorty, "Cosmopolitanism without Emancipation:

A Response to Jean-Francois Lyotard" (1985), in *Objectivity, Relativism, and Truth: Philosophical Papers* (Cambridge: Cambridge University Press, 1991), 1:211–222; Rorty, "Habermas and Lyotard on Postmodernity" (1984), in *Essays on Heidegger and Others: Philosophical Papers* (Cambridge: Cambridge University Press, 1991), 2:164–175. See their brief exchange in "Discussion entre Jean-Francois Lyotard et Richard Rorty," *Critique* 41 (May 1985): 581–584, and the useful overview by Vincent Descombes, "Les mots de la tribu," *Critique* 41 (May 1985): 418–444. Lyotard's subsequent reflections can be found in an interview, Jean-François Lyotard and Gilbert Larochelle, "That Which Resists, After All," *Philosophy Today* 36 (Winter 1992): 402–427, esp. 405–406.

19. See Richard Rorty, *Philosophy and the Mirror of Nature* (Princeton, NJ: Princeton University Press, 1979), esp. 78–79, 257–311; and Rorty, *Consequences of Pragmatism* (Minneapolis: University of Minnesota Press, 1982), esp. xiii–xlvii, 110–138, and 211–232.

20. Fredric Jameson, *The Political Unconscious: Narrative as a Socially Symbolic Act* (Ithaca, NY: Cornell University Press, 1981); Jameson, foreword to *Postmodern Condition*, vii–xxi; Stephen J. Greenblatt, "Towards a Poetics of Culture" (1986), reprinted in Greenblatt, *Learning to Curse: Essays in Early Modern Culture* (New York: Routledge, 1990), 151. Greenblatt mentions, without citation, Wolfgang Iser as another source of the trope of "oscillating discourses." We should read this essay against two more recent works in the same volume, the introduction, 1–15, and "Resonance and Wonder," 161–183.

21. Clifford, *Predicament of Culture*. For the "monotonous alternation" of the bad infinity, see Georg W. F. Hegel, *Science of Logic*, trans. A. V. Miller, (Atlantic Highlands, NJ: Humanities Press International, 1989), 137–143, 150–154.

22. Jacques Derrida, *Of Grammatology*, trans. Gayatri Spivak (Baltimore: Johns Hopkins University Press, 1976), 24–27, 131; Derrida, "The Pit and the Pyramid: Introduction to Hegel's Semiology" (1968), in *Margins of Philosophy*, trans. Alan Bass (Chicago: University of Chicago Press, 1982), 69–108. Derrida's counterintuitive comment brings out the ambiguities in Lévi-Strauss. Though the anthropologist associates history with enslavement, Derrida's suggestion that this calls forth the possibility of history as liberation resonates with Lévi-Strauss's hope that research might recover an "historical dimension" for pre-Columbian America.

23. There is irony aplenty in *The Predicament of Culture*, but the denunciations (or celebrations) of it as a study in skepticism strike me as overwrought. For different readings, see Frances E. Mascia-Lees and Patricia Sharpe, "Culture, Power, and Text: Anthropology and Literature Confront Each 'Other,'" *American Literary History* 4 (Winter 1992): 678–696; P. Steven Sangren, "Rhetoric and the Authority of Ethnography: 'Postmodernism' and the Social Reproduction of Texts," *Current*

Anthropology 29 (June 1988): 405–424; Paul Rabinow, "Representations Are Social Facts: Modernity and Post-Modernity in Anthropology," in Clifford and Marcus, *Writing Culture*, 234–260; and Arnold Krupat, *Ethnocriticism: Ethnography, History, Literature* (Berkeley: University of California Press, 1992), 101–126.

24. Clifford, "Identity in Mashpee," in Clifford, *Predicament of Culture*, 277, 289. See the different accounts of the case in Paul Brodeur, *Restitution: The Land Claims of the Mashpee, Passamaquoddy, and Penobscot Indians of New England* (Boston: Northeastern, 1985); Francis G. Hutchins, *Mashpee: The Story of Cape Cod's Indian Town* (West Franklin, NJ: Amarta, 1979); and Jack Campisi, *The Mashpee Indians: Tribe on Trial* (Syracuse, NY: Syracuse University Press, 1991).

25. Clifford, *Predicament of Culture*, 289.

26. Ibid., 302, 317.

27. Ibid., 329.

28. Ibid., 14, 333. See also Campisi, *Mashpee Indians*, esp. 14–15, 43–45; and Brodeur's account, in *Restitution*, 59, 60, of the coverage by the *Wall Street Journal*.

29. Clifford, *Predicament of Culture*, 342, emphasis in the original.

30. Despite my criticisms of Clifford's narrative coding, I do not agree with Walter Benn Michaels that "culture" in general, and *The Predicament of Culture* in particular, reify essentialist (and racialist) notions of subjectivity. See Michaels, "Race into Culture: A Critical Genealogy of Cultural Identity," *Critical Inquiry* 18 (Summer 1992): 655–865; and the ensuing debate: Daniel Boyarin and Jonathan Boyarin, "Diaspora: Generation and the Ground of Jewish Identity," *Critical Inquiry* 19 (Summer 1993): 693–725; Avery Gordon and Christopher Newfield, "White Philosophy," *Critical Inquiry* 20 (Summer 1994): 737–757; and Walter Benn Michaels, "The No-Drop Rule," *Critical Inquiry* 20 (Summer 1994): 758–769.

31. Jacques Derrida, "Différance" (1968), in Bass, *Margins of Philosophy*, 11; Derrida, "Structure, Sign, and Play in the Discourse of the Human Sciences" (1966), in *Writing and Difference*, trans. Alan Bass (Chicago: University of Chicago Press, 1978), 293. See also Paul de Man's critique of Derrida in "The Rhetoric of Blindness," in *Blindness and Insight: Essays in the Rhetoric of Contemporary Criticism*, 2nd ed. (Minneapolis: University of Minnesota Press, 1983), esp. 120–122.

32. For a sense of recent directions, compare Philip Pomper et al., eds., *History and Theory, Theme Issue 34: World Historians and Their Critics* (1995); Gyan Prakash, ed., *After Colonialism: Imperial Histories and Postcolonial Displacements* (Princeton, NJ: Princeton University Press, 1995); Bruce Mazlish and Ralph Buultjens, eds., *Conceptualizing Global History* (Boulder: Westview Press, 1993); Ranajit Guha, *History at the Limit of World-History* (New York: Columbia University Press, 2002); and Bruce Mazlish, *The New Global History* (London: Routledge, 2006). At the moment, *global* is replacing *world* as the adjective of choice, but despite the wars

of nomination, courses, textbooks, and research centers have proliferated. As of this writing, at least three English-language journals attempt to define the new field: the *Journal of World History, New Global Studies,* and the *Global History Review.* See also the brief genealogy traced out in Alan Megill, "Globalization and the History of Ideas," *Journal of the History of Ideas* 66 (2005): 179–187. Susan Buck-Morss, in *Hegel, Haiti, and Universal History* (Pittsburgh: University of Pittsburgh Press, 2009), attempts to recuperate early Hegel's master-and-slave dialectic for a new universal history.

33. Francis Fukuyama, *The End of History and the Last Man* (New York: Free Press, 1992). See also his earlier article "The End of History?" *National Interest* 18 (Summer 1989): 3–18. Of the many commentaries on Fukuyama, perhaps the best is Perry Anderson, "The Ends of History," *A Zone of Engagement* (London: Verso, 1992), 279–375.

34. Immanuel Kant, "Idea for a Universal History from a Cosmopolitan Point of View," in Lewis White Beck, ed., *On History* (Indianapolis: Bobbs-Merrill, 1963), 11–26; Kant, "An Old Question Raised Again: Is the Human Race Constantly Progressing?" in Beck, *On History,* 137–154; Lyotard, *Differend,* 154–181. I cannot do justice to Lyotard's reading of Kant here, but I should mention three points. First, the sign of history becomes the occasion for reading the *Third Critique* and the sublime into Kant's (and Lyotard's) reading of world politics. Second, Lyotard emphasizes the resonance of "event" *(Begebenheit)* and, in one of Kant's drafts, finds him using *Ereignis,* a usage that allows Lyotard to situate his reading against Heidegger. Finally, the suggestion that the metanarratives of modernity have been effectively falsified (strange affinities here with logical positivism) has some resonance with his statement, in "Apostil au narratives" (1986), that metanarratives differ from myths in locating their resolution in some imagined future. See his *Le Postmoderne expliqué aux enfants* (Paris: Éditions Galilée, 1986), 38.

35. Kant, "Idea for a Universal History," 31; Fukuyama, *End of History,* 130; Rorty, "Cosmopolitanism without Emancipation," 219.

36. Fukuyama, *End of History,* 215, 234, 244. Richard Rorty discusses Fukuyama in "The End of Leninism and History as Comic Frame," in Arthur M. Meltzer et al., eds., *History and the Idea of Progress* (Ithaca, NY: Cornell University Press, 1995), 211–226.

37. In the field I know best, Native America, an obvious example is Keith Basso, *Wisdom Sits in Places: Landscape and Language among the Western Apache* (Albuquerque: University of New Mexico Press, 1996).

38. Joy Harjo, "Grace," *In Mad Love and War* (Middletown, CT: Wesleyan University Press, 1993), 1.

FIVE. ON THE EMERGENCE OF *MEMORY* IN HISTORICAL DISCOURSE

1. Since this essay first appeared in 2000, the bibliography has become truly unmanageable. I have lightly revised the original essay, but I have not attempted even to list the more recent literature. For a sense of recent directions, compare Maria Cambiaghi, "Storia, Memoria, Cultura: Intervista ad Aleida Assmann," posted by Iperstoria at www.isolateatro.it/arse_fucine_stridenti/ospiti/mara_cambiaghi/storia_memoria_cultura.htm, accessed April 2009; Wulf Kansteiner, "Finding Meaning in Memory: A Methodological Critique of Collective Memory Studies," *History and Theory* 41 (May 2002): 179–197; the first issue of the journal *Memory Studies* 1 (2008), ed. Andrew Hoskins et al.; Jeffrey Andrew Barash: "Qu'est-ce que la mémoire collective? Réflexions sur l'interprétation de la mémoire chez Paul Ricoeur," *Revue de Métaphysique et de Morale* 50 (2006): 185–195; Allan Megill, *Historical Knowledge, Historical Error: A Contemporary Guide to Practice* (Chicago: University of Chicago Press, 2007), 17–59; and Gavriel Rosenfeld, "A Looming Crash or a Soft Landing? Forecasting the Future of the Memory 'Industry,'" *Journal of Modern History* 81 (March 2009): 122–158.

2. Jeffrey K. Olick and Joyce Robbins, "Social Memory Studies: From 'Collective Memory' to the Historical Sociology of Mnemonic Practices," *Annual Review of Sociology* 22 (1998): 105–140; Maurice Halbwachs, *Les cadres sociaux de la mémoire* (Paris: Librairie Félix Alcan, 1925). See also his *La topographie legendaire des évangiles en terre saint: Étude de mémoire collective* (Paris: Presses universitaires de France, 1941); and *La mémoire collective,* rev. ed. (1950; Paris: Michel Albin, 1997).

3. Yosef Hayim Yerushalmi, *Zakhor: Jewish History and Jewish Memory* (1982; reprint, Seattle: University of Washington Press, 1996), 94; Pierre Nora, "Entre mémoire et histoire," in Pierre Nora, ed., *Les lieux de mémoire* (Paris: Gallimard, 1984), 23–43. The translation of the essay appeared as "Between Memory and History: *Les lieux de mémoire,*" in Natalie Zemon Davis and Randolph Starn, eds., "Memory and Counter-Memory," special issue, *Representations* 26 (Spring 1989): 7–25. Compare Pierre Nora's earlier essay, "La Mémoire collective," in Jacques LeGoff, ed., *La nouvelle histoire* (Paris: Retz CEPL, 1978), 398–401.

4. On theory and the "historicist" turn in the 1980s, compare the accounts in Michael Roth, *The Ironist's Cage: Memory, Trauma, and the Construction of History* (New York: Columbia University Press, 1995), 2; Michael J. Hogan, "Hiroshima in History and Memory: An Introduction," in Michael J. Hogan, ed., *Hiroshima in History and Memory* (Cambridge: Cambridge University Press, 1996), 4; and Andreas Huyssens, *Twilight Memories: Marking Time in a Culture of Amnesia* (New York: Routledge, 1995), 5. The most thorough semantic history of *postmodernism* is Perry Anderson, *The Origins of Postmodernity* (London: Verso, 1998).

5. Alon Confino, "Collective Memory and Cultural History: Problems of Method," *American Historical Review* 5 (December 1997): 1386; Allan Megill, "History, Memory, and Identity," *History and the Human Sciences* 11 (August 1998): 37–38. Memory did not become a defining feature of the New Cultural History (which has replaced its earlier incarnation as New Historicism, a.k.a. cultural poetics) until very recently. It is not a key word in any of the essays gathered in Lynn Hunt, ed., *The New Cultural History* (Berkeley: University of California Press, 1989).

6. We should not infer, as Martin Broszat does, that peoples obsessed with "mythic remembrance" are introducing bias into an "objective" or "rational" historiography; see Martin Broszat, "A Plea for the Historicization of National Socialism" (1985), translated in Peter Baldwin, ed., *Reworking the Past: Hitler, the Holocaust and the Historian's Controversy* (Boston: Beacon, 1990), 77–87; Martin Broszat and Saul Friedlander, "A Controversy about the Historicization of National Socialism," in Baldwin, *Reworking the Past*, 102–134; Friedlander, *Memory, History, and the Extermination of the Jews of Europe* (Bloomington: Indiana University Press, 1993), 85–101; and Jörn Rüsen, "The Logic of Historicization: Metahistorical Reflections on the Debate between Friedlaender and Broszat," *History and Memory* 9 (Fall 1997): 113–145.

7. Consider the fate of Michel Foucault's usage: Natalie Zemon Davis and Randolph Starn's introduction to the *Representations* special issue invoked Foucault's *countermemory:* "for Michel Foucault counter-memory designated the residual or resistant strains that withstand official versions of historical continuity" (2). But few writers today use *countermemory;* it would be redundant; see Michel Foucault, *Language, Counter-Memory, Practice,* ed. Donald F. Bouchard (Ithaca, NY: Cornell University Press, 1977), 139–164. Predictably enough, however, *postmemory* is already appearing; see Marita Sturken, "Imaging Postmemory/Renegotiating History," *Afterimage* 26 (May–June 1999): 10–12.

8. See, for instance, Joyce Appleby, Lynn Hunt, and Margaret Jacob, *Telling the Truth About History* (New York: Norton, 1994), 258–259. I used the word in such ways in my first book, *Frontiers of Historical Imagination: Narrating the European Conquest of Native America, 1890–1990* (Berkeley: University of California Press, 1997), 293.

9. Abraham Lincoln quoted in Michael Kammen, *Mystic Chords of Memory: The Transformation of Tradition in American Culture* (New York: Vintage, 1991).

10. Michael Schudson, *Watergate in American Memory: How We Remember, Forget, and Reconstruct the Past* (New York: Basic Books, 1992), 51. Compare Michael Schudson, "Dynamics of Distortion in Collective Memory," in Schudson, ed., *Memory Distortion: How Minds, Brains, and Societies Reconstruct the Past* (Cambridge, MA: Harvard University Press, 1995), 353–373.

11. The quote is from D.R. Price-Williams, "Memory," in Julius Gould and William L. Kolb, eds., *A Dictionary of the Social Sciences* (New York: Free Press, 1964), 422, 423. See James Mark Baldwin, ed., *Dictionary of Philosophy and Psychology* (New York: Macmillan, 1902), 2:65–67; Paul Monroe, *A Cyclopedia of Education* (New York: Macmillan, 1913), 4:191–193; Foster Watson, ed., *The Encyclopedia and Dictionary of Education* (London: Pitman, 1922), 3:1070–1071; Frederick C. Bartlett, *Remembering* (Cambridge: Cambridge University Press, 1932); Paul Edwards, ed., *The Encyclopedia of Philosophy* (New York: Collier Macmillan, 1967), 5:265–274; Bennett B. Murdock Jr., "Memory," in Lee C. Deighton, ed., *The Encyclopedia of Education* (New York: Macmillan, 1971), 6:298–303. Edwin R. Seligman, ed., *International Encyclopedia of the Social Sciences* (New York: Macmillan, 1933), did not index the word. More recently, Martin A. Conway, "Memory," in Adam Kuper and Jessica Kuper, eds., *The Social Science Encyclopedia*, 2nd ed. (New York: Routledge, 1996), 527–528, rehearses the usage associated with experimental psychology.

12. Raymond Williams, *Keywords: A Vocabulary of Culture and Society* (Oxford: Oxford University Press, 1976).

13. *Oxford English Dictionary*, 2nd. ed. (Oxford: Oxford University Press, 1989), 9:596–598. In Samuel Johnson's *Dictionary of the English Language*, 6th ed. (London: A. Millar, 1785), *memory* as material object is listed fourth, and the example comes from *King Lear:* "Be better suited; / These weeds are memories of those worser hours."

14. Richard Terdiman, *Present Past: Modernity and the Memory Crisis* (Ithaca, NY: Cornell University Press, 1993); Ian Hacking, *Rewriting the Soul: Multiple Personality and the Sciences of Memory* (Princeton, NJ: Princeton University Press, 1995); Matt K. Matsuda, *The Memory of the Modern* (Oxford: Oxford University Press, 1996). Some of the best studies treat earlier periods: see Francis P. Yates, *The Art of Memory* (London: Routledge, 1966); Janet Coleman, *Ancient and Medieval Memories: Studies in the Reconstruction of the Past* (Cambridge: Cambridge University Press, 1992); and Mary Carruthers, *The Book of Memory: A Study of Memory in Medieval Culture* (Cambridge: Cambridge University Press, 1991).

15. Matsuda, *Memory of the Modern*, 15, 17.

16. Patrick H. Hutton, *History as an Art of Memory* (Hanover, NH: University of Vermont Press, 1993). See also Patrick H. Hutton, "Mnemonic Schemes in the New History of Memory," *History and Theory* 36 (October 1997): 378–91. On the philosophical history of memory, compare Jeffrey Andrew Barash, "The Sources of Memory," *Journal of the History of Ideas* 58 (October 1997): 707–717. For a fuller Annales account, see Jacques Le Goff, *History and Memory*, English language edition, trans. Steven Rendall and Elizabeth Claman (1977; reprint, New York: Columbia University Press, 1992).

17. Amos Funkenstein, *Perceptions of Jewish History* (Berkeley: University of California Press, 1993), 3, 6. See Saul Friedlander's gloss of these passages in his *Memory, History, and the Extermination of the Jews of Europe*, viii.

18. Funkenstein, *Perceptions of Jewish History*, 6.

19. Georg W. F. Hegel, *Lectures on the Philosophy of World History: Introduction, Reason in History*, trans. H. B. Nisbet (Cambridge: Cambridge University Press, 1975), 12, 135–137. The passage is one of the few that we have in Hegel's own hand from his 1830 lectures. Compare the account of *Erinnerung* in the thought of Herbert Marcuse in Martin Jay's *Marxism and Totality: The Adventures of a Concept from Lukacs to Habermas* (Berkeley: University of California Press, 1984), 220–240.

20. Philip Gleason, "Identifying Identity: A Semantic History," *Journal of American History* 69 (March 1983): 910–931; Reinhart Koselleck, *Futures Past: On the Semantics of Historical Time*, English language edition, trans. Keith Tribe (1979; reprint, Cambridge, MA: MIT Press, 1985).

21. Roth, *Ironist's Cage*, 8–9; Davis and Starn, introduction to *Representations*, 26, 2; Appleby, Hunt, and Jacob, *Telling the Truth About History*, 258; Hacking, *Rewriting the Soul*, passim. Compare Randolph Starn, "Memory and Authenticity," *Studies in Twentieth Century Literature* 23 (Winter 1999): 191–200.

22. Funkenstein, *Perceptions of Jewish History*, 7–9. Among the many discussions of Halbwachs, several stand out: compare Noa Gedi and Yigal Elam, "Collective Memory—What Is It?" *History and Memory* 8 (Fall 1996): 30–50; Susan Crane, "Writing the Individual Back into Collective Memory," *American Historical Review* 102 (December 1997): 1372–1385; Confino, "Collective Memory and Cultural History"; Jay Winter and Emmanuel Sivan, "Setting the Framework," in Winter and Sivan, *War and Remembrance in the Twentieth Century* (Cambridge: Cambridge University Press, 1999), 6–38; and Iwona Irwin-Zarecki, *Frames of Remembrance: The Dynamics of Collective Memory* (New Brunswick, NJ: Transaction, 1994).

23. James Young, *The Texture of Memory: Holocaust Memorials and Meaning* (New Haven, CT: Yale University Press, 1993), xi. Little work on memory in cultural history engages experimental psychology or brain science. For exceptions, see Schudson, *Memory Distortion;* and the brief surveys in David Thelen, "Memory and American History," *Journal of American History* 75 (March 1989): 117–129; and Winter and Sivan, "Setting the Framework."

24. Young, *Texture of Memory*, x, 1. Thus Peter Novick, in *The Holocaust in American Life* (Boston: Houghton Mifflin, 1999), 3, 4, finds *social unconscious* too squishy for a cultural history of Holocaust commemoration in America, but imagines *collective memory* as a rigorous alternative.

25. Emily Mitchell, "Thanks for the Memoirs," *Time*, April 12, 1999, 1–5. Mitchell referred readers to Louise DeSalvo, *Writing as a Way of Healing* (New

York: HarperOne, 1999). I do not wish to venture any further into this territory; I find it depressing, and readers might object that I am stacking the deck in favor of my argument by citing this sort of literature. We should note, though, that out of this corner of the discourse comes the quaint academic notion that introducing first-person and confessional mode into one's monographs is an important means of deconstructing bourgeois subjectivity. For discussions of the return of first-person, see H. Aram Veeser, ed., *Confessions of the Critics* (New York: Routledge, 1996).

26. James Berger, "Worlds of Hurt: Reading the Literatures of Trauma," *Contemporary Literature* 38 (Fall 1997): 569–583. In his *After the End: Representations of Post-Apocalypse* (Minneapolis: University of Minnesota Press, 1999), 106–130, James Berger claims that the apocalyptic moments in Jacques Derrida's earlier writings represent the return of repressed memories of the Holocaust. More recently, Derrida took up *memory* and *mourning* as key words for his "spookology," *Specters of Marx: The State of the Debt, the Work of Mourning, and the New International,* English language edition, trans. Peggy Kamuf (1993; reprint, New York: Routledge, 1994).

27. Michael M. J. Fischer, "Ethnicity and the Post-Modern Arts of Memory," in James Clifford and George Marcus, eds., *Writing Culture: The Poetics and Politics of Ethnography* (Berkeley: University of California Press 1986), 196–198; Stephen A. Tyler, "Post-Modern Ethnography: From Document of the Occult to Occult Document," in Clifford and Marcus, *Writing Culture,* 122–140. Compare the usage in George Lipsitz, *Time Passages: Collective Memory and American Popular Culture* (Minneapolis: University of Minnesota Press, 1990).

28. Nora, "Between Memory and History," 9; Ashis Nandy, "History's Forgotten Doubles," *History and Theory: World Historians and Their Critics* 34 (1995): 44; Werner Sollors quoted in Genevieve Fabre and Robert O'Meally, introduction to Genevieve Fabre and Robert O'Meally, eds., *History and Memory in African-American Culture* (Oxford: Oxford University Press, 1994), 7–8. See also most of the essays in this anthology, especially Vévé Clark, "Performing the Memory of Difference in Afro-Caribbean Dance: Katherine Dunham's Choreography, 1938–97," 188–204. The reception in the United States of Nora's sites of memory as a potential postcolonial discourse is more than a bit ironic, since, as David A. Bell notes in "Realms of Memory," in its French context Nora's essay is more nearly a conservative plaint about the fragmentation of French identity (*New Republic,* September 1, 1997, 32–36).

29. Marita Sturken, *Tangled Memories: The Vietnam War, the AIDS Epidemic, and the Politics of Remembering* (Berkeley: University of California Press, 1997), 3–5, 15–17. Compare Lipsitz, *Time Passages,* and Norman M. Klein, *The History of Forgetting: Los Angeles and the Erasure of Memory* (London: Verso, 1997). The

language here owes much to Lyotard's contrast of "local" and "master" narrative. See my "In Search of Narrative Mastery: Postmodernism and the People without History," *History and Theory* 34 (December 1995): 275–298.

30. Schudson, *Watergate in American Memory,* 5.

31. We should also mention the German *Historikerstreit,* which was well publicized in the United States, although it turned more upon confrontations with German conservatives than upon confrontations with epistemic "radicals." The *Historikerstreit* did frame the 1990 conference at UCLA featuring Hayden White and Jacques Derrida, and the proceedings of that conference are partially reprinted in Saul Friedlander, ed., *Probing the Limits of Historical Representation: Nazism and the "Final Solution"* (Cambridge, MA: Harvard University Press, 1992). Although Americans have been prominent in these debates, much of the language depends upon a specifically German resonance, as in the frequent invocation of a "rational historiography." As Michael Burleigh notes, in the German academy the invocation of social-scientific objectivity has frequently served as a tacit critique of work that is "too emotive" or "too Jewish." See Burleigh, "From the Great War to Auschwitz," *Times Literary Supplement,* May 10, 1996, 7.

32. Friedlander, *Memory, History, and the Extermination of the Jews of Europe;* Roth, *Ironist's Cage;* Dominick LaCapra, *History and Memory after Auschwitz* (Ithaca, NY: Cornell University Press, 1998). LaCapra's book extended his work in *Representing the Holocaust: History, Theory, Trauma* (Ithaca, NY: Cornell University Press, 1994).

33. See the discussion in Steven E. Ascheim, "On Saul Friedlander," in *Passing into History: Nazism and the Holocaust beyond Memory: in Honor of Saul Friedlaender on His Sixty-fifth Birthday,* special issue, *History and Memory* 9 (Fall 1997): 11–46. Compare the psychoanalytic language in Friedlander's earlier books: *History and Psychoanalysis: An Inquiry into the Possibilities and Limits of Psychohistory* (New York: Holmes and Meier, 1978), and *L'antisémitisme nazi; Histoire d'une psychose collective* (Paris: Éditions du Seuil, 1971).

34. Dominick LaCapra, *Soundings in Critical Theory* (Ithaca, NY: Cornell University Press, 1989), 36. In *History and Memory after Auschwitz,* LaCapra cites chapter 2 of *Representing the Holocaust,* where page 46, note 5, refers us to his essay in *Soundings.* There is no imaginable empirical test of the claim that the world is transference, since any test will be a transferential product and so likely to suffer from denial. LaCapra even suggests that we might define both historicism and positivism as "denial of transference."

35. LaCapra, *History and Memory after Auschwitz,* 20.

36. See LaCapra's useful remarks on the word itself in *Writing History, Writing Trauma* (Baltimore: Johns Hopkins University Press, 2001), 160–161.

37. Friedlander, *Memory, History, and the Extermination of the Jews of Europe,* x, 53, 58, 61, 102, 131, 134. LaCapra, *History and Memory after Auschwitz,* 6–7, 26–27, glosses Friedlander's argument as a claim that the Shoah is "incommensurable" with other events, but LaCapra is fuzzy on what that means. As a strong claim, it would be incoherent: One could not claim that the Holocaust was the most radical genocide in history and simultaneously claim that it was incommensurable with other events. To describe the Nazi murder of European Jews as a limit-event implies some common measure, since it must exceed ("transgress," "go farther than") the others. LaCapra backs away from this position on pages 192–195. Part of what is at issue is that Friedlander is trying to appropriate postmodern poetics to finesse the frustrated question of the "exceptionality" versus the "normality" of the Holocaust. That issue is neatly parsed in Wulf Kansteiner, "From Exception to Exemplum: The New Approach to Nazism and the 'Final Solution,'" *History and Theory* 33 (May 1994): 145–170.

38. Friedlander, *Memory, History, and the Extermination of the Jews of Europe,* 134; Maurice Blanchot, *The Writing of the Disaster,* English language edition, trans. Ann Smock (1980; reprint Lincoln: University of Nebraska Press, 1995), 42, 47, italics in original.

39. Roth, *Ironist's Cage,* 65. See Stephen Bann, "Mourning, Identity, and the Uses of History," *History and Theory* 37 (1998): 94–101.

40. Theodor W. Adorno, "The Meaning of Working Through the Past" (1959), in *Critical Models: Interventions and Catchwords,* trans. Henry W. Pickford (New York: Columbia University Press, 1963), 89–103, is sometimes cited as an early example of the new vocabulary, but Adorno's language seems less clinical than much of our current usage. Again, translation is a problem, since *aufarbeiten, durcharbeiten, verarbeiten,* and a host of related German terms tend to collapse into *working through* in English-language discussions. Compare the very different semantics in Russell Jacoby, *Social Amnesia: A Critique of Contemporary Psychology from Adler to Laing* (Boston: Beacon, 1975), a book written before the rise of memory talk in cultural history. For a sampling of the expanding literature that takes *trauma* and *memory* as key words, see Cathy Caruth, *Unclaimed Experience: Trauma, Narrative, and History* (Baltimore: Johns Hopkins University Press, 1996); Caruth, ed., *Trauma: Explorations in Memory* (Baltimore: Johns Hopkins University Press, 1995); Paul S. Applebaum, Lisa A. Uyehara, and Mark R. Elin, *Trauma and Memory: Clinical and Legal Controversies* (New York: Oxford University Press, 1997).

41. Roth, *Ironist's Cage,* 16–17, 179, 211, 226.

42. Ibid., 12.

43. LaCapra, *History and Memory after Auschwitz,* 12, 13n4, 179. The demonization is the more surprising coming from LaCapra, since he has given us some

of the best and most reflexive intellectual history of recent years and has been withering in his criticism of such tactics when practiced by social historians.

44. Charles Maier, "A Surfeit of Memory?" *History and Memory* 5 (1993): 136–151; Gleason, "Identifying Identity"; Richard Handler, "Is 'Identity' a Useful Cross-Cultural Concept?" in John R. Gillis, ed., *Commemorations: The Politics of National Identity* (Princeton, NJ: Princeton University Press, 1994), 27–40.

45. Sande Cohen, *Passive Nihilism: Cultural Historiography and the Rhetorics of Scholarship* (New York: St. Martin's Press, 1998), points toward such a reading, except that Cohen seems to imagine memory as a continuation of Historicism writ large.

SIX. REMEMBRANCE AND THE CHRISTIAN RIGHT

1. Jannell, McGrew, "Ten Commandments Monument on Tour," *Montgomery Advertiser,* July 20, 2004; Amber Mobley, "Ten Commandments Monument Tour Visits Bossier City," *Shreveport Times,* November 16, 2004; Ted Parks, "Ten Commandments Monument Begins National Tour at Site of 'Monkey Trial,'" *Associated Baptist Press News,* August 4, 2004; Union of Orthodox Rabbis and RAA joint statement, "Two Major Rabbinical Groups Support 'Ten Commandments' Judge Roy Moore," at www.orthodoxrabbis.orguor_judge_moore030815.htm, accessed April 2007; Roy Moore, with John Perry, *So Help Me, God* (Nashville, TN: Broadman and Holman, 2005). The CRA 2004, now renamed the Constitution Restoration Act of 2005, HR 1070, S.520, says that the courts shall have no jurisdiction in cases of action against any public official for "acknowledgement of God as the sovereign source of law, liberty or government."

2. Pope John Paul II, *Memory and Identity: Conversations at the Dawn of a New Millennium* (Rome: Rizzoli, 2005). For the genealogy in this paragraph, see my "On the Emergence of *Memory* in Historical Discourse," *Representations* 69 (Winter 2000): 127–150.

3. See, for instance, the chirpy tone of Roy Rosenzweig and David Thelen, *The Presence of the Past: Popular Uses of History in American Life* (New York: Columbia University Press, 1998), in which coin-collecting and Civil War reenactments are taken as evidence of serious engagement with the past on a moral, if not epistemic, par with peer-reviewed professional historiography. But see also the critical comments in Michael Kammen, "Carl Becker Redivivus: Or, Is Everybody Really a Historian?" *History and Theory* 39 (2000): 230–243; and David Hollinger, "Banality and Enigma," *Journal of American History* 81 (December 1994): 1152–1156.

4. The observation has become common among the few major twenty-first-century historians in the United States who treat such issues. See especially

David Hollinger, "The 'Secularization' Question in the United States in the Twentieth Century," *Church History* 70 (March 2001): 132–143; Hollinger, "Why Is There So Much Christianity in the United States? A Reply to Sommerville," *Church History* 71 (December 2002): 858–864; Jon Butler, "Jack-in-the-Box Faith: The Religious Problem in American History," *Journal of American History* (March 2004): 11357–11378.

5. *Christian Right* is notoriously squishy, but I use that phrase, or alternatively, "Christian conservatives," partly because of the emergence of a public style of Christianity in which positions on policy issues—abortion, religious schools, faith-based welfare, evolution, etc.—have grown arguably more important than doctrinal cleavages. Today, it is something of a cliché for students of the topic to observe that conservative Catholics and Protestants are in many ways much closer to each other than to liberal members of their respective faith communities. Where appropriate, I distinguish among liberals, fundamentalists, evangelicals, etc. Most studies of the Christian Right use World War II as a dividing line between an openly anti-Semitic "old" Right and a newer set of movements. Compare Ernest R. Sandeen, *The Roots of Fundamentalism: British and American Millenarianism, 1800–1930* (Chicago: University of Chicago Press, 1970); Leo P. Ribuffo, *The Old Christian Right: The Protestant Far Right From the Great Depression to the Cold War* (Philadelphia: Temple University Press, 1983); Timothy P. Weber, *Living in the Shadow of the Second Coming: American Premillennialism, 1875–1925* (Oxford: Oxford University Press, 1979); Clyde Wilcox, *God's Warriors: The Christian Right in Twentieth-Century America* (Baltimore: Johns Hopkins University Press, 1992); Mark J. Rozell and Clyde Wilcox, *Second Coming: The New Christian Right in Virginia Politics* (Baltimore: Johns Hopkins University Press, 1996); Paul Boyer, *When Time Shall Be No More: Prophecy Belief in Modern American Culture* (Cambridge, MA: Harvard University Press, 1992); Michael Lienesch, *Redeeming America: Piety and Politics in the New Christian Right* (Chapel Hill: University of North Carolina Press, 1993); Lisa McGirr, *Suburban Warriors: The Origins of the New American Right* (Princeton, NJ: Princeton University Press, 2001); Brenda E. Brasher, *Godly Women: Fundamentalism and Female Power* (New Brunswick, NJ: Rutgers University Press, 1998); James Gilbert, *Redeeming Culture: American Religion in an Age of Science* (Chicago: University of Chicago Press, 1997); and Patrick Allitt, *Catholic Intellectuals and Conservative Politics in America, 1950–1985* (Ithaca, NY: Cornell University Press, 1993). Ralph Reed, *Active Faith: How Christians Are Changing the Soul of American Politics* (New York: Free Press, 1996), gives an insider's view. Jon Butler, *Awash in a Sea of Faith: Christianizing the American People* (Cambridge, MA: Harvard University Press, 1990), remains a standard introduction to Christianity and American history.

6. Lawrence Pazder, *Michelle Remembers* (1977; reprint, New York: Vintage, 1980); Harvey M. Thigpen et al., *The Three Faces of Eve* (1952; reprint, New

York); Flora Rheter Schreiber, *Sybil* (1973; reprint, New York: Warner Bros., 1974); Nunnally Johnson, dir., *Three Faces of Eve* (20th Century Fox, 1957); Daniel Petrie, dir., *Sybil* (NBC, 1976). For the quotes from Pazder and the law enforcement agent, see Denna Allen and Janet Midwinter, "Michelle Remembers: The Debunking of a Myth," *The Mail on Sunday* (London), September 30, 1990. Allen and Midwinter's investigation located the original family, Michelle's ex-husband, and a variety of community members, all of whom denied the story.

7. The most thorough account of the McMartin events was recorded by the journalists Paul Eberle and Shirley Eberle, *The Abuse of Innocence: The McMartin Preschool Trial* (New York: Prometheus, 1993). But a host of other studies also treat the McMartin case en route to larger discussions of the phenomenon of satanic ritual abuse. Among the many journalistic accounts, see especially Debbie Nathan and Michael Snedeker, *Satan's Silence: Ritual Abuse and the Making of a Modern American Witchhunt* (New York: Basic Books, 1995); Dorothy Rabinowitz, *No Crueler Tyrannies: Accusation, False Witness and Other Terrors of Our Times* (New York: Free Press, 2003); and Jeffrey Victor, *Satanic Panic: The Creation of a Contemporary Legend* (Chicago: Open Court, 1993). For skeptical accounts by scholars who also participated in other satanic ritual abuse trials, see Elizabeth Loftus and Katherine Ketcham, *Witness for the Defense: The Accused, the Eyewitness and the Expert Who Puts Memory on Trial* (New York: St. Martin's Press, 1991); Loftus and Ketcham, *The Myth of Repressed Memory: False Memories and Allegations of Sexual Abuse* (New York: St. Martin's Press, 1994); and Richard Ofshe and Ethan Watters, *Making Monsters: False Memories, Psychotherapy, and Sexual Hysteria* (New York: Scribner's, 1994).

8. The best account is Lawrence Wright's prizewinning 1993 reportage, reworked as his book, *Remembering Satan: A Case of Recovered Memory and the Shattering of an American Family* (New York: Alfred A. Knopf, 1994).

9. Ibid., 180–181. D. Corydon Hammond, "Hypnosis in MPD: Ritual Abuse," transcript at www.whale.to/b/greenbaum.html, accessed April 2007. What appears to be a transcript of the speech (corresponding to the accounts given by viewers and listeners of the other tapes) has been posted at a variety of sites (pro and con) in the repressed/recovered memory wars. Wright credits Sherrill A. Mulhern for the suggestion that the Greenbaum rumor originated in the 1989 Lisa Steinberg case in New York City. But the name also suggests Adolf Gruenbaum, a philosopher known for his antitheistic writings and suspicions of depth psychology. See, for instance, Adolf Gruenbaum, *The Foundations of Psychoanalysis: A Philosophical Critique* (Berkeley: University of California Press, 1984).

10. For a skeptical account of the False Memory Foundation, see Mike Stanton, "U-Turn on Memory Lane," *Columbia Journalism Review* (July–August 1997), accessed at http://archives.cjr.org, accessed April 2007. Alan W. Scheflin,

"Ground Lost: The False Memory/Recovered Memory Therapy Debate," *Psychiatric Times* 16 (November 1999), at www.psychiatrictimes.com/p991137.html, accessed April 2007, offers a quick overview of what some in the community see as a backlash by anti-Freudians. For recent literature produced by the organizations, see especially Stephen J. Ceci, ed., *Jeopardy in the Courtroom: A Scientific Analysis of Children's Testimony* (Washington, DC: American Psychological Association, 1999); Ceci and Helene Hembrooke, eds., *Expert Witnesses in Child Abuse Cases: What Can and Should Be Said in Court* (Washington, DC: American Psychological Association, 2001); and American Psychiatric Association, *Diagnostic and Statistical Manual of Mental Disorders, DSM-IV-TR*, 4th ed. (Arlington, VA: American Psychiatric Association, 2000). See also David Brown et al., *Memory, Trauma, Treatment, and the Law* (New York: W.W. Norton, 1998).

11. Marita Sturken, "The Remembering of Forgetting: Recovered Memory and the Question of Experience," *Social Text* 57 (Winter 1998): 103–125.

12. Gary North, *None Dare Call It Witchcraft* (New Rochelle, VA: Arlington House, 1976), 7–8, 14. Compare the premillennialist account in Hal Lindsey, *Satan Is Alive and Well on Planet Earth* (Grand Rapids, MI: Zondervan, 1972). Bernard McGinn, *Antichrist: Two Thousand Years of the Human Fascination with Evil* (San Francisco: HarperSanFrancisco, 1994), is a good introduction to Antichrist narrative.

13. The standard account remains William R. Hutchison, *The Modernist Impulse in American Protestantism* (Durham, NC: Duke University Press, 1992). For the flight from Princeton, see Darryl G. Hart, *Defending the Faith: J. Gresham Machen and the Crisis of Conservative Protestantism in Modern America* (Baltimore: John Hopkins University Press, 1994); and Bradley J. Longfield, *The Presbyterian Controversy: Fundamentalists, Modernists, and Moderates* (New York: Oxford University Press, 1991). The best account by a historian sympathetic to the conservatives remains George Marsden, *Fundamentalism and American Culture: The Shaping of Twentieth-Century Evangelicalism, 1870–1925* (New York: Oxford University Press, 1980). For an evangelical historian's view of old school Princeton theology, see Mark A. Noll, *The Princeton Theology, 1812–1921* (Grand Rapids, MI: Baker, 1983).

14. Rousas J. Rushdoony, *By What Standard?* (1959; reprint, Philipsburg, NJ: Presbyterian and Reformed, 1965). Most of Van Til's book-length studies appeared later in the sixties and in the seventies. But see two of his most important earlier works, *The New Modernism: An Appraisal of the Theology of Barth and Brunner* (Philadelphia: Presbyterian and Reformed, 1946); and *The Defense of the Faith* (Philadelphia: Presbyterian and Reformed, 1955).

15. Rousas J. Rushdoony, *Bread Upon the Waters: Columns from the California Farmer* (n.p., 1969); Rushdoony, *The Messianic Character of American Education*

(Nutley, NJ: Presbyterian and Reformed Publishers, 1963). There are no sound sources for Rushdoony's biography. The best seems to be the obituary by his son-in-law: Gary North, "R.J. Rushdoony, R.I.P.," *Gary North Archives*, at www.lewrockwell.com, accessed April 2007. Rushdoony's family name is elsewhere spelled "Roushdouni" or "Rushdooney." For Rushdoony's recollections of Kantorowicz and Hutston, see "Interview with R.J. Rushdoony," *Contra Mundum* 13 (Fall 1994), reprinted at the conservative website www.freerepublic.com, accessed April 2007. There is considerable internal evidence in Rushdoony's writings that he at least studied Kantorowicz's works, especially his classic *The King's Two Bodies: A Study in Mediaeval Political Theology* (Princeton, NJ: Princeton University Press, 1957). Rushdoony's recuperation of early mediaeval political life seems to owe a great deal to Kantorowicz's account of "Christ-centered kingship," itself citing George Huntston Williams's *Norman Anonymous of 100 A.D.: Toward the Identification and Evaluation of the So-Called Anonymous of York* (Cambridge, MA: Harvard Theological Studies, 1951). Rushdoony had left the Pacific Institute of Religion by the time Williams completed his dissertation, but the connection itself appears sound. See also Rushdoony's later polemic against liberal theological readings of Christian art (especially as developed at Pacific) in R.J. Rushdoony, "The Meaning and Greatness of Christian Art" (1983), posted at www.artsreformation.com, accessed April 2007. I do not know if Rushdoony was aware of the controversial rumors that Kantorowicz (a conservative nationalist in Weimar prior to fleeing Nazi Germany) had been a Nazi sympathizer in the early 1930s.

16. Rousas J. Rushdoony, *This Independent Republic: Studies in the Nature and Meaning of American History* (1964; reprint, Nutley, NJ: Presbyterian and Reformed Publishers, 1969), viii, emphasis in the original. See also his sequel, *The Nature of the American System* (Nutley, NJ: Presbyterian and Reformed Publishers, 1965).

17. Rushdoony, *The Biblical Philosophy of History* (1969; reprint, Nutley, NJ: Presbyterian and Reformed Publishers, 1974), 5, 7.

18. Rushdoony, *Institutes of Biblical Law* (Nutley, NJ: Presbyterian and Reformed Publishers, 1973). The Chalcedon Foundation was established in 1965 and began issuing a monthly report, largely written and edited by Rushdoony. The reports have been collected in Rushdoony, *The Roots of Reconstruction* (Vallecito, CA: Chalcedon, 1990).

19. "Interview with R.J. Rushdoony." Rushdoony had elaborated on the moral meanings of restitution in his earlier book *Politics of Guilt and Piety* (Nutley, NJ: Presbyterian and Reformed Publishers, 1970), 340, emphasis in the original: "The essence of justice in biblical law is *restitution*.... Restitution involves the principle of restoration, the restoration of Godly order."

20. Rushdoony, *Biblical Philosophy of History*, 113, 115; Rushdoony, *This Independent Republic*, 1.

21. "Interview with R.J. Rushdoony"; Michael Kitada, "Burden of Wealth," *Orange County Register,* August 8, 2004; Max Blumenthal, "Avenging Angel of the Religious Right," www.salon.com, January 6, 2004, accessed April 2007; "The 25 Most Influential Evangelicals in America," *Time,* January 30, 2005.

22. Most historians of prophetic Christianity in North America distinguish between premillennial and postmillennial approaches to Protestant eschatology. Certain strains of premillennialism, which held that Christ would return before the millennium, tended to shy away from worldly politics. Postmillennialism, on the other hand, could appear to underwrite a variety of social improvement projects, and postmillennialism was frequently associated with a modernist moment in mainstream theology. Hutchison's *Modernist Impulse in American Protestantism* remains the standard account for mainline theology. I am not arguing that doctrinal shifts are the primary causal factor in the embrace of political activism by new eschatological movements. Indeed, I doubt that a majority of self-professed believers outside of the seminaries (now or in other historic periods) could competently and consistently articulate the differences between pre- and postmillennial interpretations of end times. The sort of social bases documented by scholars like Boyer, *When Time Shall Be No More,* clearly worked to create a setting in which reconstruction and other extremist movements could emerge.

23. The Falwell-Rushdoony exchange is summarized in Walter Olson, "Invitation to a Stoning," *Reason* (November 1988), at http://reason.com/9811, accessed April 2007. It apparently appeared in the policy publication of Paul Weyrich's Heritage Foundation, but I have not succeeded in accessing any of the foundation's 1980s publications. As of May 2005, www.heritagefoundation.org linked to a variety of smoother dominionist Web sites, but not to Chalcedon. On Titus and CBN, see Marc Davis, "ABA Grants Accreditation to Regent Law School," *Virginian-Pilot,* August 7, 1996. Titus has denied being a reconstructionist, by which he apparently means that he denies believing in a strict or literalist application of Old Testament law. Rushdoony and other Christian reconstructionsts are denounced in Ralph Reed, *Active Faith: How Christians Are Changing the Soul of American Politics* (New York: Free Press, 1996). For Bahnsen and Westminster, see Greg L. Bahnsen, *Theonomy and Christian Ethics,* rev. ed. (1977; n.p.: Covenant House, 1984)—the title of this book varies in other editions; Bahnsen, *By This Standard: The Authority of God's Law Today* (Tyler, TX: Institute for Christian Economics, 1985). Bahnsen's work provoked a variety of responses at Westminster. See William S. Barker and W. Robert Godfrey, *Theonomy: A Reformed Critique* (Grand Rapids, MI: Zondervan, 1990). The "core" reconstructionist movement, composed of a variety of writers with sometimes conflicting doctrine, has a strong Web presence but is not part of the public face of dominionism; it spends much of its time assailing the better-known institutions for lack of rigor. Among

the more important sites are Bahnsen's organization, www.sccs.org, and its affiliated publishing site, www.cmfnow.com; www.forerunner.com (associated with Jay Grimstead, whose Coalition on Revival attempted to pull reconstructionists, dominionists, and other conservatives into dialogue); Gary North's writings, many of which are posted at www.lewrockwell.com; and Gary DeMar's organization, www.americanvision.org. We still do not have a sound scholarly account of the movement, but see Frederick Clarkson, "Theocratic Dominionism Gains Influence," *Public Eye Magazine* 8 (March–June 1994), posted at www.publiceye.org, accessed April 2007.

24. David Brody, "Washington, D.C.: Remembering our Christian Heritage," www.cbn.com/CBNNews/News/040702a.asp, accessed April 2007. See also the 700 Club, "Cape Henry, a Christian Nation," also at www.cbn.com, or any of a host of other stories.

25. The 700 Club, "David Barton on the Foundations of American Freedom," www.cbn.com/700club/features/david_barton_foundations0207.asp, accessed April 2007.

26. David Barton, *The Myth of the Separation of Church and State,* revised and reprinted as *Original Intent: The Courts, the Constitution, and Religion* (n.p.: WallBuilders, 1997). See also the Web site www.wallbuilders.org. On Barton, see Rob Boston, "Who Is David Barton and Why Is He Saying Such Awful Things About Separation of Church and State?" *Church & State* 46 (April 1993): 8–12; and Deborah Caldwell, "David Barton and the 'Myth' of Church-State Separation," n.d., at www.beliefnet.com, accessed April 2007.

27. Jeff Wright, "Lecturer Exhorts Pastors to Activism," *Eugene Register-Guard,* July 21, 2004.

28. David D. Kirkpatrick, "Putting God Back Into American History," *The Nation,* February 27, 2005, 1; Andy Sher, "Texas GOP Leader Takes Frist on Religious Tour," *Chattanooga Times Free Press,* April 12, 2005.

29. Nora is cited in Jay Winter, "The Generation of Memory: Reflections on the 'Memory Boom' in Contemporary Historical Studies," *GHI Bulletin* 27 (Winter 2001), at www.ghi-dc.org, accessed April 2007.

30. Winter, "Generation of Memory."

AFTERWORD

1. Hans Meyerhoff, introduction to Meyerhoff, ed., *The Philosophy of History in Our Time* (New York: Doubleday Anchor, 1959), 22–23. Compare the narrative in Carlo Antoni, *From History to Sociology: The Transition in German Historical Thinking,* trans. Hayden V. White (Detroit: Wayne State University Press, 1959). See also the review by Bruce Mazlish, *History and Theory*

1 (1961): 219–227, notable for its especially vicious critique of the translator's introduction.

2. Richard Wolin, *The Seduction of Unreason: The Intellectual Romance with Fascism from Nietzsche to Postmodernism* (Princeton, NJ: Princeton University Press, 2006). For an introduction to the Sokal–*Social Text* affair, see the collection put together by the journal *Lingua Franca:* Alan Sokal et al., *The Sokal Hoax: The Sham That Shook the Academy* (Lincoln: University of Nebraska Press, 2000).

3. It is not so much that there has been a conscious movement to smuggle the sacred back into the campus history classroom, although a few brave souls have openly called for academics to recognize appeals to supernatural forces as valid warrants for truth claims in histories written by Native Americans, for example. Well intentioned as such proposals may be, it is not in the strategic interest of religious minorities to open up the discourse of professional historians to the supernatural—in a nation as overwhelmingly Christian and devout as the United States, the outcome would not be the sort of warm, fuzzy, "many paths to God" spiritual affirmation that sometimes passes as religious investment in college towns. See Richard White, "Using the Past: History and Native American Studies," in Russell Thornton, ed., *Studying Native America: Problems and Prospects* (Madison: University of Wisconsin Press, 1998), 217–243, for a useful discussion.

4. One of the most systematic attempts to create a language of "the threshold" is the work of Paul Ricoeur. See especially *History and Truth,* English language edition, trans. Charles A. Kelby (1964; reprint, Evanston, IL: Northwestern University Press, 1965); *Time and Narrative,* vols. 1–3, English language edition, trans. Kathleen McLaughlin and David Pellauer (1983–85; reprint, Chicago: University of Chicago Press, 1985–88).

5. François Cusset, *French Theory: How Foucault, Derrida, Deleuze & Co. Transformed the Intellectual Life of the United States,* English language edition, trans. Jeff Fort et al. (2003; reprint, Minneapolis: University of Minnesota Press, 2008), 333. Compare Jean-Philippe Mathy, *Extreme-Occident: French Intellectuals and America* (Chicago: University of Chicago Press, 1993); and for an argument about the linguistic turn in French historiography, see Gerard Noiriel, *Sur la "crise" de l'histoire* (Paris: Éditions Gallimard, 2005).

Index

Text: 10/14 Palatino
Display: Univers Condensed Light, Bauer Bodoni
Compositor: Toppan Best-set Premedia Limited
Printer and binder: Maple-Vail Book Manufacturing Group